Also available at all good book stores

9781785316470

9781785313929

9781785315466

9781785316265

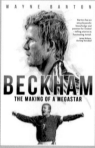

9781785316760

9781785318573

9781785318436

9781785315541

9781908051783

THE
SUNSHINE
Kids
THE AUTOBIOGRAPHY OF
RAFAEL & FABIO
DA SILVA

THE SUNSHINE *Kids*

THE AUTOBIOGRAPHY OF
RAFAEL & FABIO DA SILVA

WITH
WAYNE BARTON

FOREWORD BY
SIR ALEX FERGUSON

pitch

First published by Pitch Publishing, 2021

Pitch Publishing
A2 Yeoman Gate
Yeoman Way
Worthing
Sussex
BN13 3QZ
www.pitchpublishing.co.uk
info@pitchpublishing.co.uk

ISBN 978 1 78531 878 8

Typesetting and origination by Pitch Publishing
Printed and bound in Great Britain by TJ Books Ltd

Contents

This book is dedicated to our
parents and to God.

Foreword by Sir Alex Ferguson

I AM writing this foreword for the two brothers Fabio and Rafael Da Silva. Every time I hear their names mentioned I smile. Of all the great players I managed, no one delighted me as much as these two young lads. Not that I put them in the lead in regard to performance, but in terms of their manner, their character and personality they took some beating.

When they first came to train with us at 14 years old, they had that quality that made them a must to sign. They were so keen to be players that they were the first out in the training ground every day. From the day they joined us, until the day I retired, they retained that habit – first out, last in, and despite the coldest of weather they never wore tracksuit bottoms! Honestly, they were gems!

Fabio was a bit unlucky in his time with us with repeated shoulder injuries, but it never took his enthusiasm away. The pinnacle of their time with United came on 12 March 2011, my wedding anniversary, which is why it will always stay in my memory. We were crippled with injuries, especially in the midfield, and I had to put Antonio Valencia, Ryan Giggs and Paul Scholes on the bench knowing they could only give me a limited amount of time on the pitch. So, the midfield was Rafa wide left, wide right was Fabio, and in the centre were John O'Shea and Darron Gibson. The climax for these two young lads was our first goal. Rafa makes a road in towards the Arsenal box, crosses, a bit of a flurry in front of their goalkeeper then from nowhere Fabio nipped in to score! What a day for them!

Of course, their team-mates loved it when they swapped identities. When I would want to talk to Rafa he would say he was Fabio and when I went to talk to Fabio, he would say he was Rafa – the players loved it.

At the end of their first season, I pulled them into my office to congratulate them on doing so well and said to them, 'Now go home and have a good rest.' Their reply was, 'No, Boss, we play every week for the village team.' Their father had built a pitch at the back of their house! Now I often wonder if this is the recipe which makes all those great Brazilian players: they never stop playing!

There are too many examples of the energy that comes from that country's players but there is one example I've referred to many times. When we played AC Milan in the second leg of the European Cup in Milan and this guy Cafu is up and down the pitch all night as if he had two hearts! The Da Silva boys had that same approach to the game. They're now at other clubs but, for me, I loved being their manager. Their enthusiasm spread right through the club.

Sir Alex Ferguson, CBE

Introduction

PEOPLE ASK us all the time what it is like to be twins. We're the same, but different. That applies to us and our journey.

European football fans think of a Brazilian upbringing, especially in Rio de Janeiro, as playing football with balls made from rolled-up socks in favelas. We grew up in Petrópolis, around 45 minutes from Rio depending on traffic, and, while we can say we had a little experience of that, it was different to the way most people imagine it. Our father grew up in that era. By the time we were born, our town was more developed and it was harder to play on the street.

We still did – in fact, that's where we learned many valuable lessons. We were five years old and playing with our brother and his friends who were seven years older than us. They didn't take it easy on us. It was very competitive. We were lucky that our brother Luiz, who we call Zerrique, was there to look out for us, but we were never afraid, and even though it was difficult we matured – in a football sense – much more quickly than other boys our age were able to. We were spotted by a local coach – not a professional coach, just a coach for a small club – who was walking past and saw how we handled ourselves against the much bigger boys. His team was for boys who were the same age as our brother's friends, but that was no problem for us.

Our father was a footballer. He never made it professionally. He felt he was good enough but when he got to the age where he had to decide to play football or get another job or career, he was put under pressure by his parents to work. At 15 he was already working, and some clubs were asking him to come and play, but his dad thought it would be too competitive and told him he had to find a different job. Becoming a footballer is a dream in Brazil but it is also very competitive. We were encouraged to play – we were just kids – but our dad never put any pressure on us to play or to stop. He taught us the skills that would help. We were both right-footed so he encouraged us to play with our left foot as well.

Our parents came from big families. That was always the way, back in those days – maybe they had nothing else to do to entertain themselves! We were a close family, bonded by our grandparents, so when we went to see them we would see everyone else. Our mum and dad were very hard-working. Seven days a week. They were housekeepers for a family who owned a mansion in Petrópolis. At the weekends, the family would come from Rio to spend time in the house, and our parents were still needed then to take care of everything. In the week, when the owners were not there, we were allowed to go in the pool. It was a taste of a different life and a bonus from the work of our mum and dad.

We grew up appreciating the value of everything because of how hard they worked. By European standards you might have said we were poor, but we always had everything we needed. Our parents are our heroes in life. From the moment we were able to work we knew we'd be working hard to try and repay them for everything they'd done for us.

Dad was very strict, but also very emotional. Zerrique got into trouble a couple of times at school and Dad wouldn't go because he would become too frustrated – he'd tell Mum to go alone. We were very young but we observed it all and learned from it. We didn't want to upset our parents in that way.

Because we were twins, we did everything together. We were so close in ability, so whenever we played football against each other – and we were as competitive as we were inseparable – it was very difficult because we were just the same. Sometimes we'd play on huge football pitches, one against one, running until we were exhausted from trying to beat each other. Usually when you play against someone else there is a difference in quality. It can become uncompetitive. It can be boring. That wasn't the case for us.

People see us and think we're so nice with each other and we love each other and that is true. When we were playing, especially in Manchester when one of us might be getting a game instead of the other, we were always very happy for who was playing and wanted him to do well. But on the training pitch, we fought for that position just as hard as we would against any other opponent.

Rafael: We've changed over the years. When I was younger, I was so calm, relaxed ...

Fabio: And I was always agitated! Now it's the other way around! It's funny. I think we just bring that out in each other. When he's calm, I want to upset him or get on his nerves, and I know that when I am relaxed, he wants to do the same.

We fought, we argued. That's part of life, part of any family. The day we wrote this we had an argument. That's what happens when you're close. Of course, when you are a twin you are closer than normal. We slept in the same bed when we were young. We shared the same bedroom when we were teenagers. Even after we went to Manchester United, we shared a room; we were allowed our own hotel rooms for games, but after a while, the club noticed we were only using one of the rooms. Sir Alex Ferguson even asked us if it was true, and why. We were honest and said we didn't need it – from then on, they only booked one room for us.

Our brother had already been to Europe to try his luck at becoming a professional. He was offered a chance by Brescia and they liked him very much. In fact, they liked him so much that they said they would even sign us up to their academy to help him settle. Everything looked like it might happen, but then there were complications in the deal when an agent asked for too much money and Brescia said no.

Zerrique was a brilliant footballer. He had more talent than us. Everyone has those stories of someone in their family who didn't make it to the top and you don't know whether to believe them. Believe us. He was fantastic. We were famous in Petrópolis for being very good at such a young age, but the locals knew he had more ability than us and they would say so.

But football is not just talent. It's about discipline and making a sacrifice. Maybe Zerrique didn't have that attitude. It's hard. It's challenging. You have to want it in a certain way. Brazil has hundreds of thousands of footballers from the streets who have all the talent in the world. It's a very small number who are able to make it professionally. First of all you need to make those sacrifices, so when your friends are going out and having a good time doing other things, you have to go to training, or stay in and stay focused. You have to be able to keep that focus if you're going through a bad spell, if the pressure is maybe getting to you and you're not playing as well as you can. The funny thing is, we learned our discipline and mental strength from a very early age thanks to Zerrique and the exposure to playing with the older boys. It wasn't easy to stay that way, but we were used to it from the age of five, and that helped.

From the age of five until 11 we played football locally for an amateur team, Boa Esperança, every day from Friday to Sunday. We loved it, of course, but we still needed to be disciplined because there were weeks when we might not feel like it, or we didn't play our best game, or we just wanted to be like other kids and stay at home and watch cartoons. And you know, our dad said to us that if we wanted to, we could. But he said he thought we were both very special and we had an opportunity that not many others had. He said he knew it might be tough sometimes, but the more we stayed with it, the more we were going to improve and the more we were going to learn. One time he said that to be a footballer, you must be a crazy man. You have to do some things that normal people don't do.

When we were eight years old we started to play futsal in Petrópolis for a team called Petropolitano. Every young boy who wants to be a footballer should play futsal; for us, it accelerated our development. Playing in tight areas and small spaces; at first we didn't like it, because we both love to run. It forces you to think more quickly and enhances your reactions and reflexes. It's a completely different environment to a full game of 11 against 11, and the ball is heavier, making it a bit more difficult to control. Futsal originated in South America but it is starting to become more popular around the world; if it is introduced to kids at the age we were then it could make a really big difference.

Football didn't originate in Brazil but everyone in the world knows how much the country loves the game. The team we supported was Botafogo, the top team in the country when we were five – the best team in the world all of the time, obviously! But because of our parents working and us playing football from such a young age, we were not able to go and watch them play.

We grew up in a golden era for the country. How could it be better? Brazil won the World Cup in 1994 and 2002 and got to the final in 1998. Players like Romário, Bebeto (who played for Botafogo in 1998), Ronaldo, Rivaldo, Ronaldinho, Kaká – some of the best players the world has ever seen. For us, specifically, Cafu and Roberto Carlos were fantastic examples. When we became full-backs, we'd be watching them all the time and then we'd be trying to copy them in training. They weren't traditional full-backs. They would try tricks, score free kicks.

In other areas of the world, the full-back is not a very fashionable position. A few years ago the former Liverpool player Jamie Carragher said nobody grows up wanting to be a Gary Neville. Maybe before you are ten years old he is right. But when you realise how competitive it is to become a professional, when you realise how you have to learn the tactical discipline of playing in defence, you have a much greater appreciation for the quality of a player like Gary.

Growing up in Brazil, the emphasis is always on scoring goals, so, even for us, we were learning to score, learning to cross and to dribble. Maybe it's different in other countries – if you don't show some attacking quality, coaches can see something in you that makes them think you'll be a good defender. In Brazil, if you don't know how to attack, they won't consider you to play at full-back.

We didn't grow up and decide to play football because we wanted to be legends for Botafogo. It wasn't that we wanted to win medals, or become the most popular, or rich, either. Our only goal – and this is something we always agreed on – was to make sure Mum and Dad didn't have to work. Dad loved football. He loved that we played football. But he couldn't come and watch us play because he was working. Our games were on weekends and those were the days when he worked the most. Dad was okay with that, even though he was frustrated at missing out on those early years of watching our development. We understood that he wanted to, he just couldn't, and he was working hard to ensure that we didn't miss out, too. That made us appreciate the opportunity we had, and made us work harder to do everything we could to make the most of it.

There's a saying, where we come from in Brazil, that rich people cannot make professional footballers. That is a reference to the desire and the hunger that you need to succeed; these are qualities you see in almost all of the top Brazilian players in history, and it's something that cannot be manufactured. You can have this in your personality, but when you learn from an early age that playing football as a professional is an opportunity that only very few have, and you understand how hard others are working to get that opportunity, it makes you appreciate that in a different way. Rich people don't want it as much as poor people. We had a motivation, a motivation bigger than any prize football has to offer, and that was to give back to our parents.

Fabio: At Boa Esperança, Rafa was a striker and I was a midfielder. In our city we were very popular. We had some very good players but my brother and I were probably the best. We'd dribble through teams. He'd pass to me, I'd pass back, he'd pass to me, I'd pass back, one of us would score. Every time.

Rafael: Because we were so well known in our city, it didn't take long for professional clubs to show an interest. The first was Fluminense, but they were based 70km away. It was impossible. Dad couldn't take us. He said he would love to, but he had no time.

Fabio: Fluminense had a big training academy and a dormitory where they housed lots of boys who stayed there over the weekends and through the week. Their scout told our dad that he would pick us up and take us there. He would do the drive that would take one and a half, maybe two, hours, maybe more in rush hour, from our house to Rio de Janeiro, twice a week so we could train. Their team were chasing the league title so they wanted us there to help them win it. He did that for six months – we did win the league, and so we were very popular and they wanted us to stay on.

Rafael: We got a lot of attention then. Botafogo said they wanted us to sign for them. Fluminense said no, we have an agreement with the family.

Fabio: Nothing was signed. But like we said, our dad is a strict guy. His word is worth much more than any paper. Dad loved Botafogo, as did we. He was crazy about them. But he had promised Fluminense, so at 11 years old, that's where we went. Fluminense had one of the most highly-regarded academies in the country, not only because of how they developed talent, but for the way of life and the way they looked after the boys.

Rafael: So we stayed in this big room with all these other boys. It was something like 14 rooms, four beds in every room. For the first three weeks, my brother cried every night.

Fabio: I did! I was 11 years old. Fourteen rooms, four beds each. We were much younger than the other boys. Because we were so highly-rated, Fluminense had come in early to make sure we stayed with them. I'm not sure it was legal! But it was a now or never situation for us. We had to take it.

Rafael: I cried too, I admit that it was hard.

We had a weekend off and went back home. Mum could see that we were scared. She said if we didn't want to go back, we didn't have to. She was sad because she saw the change in us. She reassured us. It was fine. We could go back home, we would have food, we would have school, we could just do what everybody else did and get a job when it was time.

Dad came to us and said, 'I'm never going to make you guys go to Fluminense. But you see these guys who work hard in the sun for 12 hours a day. You can go to school and there is no guarantee at all that you will get a good job. In football, it is clear to see you are two of the better players. You can stay there and try. It will be hard for now. But you will get used to it and I am sure you will fall in love with it.' And he was right. We went back, and in just a little time, we loved it so much it was hard to go back home! Everybody loved us at the club and we loved them.

We don't think our parents could have imagined how well it would go for us, but they probably also didn't know just how much their conversations influenced us to give it another try. That's why we say they're our heroes. They could have put pressure on us to obligate us to go, or not to go. They gave us the choice and they gave us the confidence to not only know we could make the choice and they wouldn't be disappointed, but also that they believed in us to do something many people would think is impossible. We're parents now. It's not an easy thing to know how to speak to your children.

Fabio: We were intelligent kids. It never got to a stage where we considered doing anything other than becoming footballers.

Rafael: Maybe if I grew up in England I would have become a golfer.

Fabio: Definitely not! He never touched a golf ball before we went to England! But we were good at school.

Rafael: You were better than me! I never had to repeat a year, at least. No, we were okay. I'd say never ten out of ten but always six out of ten. We never had any problems.

Our brother told us that we had to stick together when we went back to Fluminense. That we had to take care of each other and, because we were the youngest, make sure none of the older boys hurt us. He didn't go to Fluminense but he had been through this sort of thing before at Atlético Mineiro and he knew that sometimes the older boys could be bullies. At 11 years old, we didn't really know what to expect, so it was good for us to be prepared.

Fabio: We changed positions at Fluminense. I was a striker now. I played there for six months. And my brother was in midfield.

Rafael: For two training sessions! I thank the coach Edgar Pereira for that, because he moved me to right-back. He was a great coach and was chosen by the national team to work with young players there too. Where we were training was the hottest area in Rio de Janeiro. The first day was bad enough, and somehow the second day was even hotter. We could not run. On one side of the training ground there were these huge trees providing some shade. I was so hot that I said to myself there was no way I could continue, so I moved myself to the right, under the trees. I stayed there all training. After the session the coach asked me if I'd ever played right-back before. I said 'yeah, yeah' – but I'm like that, he could have asked me if I'd ever played goalkeeper and I'd have said yes. He told me to train there the next day. That was me, forever, at right-back. It was a good coach, and a good tree.

Fabio: Maybe it was the tree, but he was a very intelligent coach. He saw how fast we were and how much we liked to run, qualities that were great for a full-back. I stayed for a lot longer as a striker, and I scored a lot of goals. There was another set of twins there, Romulo and Juan. Identical twins, just like us, in the same team. This is all true. One played full-back and one played in midfield. These boys were fantastic. Physically they were unbelievable. In training they're at the front all the time. Me and my brother were fast and had a lot of energy but these guys were something else. It was too much. It *was* too much. We found out that they had fake IDs. They were three years older than us. That kind of thing happened quite often in Brazil. They were expelled from the club.

The coach tried everyone at left-back to replace one of the twins but couldn't find anyone suitable. We had a lot of good strikers in our team, so for a few games, the coach always had to leave a really good player on the bench and bring him on. I was strong on my left side because of the way that our dad had taught us. Coach Edgar was thinking of how he'd moved my brother and asked me if I had ever thought about playing left-back. I was a little reluctant. 'No, no, please don't move me!' But he asked me to try it for one game. He wanted to try and play with all of his best players on the pitch. And I enjoyed playing the full game. I grew to enjoy it. I was more adaptable than my brother, I could play in a lot of different positions, and sometimes played in midfield and the centre of defence.

Good things were happening but we didn't have goals like normal players. It wasn't as if we dreamed of playing in Europe or even playing for Brazil. We just wanted to become professional footballers to make money for our parents. We weren't driven by ambitions to win trophies or to play in the Champions League or anything. But one thing we both had was a competitive streak, to win every time we played at everything. As soon as Manchester United became involved, everything changed.

We knew from day one that we might not be able to play together forever. It was rare to become a professional footballer. Even rarer to do it as twins. Even rarer to do it on the same team. Our parents said to us that we must prepare for that day. They said it was a good thing we had stayed together for as long as we had, but prepared us, saying that we were so similar as players that we would probably have to find different clubs if we were going to be professionals. Every year when Fluminense would tell some boys they weren't good enough and they wouldn't be staying, we prepared for it to be us. Luckily, we were always kept on, and we were able to keep our progression going.

The story goes that we were scouted at the Nike Cup in 2005 but John Calvert, Manchester United's South American scout, 'found' us earlier than that, when we were about 12. There were a lot of good young players in our team that he liked. There was us, Maicon Bolt, a striker, and Arthur, a centre-back. John really liked us and wanted United to take a closer look at us.

Fluminense were with Adidas. The Nike competition was just for Nike teams, so John persuaded them to change the format so the best teams could compete. It was so competitive that local teams had to play against each other to qualify. Even though John had done that for us, there was no guarantee we would qualify. Corinthians were the favourites. John was right, though – we were good enough to get through, and that enhanced our reputation locally.

We would never say we were the best players locally, or even on our team, but we were two of the best, and of course it helped us that we were twins because we were distinctive. That had helped us the entire way through. *Ah, the twins. Yeah, they're the best in the street. In the neighbourhood. In the town. In the team. The twins.* So maybe we were the best in the street, in our town. But when we arrived at Fluminense there were some amazing players. The standard was very high. So was the level of competition at the Nike Cup. If all went well, we might be offered a deal by a European club, so it was time to prepare to be without each other again.

As it turned out we didn't separate properly until January 2014, when we were 23. Although that was a very upsetting time as far as leaving Manchester United was concerned, from the perspective of us being on our own, it was a good time for us to learn to be apart.

We did more together than we expected we would, and more than anyone could have predicted. We could never have imagined we were about to be involved in one of the most successful periods in English football history.

Destination Manchester

IT'S TRUE that in 2005 our life started to change. When we were young boys we didn't ever think about leaving Brazil. But in 2005 we left the country for the first time to play in a tournament in Spain. The flight was terrible; turbulence all the way. It was the first time we ever got on a plane and it was the worst flight of our life. In Spain we were playing in a young Brazil team, but against clubs like Barcelona. This was also the first time we realised there was a different kind of pressure. There were scouts from around the world watching these games. This was a difficult tournament for us, and we didn't really do ourselves justice.

Even as a 14-year-old there is a big weight of expectation on your shoulders when you pull on the shirt of Brazil. We were probably being considered for selection anyway but it helped that Edgar Pereira was now involved with the youth selection for the country, because of how well he'd done at

Fluminense. Soon after the trip to Spain we were called up to play in a tournament in China – the Nike Cup.

The flight to Hong Kong from Brazil was twice as long as it had been to Spain. It took a full day to get there. Thankfully, the journey wasn't so bad. At the hotel they did everything to make us feel at home, so we were eating food we were familiar with and although we did go out a few times, we didn't see too much of Hong Kong – just enough to make us appreciate that this was a completely different culture and lifestyle to what we were used to. We weren't there as tourists, though. We were there to play football. Even then there was the pressure. After all, it felt as if the tournament had been changed just for our benefit, and so we had better win it or it could have been embarrassing. The tournament had even been renamed the 'Manchester United Cup', maybe because United were doing their pre-season tour in the area at the same time.

Rafael: There was an opening ceremony where all of us got to meet Eric Cantona. This was our first introduction to a man we didn't even recognise as a legend of Old Trafford. No ignorance on our part – he retired from playing before we had internet. We had one small television in the house and we were allowed to watch cartoons and that was it. We played football – we didn't watch it, unless it was Brazil who were playing. The first great French player I remembered was Zinedine

Zidane, for what he did in the 1998 World Cup against Brazil. Zidane is the greatest ever. We just had no idea what Cantona meant to football, what he meant to Manchester; of course, we would find out.

We played against Paris Saint-Germain in the first game and lost. It was so disappointing. The games were short – 20-minute halves. It was tough to get into a rhythm, to get into the game. The humidity also made it very uncomfortable. In the second game we played against a Swedish team, Brommapojkarna, and, to be honest, we were expected to defeat them comfortably. They were a good team – they qualified for the tournament, so they definitely had quality – but there was a difference between them and teams like Manchester United, Inter Milan, Arsenal, Borussia Dortmund, and ourselves. We were among the favourites. But we found it difficult in these games. Although we won – and then again against South African team Moroka Swallows – we went into our last group match against Tai Po knowing that if we didn't win we'd be out of the competition.

We have a close friend, Leonardo Barcellos. He didn't make it as a professional but he was in our Fluminense team and we sometimes joke with him that he saved our careers. We were having a dreadful game against Tai Po and were almost certain to be eliminated. The rain was pouring, our shirts were stuck to our skin and they were defending so well that everything we were trying was useless. The first half ended goalless. We've played ten, maybe 15 minutes of the second half and we can't even get a shot on goal. Nothing is coming off. We're too anxious to relax. Then Leonardo hits a long pass. Even that goes wrong. This time, though, a wrong makes a right – at least as far as we're concerned. The pass flies over the goalkeeper and into the top corner of the net. It looks like one of the greatest goals. It feels like that for us. Instantly, our mood is transformed. That goal comes so close to the end of the game and we switch into another gear, scoring two more times to win 3-0.

Okay, so maybe Leonardo didn't save our careers, but it felt like that at the time. He was very unlucky. In the next game, we play Pumas of Mexico. We put in a really good performance and win 2-0, but Leonardo was involved in a tackle in which the other boy suffered a broken leg. It's an accident; it's tough, especially when you're young, and even for the player who makes the tackle, because they have to live with it. But it was a fair challenge – which was more than could be said for the game against Estudiantes in the semi-final, a game as competitive as you can imagine for teams from Brazil and Argentina facing each other, even at that level. The aggression can cause you to lose your concentration. Not for us that day – we won 1-0 and got to the final where we played PSG, the team we lost to in the very first game.

Revenge plays on your mind, even as a kid. Again, you could do without the distraction, but this is human nature, and this wasn't a normal situation. We're playing in a tournament with some of the biggest teams in the world. You hear stories about scouts from this or that team watching you – you know for sure they're watching you in these games. It's a series of games over three or four days that has the capability of changing your entire future. It wasn't overnight, but it had gone from us being well-known in the area in which we lived, to then playing for our country, and then hearing stories about Real Madrid wanting to sign us on top of this preliminary contact we'd been having with Manchester United: the two biggest clubs in Europe. Suddenly, your friends and parents and coaches telling you how good you are feels like reassurance instead of a compliment. It was great for a while, being so distinctive and well-known because of the simple fact we are twins. But you then are *expected* to do well and that is a different feeling for a young teenager to handle. Emotionally it was tough but all of the good advice we had from our parents and brother helped us in these moments.

Before the final, John Calvert came to talk to us. He said that whatever happened, Manchester United would still like to take us on trial. We didn't know this at the time, but United were arranging a deal with Fluminense. John's words did help take the pressure away from us. We were nowhere near as tense or anxious, or concerned about making a mistake, as we had been in the first game against PSG. We won 1-0, and our performance was much better this time around.

It would be wrong to say we *expected* United to make contact. We hoped they would, and we didn't know when it would happen if it did. Within a couple of weeks of the Nike Cup ending, the relationship between the clubs was made formal and we were told that over the next few months, United might take some of us on trial.

What we did not expect was for an Arsenal representative to come in and make an offer. And they offered a lot of money – but to the wrong person. Instead of approaching Fluminense, they went straight to our dad, and he – as a man of integrity and principle – refused to discuss it with them, and said they should talk to our club instead. They might have done, but we never heard any more about it.

Rafael: I went to Manchester first. It was strange to be by myself. Well, it was me and Arthur, but it was the first time being away from my brother and my family. I think I stayed in the Lowry.

Fabio: To be honest, when he was gone, I wasn't thinking that I wished I was there. But then he came back and started to talk about it and I was desperate to go. It was crazy.

Rafael: When I first went to Manchester, they said it was for training, not for a trial. After it went well, they said they would be interested in bringing me back. I was scared, because they didn't speak about my brother. We arrived back in Brazil and the guy who was with us saw that I was worried and he said, 'It's okay, we want your brother as well. Next time you will come with him.' I was so relieved and so happy.

Fabio: From then on, it was usually all four of us. Us, Maicon Bolt and Arthur. The first day I remember walking into Carrington with John Calvert, and going straight to Sir Alex's office to meet him. I'm nodding like I understand what he is saying. John is translating everything. To be honest, I was just a little overawed by it all. But United were always showing they were keen to sign us, even when we weren't there. One day when we were back home in Brazil I got a call on my cell phone. Zero zero zero zero zero. Where the hell is this call from? It said Europe – I've never had a phone call from Europe before. 'Olá!' The voice on the other end is friendly but unfamiliar. 'It is Cristiano!' I thought somebody was taking the piss. Sir Alex has convinced Cristiano Ronaldo to call us to tell us to come to Manchester. Cristiano had been on holiday to Rio a few times so was comfortable speaking Brazilian Portuguese – we didn't know any other language, we hadn't even started learning English yet.

When we were in England, every morning, Ruud van Nistelrooy would make sure he welcomed us. 'Bom dia!' For a professional to show that sort of attention was great, but Ruud was bigger than just a professional, he was one of the greats. Perhaps he'd been told to be friendly, like Cristiano, but the impression we got was that their welcomes were genuine. They had been in our position once, as young players moving to this big club in a different country.

Manchester United are known as a club who bring through their own players, most of them local. When we were on trial, there were so many players there who went on to become well-known in England. Danny Welbeck, Fraizer Campbell, Danny Drinkwater, Tom Cleverley. Febian Brandy was also very helpful to us and went out of his way to help us settle. We were popular boys in Brazil, well-liked by our team-mates, and fortunately we would become well-liked in Manchester, too. But not everybody was welcoming. The Eckersley brothers – local players, full-backs themselves – smashed us at every single opportunity they got. Welcome to Manchester. It wasn't exactly hate, but they weren't happy with us being there, and that was only natural. It sometimes felt like they wanted to kill us.

When it comes to talent – pure talent – then the players we played with in Brazil were just as good as those at United. Probably better in a lot of cases. But what we found in England was discipline and hard work. Full-backs, for example. They stayed in position much more often in England. Even at 16. In Brazil, you're up and down the byline, you just want to assist or score goals. In England they're in position, defending first. One of the first things you notice is that everyone is working as hard as they possibly can to make the most of the opportunity they have.

As soon as we had a taste of Manchester it felt very serious. We went on trial, we went to train, we signed contracts there – it was never a case of going there for a holiday. This was an opportunity at one of the world's biggest clubs and we were not going to use that chance just to go sightseeing or clothes shopping. That competitive spirit came out again. We wanted to prove that we belonged. That we could contribute.

We didn't speak English when we first arrived but it was easy to tell that Paul McGuinness, the youth team coach, was going to be very important for us, just as important as the manager in those early days. Everything he said, John Calvert translated for us. The messages were brilliant. We would always be challenged to do something. After coming off the training pitch exhausted following the morning sessions, Paul would ask, 'Right boys, time for some technical training?' And we would be enthusiastic, hiding our tiredness. 'Of course!' Everything they asked, we said yes. It didn't matter what it was. Yes, we would do it. We were desperate to impress them.

Even if we didn't want to do it, even if we were tired. Yes, every time. We needed to impress at every opportunity. We didn't want it to look like we couldn't do it.

Fabio: We would get included in first team training. The very first session, my very first involvement, I can remember it like it was yesterday. I played a lot of video games when I was younger. I lost count of how many times I had played as, and played against, Rio Ferdinand, Ryan Giggs, Wayne Rooney, Cristiano, all of these wonderful players on the video games. Here they were in the flesh. I was actually playing with them. First moment. The ball is coming towards me in the air. Paul Scholes is coming towards me on the ground. He's giving me a welcome like the Eckersley brothers – he's letting me know that I shouldn't expect to take it easy. This is my first touch – the truth is, I didn't know what to do, I almost froze. But the ball bounced on to my foot, a perfect bounce, and it goes over his head. I instinctively move to pass it. It looks like the most amazing piece of skill. Everyone goes wild – I can remember Rio screaming at it. The truth is, it's a complete accident! I was lucky Scholes didn't smash into me.

It was so competitive at United then. All the way through the club. The first team was becoming the best in England again but the reserve side was also very talented – Gerard Piqué and

Jonny Evans in defence, Fraizer Campbell and Giuseppe Rossi up front scoring lots of goals. The youth team – the team we would have been playing in if we were allowed – got to the FA Youth Cup final in 2007. It was a very strong time. The reason we weren't allowed to play was because we were from Brazil and didn't turn 18 until July 2008, so United were doing whatever they could to get us registered and playing as soon as possible. That included looking into getting Portuguese passports, and we were open to that, although truthfully – even though we might have said differently when we were younger – we always really wanted to play for Brazil. That was our country, that was our place. Our dad would not have been happy.

United proved they were willing to wait when they made a deal with Fluminense to sign us in February 2007. We were represented by Cassiano Pereira, an agent who, to be truthful, is more of a friend now. He had our best interests at heart and, as a businessman, knew how to deal with negotiations. United did not offer the biggest wages then – it was probably less than what Arsenal had offered – but it was much more than what we were used to in Brazil.

Rafael: I can remember the reaction of my parents when we were all told of the offer. They leaned back in their chairs – it was hilarious, like one of those WTF? memes – because they were so stunned. It wasn't just the money, it was the commitment for a period of time, the commitment to moving. It was an offer that would change the life of our family.

Fabio: We were like, 'Sign, sign!' But Cassiano is cool and says, 'No, you are interesting the top clubs, Real Madrid, Arsenal, they can offer more.' He was looking after us – but he knew that we were desperate to sign, and would have signed for the offer that was given, so he worked it out with United.

A couple of weeks after we signed that contract, we played in the South American Under-17 Championship in Ecuador. Our team was very good. We had Alex Teixeira and our club-mate Maicon Bolt with us but the player every single one of us thought was destined to be brilliant was Lulinha. At Fluminense there was a player called Walandy who we shared the same expectation about. Every generation has them – Brazil always seems to have several.

Rafael: Lulinha scored 12 goals but because my brother scored seven, and was a full-back, everyone gave a lot of attention to him. And he deserved it. For me, I defended more often, and in Brazil, if a player spends more time defending than attacking – even if you're a defender! – then it can be a negative thing. They think you are not so good.

Fabio: But without you providing the security, shape and balance in defence, I do not have the freedom to run basically like a left-winger, and score all those goals. One cannot happen without the other. It is right, the reputations of the more defensive players suffer, but it isn't necessarily fair.

Before we played in the Eight Nations tournament in South Korea – which was a warm-up event for the Under-17 World Cup there a few weeks later – we had a new coach, Luis Antonio Nizzo. We won the Eight Nations, on penalties against Nigeria, but it didn't feel the same as with Edgar Pereira. We had such a special relationship with him. Nizzo wasn't a bad coach – it was just different. When we went back to Ecuador to play in the Pan American games a couple of weeks after the Eight Nations it was clear our travelling was catching up with us. Against the host nation we tired in the second half, conceding three goals and losing 4-2. We were knocked out in the group stage.

We had another long flight back to South Korea for the Under-17 World Cup in August. It started well. We won 7-0 against New Zealand and 6-1 against North Korea. That was not reflective of the quality in this competition. England had Danny Welbeck, who we knew now from spending time with him at United. Belgium had Eden Hazard in their squad.

Germany had the brilliant Toni Kroos. Spain's squad included David de Gea and Pedro. We came up against Ghana in the round of 16. This squad featured no players who would go on to earn a full international cap but it seemed as if they were all taller than us, faster, stronger, with more energy on the day. They beat us 1-0. Maybe they were better – maybe we were exhausted. Maybe it was the new coach. No excuses. We should have done better. It was embarrassing.

Rafael: Both of us are pretty poor losers, but I'm worse. We were tired but the first thing you want to do is to play football again to win and make it better.

As soon as we returned to Fluminense, though, we discovered they had changed their mind about the deal with Manchester United. They weren't happy with it – maybe they wanted more money. They can't break the deal, though. So the solution is that we can't train or play until we go to Manchester, which is almost a year away. This is a crazy and frustrating time for us. Since the age of 11, the maximum time we have spent without being around competitive football either in games or in training has been a month. It was confusing for us – all we wanted to do was play. We never held back, we'd give our all for Fluminense if only we were allowed to. The politics of transfers has little to do with us; we were just kids.

It is strange, because we started writing this story in the summer of 2020, at a time when the coronavirus has forced many countries around the world to quarantine, and almost all of sport stopped. This was a familiar feeling for us, but it was unwelcome. There are things in life and in sport you cannot help. In football you get injuries and suspensions and miss games. This is normal. It is not normal to be in the situation where you are fit and willing to play, and there is nothing stopping you, but you can't.

We loved our time with Fluminense but it is clear this wasn't the best way for things to end. We maintained contact and communication with Manchester United and when Fluminense made it clear we wouldn't be considered to play, the clubs agreed that we could go to Manchester in January 2008, a few months before our contract started. It wasn't a good thing to miss football but we did have the opportunity to prepare to move to England as a family which was a good thing.

Fabio: I had been with my girlfriend Barbara since I was 15 and she was 14. We were very close and I couldn't think of moving to Manchester without her coming too. So I had to talk to her father – and as a 17-year-old, you can imagine how scary that was, to tell her father that I wanted to move thousands of miles away, take his little girl halfway across the world. I can imagine how I would react in his position. I explained how I felt about her, that my family was going to be there too. Eventually he said he would consider it. It was not an easy decision for him, but he said he would allow it if Barbara and I got married.

He was concerned about the lifestyle footballers have. He thought about the reputation that comes with more money, and the idea of more girls being interested. But, if I could commit to marrying his daughter, he would see how serious I was, and she would also have some security in case anything did go wrong. I was happy to do that, not just because it would mean that we could go to Manchester together, but because I did, and do, love her and I wanted to spend my life with her. It was important to me to get her father's blessing because of the respect I have for him, and I think by going through with getting married, even though we were so young, I earned his respect too.

Rafael: Because all of our family were going to move to Manchester, it meant we had started to already fulfil our ambition of providing for our parents. They could move with us and they wouldn't have to work. We were so proud of this but one thing we didn't realise was how deeply that would affect our dad, for a long time, and not in a good way. Because he is so proud, because he worked every single day of his life, and because of the sacrifice he has given for us to progress with our life, he found the idea of his young sons providing for him very difficult and even embarrassing. In fact, for a while, he was so down that I don't think it is exaggerating to say he was depressed. It was difficult for us to understand – a time when we were so excited, and he was excited for us, but for different reasons.

As a football lover, he was so proud that we were going to play for one of the world's biggest clubs. But he struggled to reconcile that with the reality of going to Manchester and not having to work to support and provide for his family. In fact, he refused to. We had to talk to the club about it because he felt so strongly. United offered him a job as a groundskeeper at Carrington. I think that made him feel much better; the funny thing was, he didn't even take the job because of the language barrier, but I do think having the option made him feel much more comfortable and accepting of the situation.

When we arrived in Manchester in January 2008, we hadn't played any football for almost five months. We were going to have to learn to kick a ball again – not exactly the best preparation when you're going to play for one of the world's biggest clubs!

Rafa – Out of Nowhere

EVERYTHING CHANGED so quickly after we moved to Manchester. It was not normal. I couldn't have predicted anything because it was crazier than anyone could have expected. Playing your first few games as a professional for the team who are champions of their country, champions of Europe, in some of the most high-intensity occasions. I can honestly say it is only when taking the time to reflect that I can truly appreciate how mad it all was. All of what I'm about to tell you happened before I could even speak the language I'm writing in to deliver the story!

We arrived in January 2008. My brothers and their wives, my mother and father. The club helped us settle into the area and not long after that, Rodrigo Possebon, who signed in the summer, stayed with us too. What can I say about the way the club helped us to settle? It felt like they did everything for us, sometimes it felt like it was only for us – maybe it was just typical of the way they helped every young player in our situation, but right from the start we were made to feel special. I can say that in those early days, the biggest reason for that was the personal help of John Calvert and Paul McGuinness. John was always there to explain and translate. I'm sure Paul worked more hours than he was supposed to just to help us. He was like a personal coach to us. We trained with the first team, sometimes – not all of the time, because they were playing in some big games. We trained with the reserve team, sometimes, but again, not all of the time, because we couldn't play. But then Paul also had extra sessions with us, and he always had the energy and enthusiasm for it as well.

Sometimes it felt like a test. He would ask my brother and me at lunch if we wanted to train in the afternoon, at 3pm. We'd know from the way he was asking that he didn't just want us to say yes, he wanted us to be as enthusiastic as he was. And maybe he wasn't enthusiastic himself, but it always seemed like he was. Because of that, even if we were tired, we became excited again to get back out there and work. I know that Paul was testing us. If we even *looked* reluctant, it might be something that would count against us. The sessions with Paul were always fun, and always competitive.

I don't have a memory like my brother of the first time I trained with the first team. But we had a few friendly games at Carrington – in the training sessions before we arrived permanently – and in the very first game I played really well and made an impression. I was told that some of the players in the senior dressing room had been talking, and that Gary Neville in particular was really angry. So I asked John, and he told me that Gary had been complaining that I'd been brought over to retire him! John was happy when he said it – so maybe it was a joke, maybe it was serious – but I remember feeling fantastic when he told me. Gary is a legend of Manchester United and he still had plenty to give at that time. I might only have been 16 when that game happened – but it was a huge boost for me.

We had already experienced most of life in Manchester before moving there. We went to Old Trafford regularly to watch the games – I think the first one I saw was against West Ham. Ruud van Nistelrooy scored. It was his last goal at Old Trafford. I can remember the atmosphere being incredible. I know people have criticised the noise there but my first few experiences of it were great. By the time I was playing regularly, the fans were used to United winning all the time. They came for the show – they knew it would finish 3- or 4-0 to United. So maybe the critics have a point. But there were some occasions when the supporters created an atmosphere like I've never heard in my life.

Ruud and the manager had a falling-out and one of the best strikers in the world moved to Real Madrid. But

United continued to get better. They were getting 70,000 in every week even without winning the league title, and to be around it when they became champions again – I was the most excited guy in the world. I would imagine playing there. I can remember saying to John when we were watching a game, 'I'm going to play on this pitch!'

John was good with his own predictions. We weren't in Manchester for the Champions League semi-final against Milan in 2007, but we watched it on television. I can't remember exactly where we were, but John was with us and said after the game, 'Look, United will be in the final next season, don't worry.' This wasn't an easy prediction. I don't think it was as obvious as John's confidence made it sound. But there was something in the way he said it which made me believe him. And when we arrived in Manchester permanently, Cristiano Ronaldo had become even better, scoring goals for fun. Seeing the guys up close in training, I shared John's belief that they would get to the final at least.

I feel so lucky that we came when we did because of the things we experienced before we even played. We would normally sit in the family stand or the directors' box for home games, but there were so many people there for the semi-final against Barcelona in 2008 that we had to find a place high up in the North Stand. I can still see Scholesy's brilliant shot flying into the net. I can remember the last 20 minutes was so strange

– the crowd was quiet, but in a weird way because the game was so close and tense. No one was thinking about shouting. It was as if they were too scared to make a sound. But we got through to the final in Moscow – it was the best game I've ever watched. Maybe it was the sense of occasion, the fact that there were two teams at the top of their game playing so well.

It reminded me of the 1994 World Cup Final between Brazil and Italy. You might not think of these as obvious choices. But the intensity of the Champions League Final was stunning to witness. Maybe the weather helped! It was raining so bad. But to see two teams working so hard, knowing that those conditions make every mistake worse. The standard, for me, was amazing. For occasion, the Brazil 1994 game matched it, but for quality, United – Chelsea was even better. For United to win it was perfect.

Well, in one way, at least. It was great to be at the club that had just won the Champions League. But after the game I was left with another thought, which wasn't so positive. How can I ever get into this team? Gary Neville was still there. Wes Brown was the right-back in the game and he had provided the assist for Cristiano's goal. John O'Shea could also play there. These were the senior players – and we've already mentioned how competitive the reserve team was.

That summer we were finally able to start playing again and we were in the reserve team dressing room. We had mostly kept to ourselves before then – we were as sociable as we could be with the language barrier. When Rodrigo arrived it helped us a lot and I think us being there helped him too. We could be natural around each other. It was difficult to be natural around guys like Cristiano and even Anderson. Ando would talk to us, but he was a big player in the first team, so we were a little bit scared – of course, we'd talk to him, but we were treating him with so much respect that we didn't even laugh and joke with him. We were just young, and we listened and were mostly quiet. It was different when Rodrigo came because he was at the same stage as us. And he was a player with a lot of qualities that you don't see in many players. I haven't seen many players who are able to strike the ball as well with both feet in the same way that Rodrigo could.

We were all picked in the squad to play a friendly against Peterborough close to the start of the season. My brother and Rodrigo were on the bench. I was picked to start. I can remember every single minute of that game. I got cramp but I played through it – there was no way I was going to come off. I can't express how desperate I was to impress everyone. You're trying your hardest, trying tricks. It's difficult, I admit, to play in a foreign country where you don't understand the language and you are told to just go out and enjoy yourself. But I did. And I know that I played well, I could feel that myself, but it was a fantastic surprise to hear everyone giving compliments after the game. The biggest one came from the gaffer – John told me that Sir Alex had told the press that I was 'sensational'. What do you say to that? Well, what I said to John was, 'See, John, I told you! I'm going to play for Manchester United!'

That was a bit of a joke, just the way that John and I talk to each other. But honestly, that game was the time I began to believe I really *could* play for United. I was feeling even better because people were praising my brother for the way he played when he came on, but almost straight after that he injured his shoulder and that meant he was going to be out of the team for some months. I was so sad for him. I was certain that he would have been with me and Rodrigo on the bench against Portsmouth in the Community Shield.

Most people see that as just a game. For us it was a medal – a chance to win a medal in my first game with the European champions. This was United's first match after winning that trophy and we were in the squad. I dreamed of coming on but maybe it came too soon – we had a bit of an injury problem at the club at the time and maybe that's why we got on the bench. Gary Neville started and he came off for Wes Brown. I got a winner's medal, because we won on penalties, but I didn't get on the pitch.

A week later, I was on the bench again for the first league game against Newcastle, and this time I did get on. As a winger! I'd never played in this position in my life. It was 1-1, there were ten minutes left and we needed to win. I can't remember what Sir Alex Ferguson said to me – I couldn't speak English, so I'd be lying if I said I could (though even when I could, it wasn't always easy to understand him!) – but I do remember him trying to say something. Probably something like, 'Enjoy!' Carlos Queiroz was a little more specific, 'Play forward, try to be creative, let's play.'

I wasn't expecting to come on and those ten minutes just went by so quickly. It was really hard to try and make an impression. We drew. I had conflicting emotions – I was of course happy to have played, but also frustrated because we didn't win, and concerned that I might not have done so well because I didn't win the game for us. When it is your first game you worry in a way that is not in proportion. It was a few weeks until I played for the first team again.

There were big matches I missed, although I could not have even expected to be selected for them so soon. It wasn't a great start to the season for us. We lost to Zenit Saint Petersburg in the European Super Cup, then in the league we lost at Anfield and drew at Stamford Bridge. At Chelsea, Cristiano came back from an injury which had kept him out at the start of the season – it was obvious we needed him. And it was obvious we needed to improve our form. Against

Middlesbrough in the League Cup, Sir Alex picked a stronger team than he usually did.

Before that game, I'd been playing in the reserves for a few weeks. The coach at that level was Ole Gunnar Solskjaer. I didn't spend as much time with him as my brother would go on to do, but I can say that I learned a lot from the experience. Ole is a good guy and a very good coach. He's also a very good man-manager. He knows how to deal with players. As a person, he's even better.

It was five weeks between my first appearance and the game against Middlesbrough, which was my first start. Maybe it helped that I had a little time to prepare and I was in my normal position, but I played well. We won 3-1, and I watched the game back many times because I wanted to see how I contributed. There was one moment I did not enjoy watching back. In the second half, Rodrigo – who was also starting for the first time – was the victim of a crazy tackle by the Middlesbrough player Emanuel Pogatetz. The result was a broken leg which would keep him out for a few months.

The impact is bigger than a few months, though. This was a reminder that talent is only a part of football. You need opportunity and you need luck, just as much as you need hard work and the natural ability. Opportunity – the injury crisis at United had given chances for me and Rodrigo to play in the team who were the best in Europe. Luck – well, just ask my brother, who would surely have benefitted from that opportunity if he hadn't been injured himself just before the season started. This was only the start of our time at Old Trafford, but who knows what sort of impact it had on our long-term futures there? I'm not the sort of person who would get scared or worried that the same thing might happen to me, but everything was moving so fast anyway that there wasn't time to worry.

My performance was enough to earn me a start in United's first European game of the season. I lined up alongside Rio Ferdinand, Nemanja Vidić and Patrice Evra. I came off with cramp in the second half and that's probably because I was so tense! It was not my best performance, I admit, though it wasn't too bad, and we won 3-0 so, really, it was perfect. Was I nervous about the match, playing for United, playing in Europe? Maybe. But I was just as nervous playing alongside these defenders.

Looking back, it seems funny, because I don't know why it was a problem. Today we are friends and I can talk to them with no problems, but as an 18-year-old, I can remember thinking, 'Fuck, this is crazy. These guys are the best defenders in the world. You have to do good, here. You have no choice.' Those were my thoughts before and after the game. When the whistle blew, it was different, and I was able to switch that off and concentrate on the game.

Rio was a big help. He played on the right side of the centre and so he was the player I was next to. From day one, Rio was the teacher, the professor. He was the master. I can't speak highly enough about how he helped me get through not only that game but all of my early matches. He knew my English was limited – I was trying – so he kept it simple:

'Right!'

'Left!'

'Go!'

'Stay!'

These were straightforward instructions. But they were coming from someone who was one of the best defenders in the world – one of his areas of expertise was timing. I was too young to even appreciate that, but old enough to trust in what he was saying.

Against Aalborg I came off for Wes Brown. Our start to the season was getting better and we were winning games convincingly now that some of the players were coming back from injury. Our squad was incredible and there were very few positions that the manager would not rotate. Maybe when fit Rio, Nemanja and Patrice would definitely start, and Cristiano was the best player in the world so of course he would, too. When I played against West Ham at home we didn't have Michael Carrick, Paul Scholes or Ryan Giggs in the team, and Michael Carrick and Wayne Rooney came off the bench. This United team had no problem scoring goals but we had added Dimitar Berbatov to the squad – a very different player to Wayne, Cristiano or Carlos Tevez. Tevez and Rooney, they ran everywhere. Berbatov, it's true, he didn't run. He just had the quality. Everyone knows about how good his first touch was. I don't think he got the credit he deserved for the timing of his passing.

What Berba did to West Ham was crazy. He didn't have the space to do it! There was no room. It was against logic. But he brings the ball down on the byline and turns the defender. I couldn't believe what I was watching. Look, I'm used to seeing outrageous skills. I'm from Brazil. The skill itself is not extraordinary. It is the ability to do it in a game like that at Old Trafford and make it look like a training session. But even then it means little without the goal. You need a goal. And he gets it – he is still calm and rolls the ball across for Cristiano to score. It was unbelievable.

It left an impression on me. Years later, when I was in training at Lyon, one of the boys showed a similar piece of skill, but we didn't score from it. I had to pull up the video of Berba right away to show him afterwards.

At the time, because I was so young and inexperienced, and because these things were happening so fast, maybe I didn't feel as if I was qualified to talk about them. It's only now, looking back, that I do. And in a funny way I was in the same position as Berba – trying to break into this great team by showing what I could bring. We needed a player like Berba because of the different qualities he had which nobody else possessed.

It was difficult for him because of how popular the other forwards were. I will say right from the start, however, that I did not really get on with Carlos Tevez. Or maybe I should say that it seemed he had a problem with me and it started from there. I don't know what it was – maybe he had an Argentina/Brazil thing – but at the start it seemed like he wasn't very good around young players. Then it seemed like it was personal. I felt like he didn't respect me. The way he would talk to me on the pitch wasn't nice. I wasn't going to answer back. I was so young and so new, and he was an established player. You don't talk back. These days, young players do stand up for themselves more. They won't stay quiet – and good for them. For me, I felt like staying quiet was the way to get through it. I definitely didn't want trouble and I didn't want to upset anyone.

He was fairly popular in the dressing room – I know Patrice liked him a lot; Cristiano talked to him, too. I never knew why he didn't like me, I didn't talk with him away from the pitch, and we just kept out of each other's way when we weren't playing. On the pitch, look, he was one of the greatest forwards in the world. He was technically fantastic and scored some great goals. It just felt like he would go out of his way to be critical about what I was doing – which was very different from the support I would receive from everyone else.

So I was trying to keep myself to myself and be as positive as possible. But you can't afford to hide at United, and every single week seemed to present a brand new, difficult challenge. My sixth game for the club was against Celtic in Scotland. Wow. Now there was a crowd that didn't seem to like any of us. They were wild – but wild in the way that you thought they might go crazy and smash everything up, especially when Giggsy scored to equalise in the last few minutes to get a draw.

A few days later I was on the bench against another team whose fans didn't like us very much. Those Arsenal supporters were happy with their players, though, who were winning 2-0. I came on for Gary Neville with 30 minutes or so to go. We needed a hero – maybe if I'd come on ten minutes earlier! I scored a goal in injury time, and even though we still lost, everyone remembers it because it was a nice strike. I took the ball on the chest and hit a clean volley with my left foot into the corner. It brought no reward for my team, but for me personally, I think it was the moment when I became a genuine first team contender.

I'd done okay in my performances – but to be fair, I hadn't played very well at Celtic, and perhaps I needed a big moment to 'arrive'. Maybe, before, I had been selected because of injuries or rotation, but I had been given this chance against Arsenal and had done very well. Every game for Manchester United is a big game, but some are bigger than others. To play in one of the biggest and have an impact: it was a moment that caused people to talk about me. 'Oh, he scored a goal, maybe he could be a Manchester United player.' Other people start to believe it. *I* start to believe it.

I think my performance did as much good for me as my goal, though. Everyone saw my attitude, how desperate I was to win. I remember running like crazy in that game, tackling everything that was in front of me. A lot of people asked me why I didn't celebrate the goal – but I was brought on to try and win the game for us. I still hoped there was time for us to get an equaliser so there was no time to waste. You are playing for yourself, yes, but you are playing for your team-mates and for your supporters who all want you to win the game. This was my personal attitude, and it was clear that the United fans appreciated it too. That was just a happy coincidence.

After the game, I must have watched the goal a hundred times!

It was a strange moment in my life. Suddenly there was a level of expectation about me. Up until this point I had been an unknown player, able to just play my natural game. Now, everybody in England knew who I was. I watched my matches back and it was easy to see after that Arsenal game that things were changing – I was thinking too much about what I was doing, and I'm sure my performances were not as good for a while. Nobody at the club was putting any pressure on me at all. They were happy for me to carry on doing what I was doing. But I was putting pressure on myself, asking myself if I was doing the things that people expected. Asking what it was that they were expecting. And I was 18, doing something not many people have ever done.

Plenty of teenagers have played for Manchester United. That's part of their history. Not many of them would have played their first games for the club just after they won the European Cup, coming from another country. Only my brother and Rodrigo could understand that – and only my brother understood how strange it was to be doing this after not being able to play any games for a year! You can call it a dream, and it was, but it was also literally like a dream. It was surreal. These were my first games as a professional footballer and they were some of the biggest you can play in football. You play for Manchester United at Old Trafford, play for them with the best player in the world, play for them in the Champions League, play at Celtic, play at Arsenal and score at Arsenal. It wasn't until I played at Celtic that I moved from the reserve team dressing room into the first team. And when I did, the club were already talking to me about a new contract – five months after we officially signed.

It all happened so quickly. And now, when I look back, I appreciate how mad that all was; but because I was so young, before I could really understand it, I felt like the pressure was physically impacting my form.

It didn't stop me enjoying it, or trying to make the most of the opportunity. In my 14th appearance I played in an occasion that would be seen as the highest moment in club competition for any Brazilian player. The Club World Cup tournament in Japan was very special for me. When it comes around, if a Brazilian team gets to the final then it is a real opportunity to show how good you are against the best in Europe. I mean, it is called the Club World Cup – and that's how seriously we treat it. It's difficult to even compare because in Brazil there isn't an equivalent to the Champions League, and then you have this tournament which feels like a level above it. So it was a real dream come true for me when I was selected to play against the Ecuadorian team Liga de Quito in the 2008 final.

To win it? Well, such a trophy is the pinnacle of a club career. It is something you work your entire life to achieve, and if you get there once it is amazing. In our team there was Edwin van der Sar who was 38 and he had won the trophy when it was known as the Intercontinental Cup. Rio was 30. These players had worked and won league titles before they won the Champions League. I won a medal the first time

I was in a United squad – maybe you don't want to count the Community Shield, but after 14 games, to become the best team in the world? Wow. It was a good memory in the middle of that difficult run of form. And it wasn't an easy game – Nemanja was sent off in the second half when it was still 0-0, but we kept our discipline at the back and Rooney scored quite late on to win the trophy. The trip to Japan was extremely memorable.

The games back home were tough. We played at home, either side of the Club World Cup trip, against Sunderland and Middlesbrough and we were made to work extremely hard for 1-0 wins. Maybe that's why I found them less enjoyable. I do remember that things started to feel better after we came back to the UK and I don't doubt that a large part of my own mood improved by my brother's return from his injury. He started to play in reserve games and I would go and watch them all – and he was making an impression. Rodrigo had also recovered much more quickly than people expected and was playing in January.

Fabio had worked very hard to get back and I'm sure it was difficult for him. But he never said that to me. He never complained. I'm sure it was hard for him to watch me getting this opportunity but he was always so supportive. It wasn't just that he came back from his injury. It was that when he played in those reserve games, he was playing amazingly, scoring goals – scoring hat-tricks! I could feel that he would be joining me soon in the first team because he was doing better than I was in the reserves. His first chance came soon after he came back, against Tottenham in the FA Cup. He played so well in that game.

One reason why United were so good at this time was because we had this perfect blend of young players, players at their peak who were among the best in the world, and players of ultimate experience. I played against one in training every day: Ryan Giggs. He was 35, had played more times for United than anyone, ever, and won more trophies in England than anyone, ever. Every single day he was coming at me, targeting me, wanting to attack me. I can't tell you how hard it was to defend against him.

Ryan was like Scholesy and Rooney. They're strange – they like and want you to tackle them. The reason why? They want to tackle you back. It's like they live for it. You can't go into a challenge against any of these guys and think you're going to tackle and get away with the ball. You know you're going to have to challenge and fight every single time. In the end they made me just like them. It became a key part of my quality as a player. No ball was ever lost as far as they were concerned. Football is not just getting the ball, dribbling and scoring amazing goals – and these three players were experts at doing that as well. I know that these training sessions shaped me as a player. It is a part of English culture, or Manchester United culture. Many years after this, when I was playing for Lyon, I made a tackle that I would make every morning at Carrington. Red card! Clearly they weren't used to that in France.

That season, out of all the world stars we had in our team, Giggsy was voted player of the year. He scored a goal at West Ham when he went around three or four of their players. I remember watching that from the other side of the pitch and feeling some sympathy for those guys who had to deal with what I faced every morning.

It seemed as if this season might even be better than United's last one. We got to the League Cup Final – I played in all of the games on the way there. In the first leg of the semi-final against Derby County we lost 1-0. Afterwards Sir Alex came into the dressing room. Many swear words – the message was that the young players would have to play in the second leg and put it right. He was right. We could play much better than we did in that game. We did – we won 4-2 to get to the final. And then most of the same kids played again because we were drawn against them in the FA Cup! We scored four in that game too. I had picked up an injury in the second game against Derby – I went to cross the ball and hit the advertising boards, and I had to come off before half-time – but I was desperate to keep my place in the team so I played through it for a couple of weeks. I even played the full game against Blackburn in February but afterwards it was obvious I needed some time out. I needed to wear a foot brace – naturally, I started to worry I'd done more damage by trying to play through it. I couldn't walk.

I missed a crucial part of the season and I was devastated. The match after Blackburn was against Inter Milan in the San Siro. The Champions League had resumed and now John O'Shea was the first choice as we won against Inter and then Porto in the quarter-final. John was a fantastic player and a brilliant professional. He had lots of experience so maybe he would have been selected ahead of me anyway – but I was sure I would have played at least some part of the League Cup Final because I'd played in all of the games before. We won that on penalties. Great for us, and I was happy, but also very sad not to play.

But when I was back in the team, I was delighted that Fabio was there too. In a year in which many great things happened, one of the best was playing with my brother for United for the first time. What an occasion to do it – the FA Cup semi-final against Everton at Wembley. The game did not live up to the occasion, however. It finished 0-0 – we should have won, but we lost on penalties. Before the game everybody was speaking about the great future of Manchester United because Sir Alex was going to play me and my brother, and also Darron Gibson, Danny Welbeck and Kiko Macheda. It might have been one of the youngest teams to ever play a semi-final. Despite our nerves and inexperience, we were the better team.

Injuries could have ruined the season for us. Kiko was in the team because he'd kept things alive. Against Aston Villa a couple of weeks earlier we'd had so many players out; Rio, Nemanja, Rooney, Berba, Scholesy. Kiko came on in the second half and won the game with a great goal that everyone still remembers to this day, and will remember for many years to come. He will remember it for all of his life. Kiko's goal was seen as a turning point but Liverpool were still chasing us for the title. We couldn't afford to slip up.

Against Spurs at home we were 2-0 down at half-time. This time, the manager was so angry I couldn't understand anything he said. But the message was clear enough to pass through any language barrier.

The atmosphere in the second half was something I'd never experienced before. The nervousness from the fans was something we could feel. All of our star attackers were back fit and on the pitch at the same time. Cristiano, Rooney, Berba, Tevez. Ten minutes of the second half went by and we couldn't get a breakthrough – until Michael Carrick was brought down and won a penalty. Cristiano took it: 2-1. WHOOSH. The noise from the crowd – it was like a tidal wave. Forget about tactics now. Forget about trying to communicate with other players on the pitch: that was no good. It was so loud. Rooney scored the equaliser. A few seconds later, Cristiano scored again. We were winning – the fans were going crazy; they knew nothing would stop us winning. I came off after that third goal and I don't even think I'd sat down before Rooney scored the fourth. We won 5-2.

I've never played in a game like that. And when I say it's something I develop a greater appreciation for as time goes on, I mean it. I still couldn't speak or read English. I didn't understand what I was watching on television. It seemed like my existence was only to train and to play football and to be with my family – which was no bad thing, but, it separated me from the awareness of just how important this period was in Manchester United's history. I didn't know just how close we were to having the best season the club had ever had. I hadn't realised when we'd lost on penalties to Everton. It was just as well – trying to take in what was happening in the moment was difficult enough.

My return to the first team was marked with the confirmation of the new contract that had been suggested five months earlier. I had also been nominated for the PFA Young Player of the Year award. But even that was not as great an honour as the manager saying that he thought I was a 'typical Manchester United player'. Of course it is a compliment that means so much to me, because of who said it and why he was saying it. But for me it was even greater because I didn't invent myself to be this way; there was no manipulation. I didn't change. I was the way I was, I played the way I always did, and for that way to be considered a natural fit for Manchester United was a wonderful feeling.

I felt like I had a chance of getting into the team when we played at Arsenal in the second leg of the Champions League semi-final. I was training really hard and I know I was being considered, but in the end, the manager kept faithful to John, and I could definitely understand that. He had the experience, he had played in the knockout games and he'd even scored in the first leg – it was a good decision by Sir Alex, even though I was disappointed.

When I think of that game I have one memory. We were winning 3-0 and I came on for the last part of the game. Ten minutes later, Darren Fletcher was sent off for a foul on Cesc Fabregas. He'd miss the final. We won at Arsenal, and with one of the best performances of that team. Cristiano scored two of the greatest goals. I speak as someone who watched that first hour from the bench and I feel sure I can say it was a historic game. And yet afterwards there was just this heavy, tremendous sadness in the dressing room. Some of the players were devastated for Fletch. I spoke of Cristiano, I spoke of Ryan, but Fletch played as well as anyone did for us that season. We all loved him. He wasn't just a great player but he was the nicest guy. It's one thing if it was a deserved red card – but it wasn't. It would be an important miss for us against Barcelona in Rome.

We had taken Arsenal apart. Cristiano's goals were just outstanding – the free kick, the breakaway goal. They were normal for him, however. That counter-attack goal was one we scored often against Arsenal. I don't know what it was about them, and we definitely didn't win every time we played against them, but when we did – and maybe I shouldn't say this so bluntly – it was *easy*. It was strange. Games at Manchester United, just like the training sessions, were so competitive. Against Arsenal it was usually comfortable. We could enjoy ourselves.

A couple of weeks later we played against them in our last home match – all we had to do was avoid defeat to win the league. We drew 0-0. Champions, in our first season with Manchester United. Personally I felt so happy that I had been able to contribute by playing in so many games. I felt a real part of it. There were so many players who could say the same that year, even if they only played once or twice. Kiko for example scored two winning goals in his first two games for the club. We needed that just as much as we needed the defenders and goalkeeper who broke defensive records for consecutive clean sheets – as much as we needed the best player in the world. And because all of those contributions had a value, I could feel that I had made an impression as well.

Even so, I had accepted that I probably wouldn't get to play in the Champions League Final against Barcelona. The manager only let us know the day before the game but I knew John had played really well and deserved to play. Sir Alex used the examples of Paul Scholes and Park Ji-sung – who had missed previous finals but had been able to play again. He said he was sure my time would come again. I was comforted by that at the time – being part of this team made you think you would be in this position for many years to come. When he said it, I realised that just one year before I had not even played a professional game. I wasn't even allowed to train in Brazil. Now here I was, a Premier League champion, a world champion at club level, and my disappointment was not playing in the Champions League Final. I could appreciate that it was an achievement to be proud of to even be on the bench.

Then the whistle blows to start the game and this right-back is sitting as a substitute, certain that he can make the difference and change the game if only he is given the chance. I'm sure even Tomasz Kuszczak, our substitute goalkeeper, is thinking the same, especially when we let in an early goal. It is natural. Every single player is thinking like that. Maybe the one player who could say that truthfully is Fletch. I can see how that game is completely different with him on the pitch. I know everyone has said that over the years – and if we think like that, imagine what it is like for Darren? Maybe it is his biggest 'what if' in football – if only he had been on the pitch, Manchester United could have won the Champions League for the second year in a row.

This was a brilliant Barcelona team. They were so good; Lionel Messi, Andres Iniesta, Xavi. I loved to watch that style of football if you play it like Barcelona could. The players were so good that every passage of play had the intention of scoring a goal. Anybody who enjoys football can love and appreciate that. Many teams play tiki-taka with the aim of ball retention in their own half. In that circumstance tiki-taka means nothing – it's pointless. Of course, it's much easier when you have the best players in the world playing it. You can try and play an attacking version of tiki-taka and if you don't have the players to break between the lines it can also come to nothing. But Barcelona did have those players. And Messi scored the second to kill the game off.

I watched that game thinking, and feeling – and this is something I still feel – that we were better than them. We should have won.

And this is how Manchester United reel you in.

How could I have imagined I would win a league title and the Club World Cup in my first year – that I would play so many times in so many important games? I was a boy with no vision of ambition in football – I did not start to play dreaming of winning trophies. And there I was, having played one of the most successful seasons in the history of Manchester United, maybe the biggest club in the world.

We were penalty kicks away from the FA Cup Final. We were unlucky in the Champions League Final. We were so close to winning everything you can win in football.

And in the end you're not celebrating. It's not quite the same as Fletch but I understand the feeling. I missed out on the League Cup Final I should have played in. If only for this. If only for that.

Manchester United had won the Premier League and played one of the greatest seasons in their history. But their internal report card read, 'Could be better.'

Fabio – Intense Times

MY FIRST year in Manchester was a different experience to that of my brother. There were times when it was very frustrating. For me, the frustration had started back when we were not allowed to play. All I wanted to do was to get on a pitch and play a competitive game and it seemed there was always something in the way to stop that happening. Then every time it seemed like it was going to happen, every time things looked to work out, something else got in the way.

We moved to Manchester – well, that took some time to adapt to, because going there for 15 days is a very different thing compared to going there to live. At least we could train. But you see the first team doing so well and it makes you dream. You look at the reserve team doing so well, a level you think you've been brought in to play, and you're frustrated that you can't take part. Then Manchester United win the European Cup. Then, instead of thinking you'll be 'adapting' for a year, you're training with the first team and being called up to play in a friendly game.

I remember Sir Alex Ferguson telling us we were going to play. I was only just 18. I was going to play some minutes in the actual first team of the European champions. I hadn't played a competitive game for a year! My brother was fantastic against Peterborough. I did okay as well. Nobody was thinking – not even us – that we would be even considered to play in the first team that year. It is difficult to express the highs and lows that I was feeling. I don't think many have been in such a position. To go from not being able to even train, to moving to Manchester from Brazil and training but not playing, to suddenly playing for the best team in the world … You could say that Peterborough changed our lives, because that was the moment when people at the club said, 'They're ready to play for Manchester United.'

Being ready and having the opportunity are two very different things. At Old Trafford there was this guy called Patrice Evra in front of me. Patrice was one of the best left-backs in the world. Maybe even *the* best. He never missed a game, not even a minute of a game. It was ridiculous. On the other side there was a potential opening for my brother. Gary Neville was near the end of his career and had a lot of injuries. Wes Brown had been the right-back in the Champions League Final but was a natural centre-back. I knew the gaffer would be fair – I knew I would get my chance. But I knew, in my heart, it was going to be a tougher challenge for me than it was for my brother.

I remember an early conversation with the gaffer. He knew I could play in different positions and so he asked us about it. It was going to be difficult enough for us to settle without competing against each other and so that's what I said. If the same question was asked today, I think both of us would have been happy saying we would compete for the same position without a problem. But then we were just 18. We both wanted to develop and we both wanted to establish ourselves and there was no way we would do that at the expense of each other. We were not in our own country. My brother is my everything and we were with each other every minute of every day. He is with me inside and outside of football. I can count on him and he can count on me. I said no, I play at left-back, Rafa goes at right-back. I know the gaffer respected that wish and they wanted us to settle too.

It didn't matter anyway. A couple of days after the Peterborough game I was swimming and hurt my shoulder. I couldn't believe it. It was my first ever injury, and a serious one, at the exact time I was finally able to play football properly again.

I put on some weight while I was out. I couldn't get used to the different food – I was trying to just eat what I liked, but for the time I was out injured I wasn't eating well. I was lucky that I was only 18 so it didn't really affect me too much, but it was still something I had to go through and learn. At the top level of football, you can't really afford to be at a disadvantage. You have to do everything properly. Maybe people will sympathise because of how difficult a time it was. I had my first ever operation in a foreign country where I didn't understand the language. There was an English girl called Laura who worked with our agent at the time and she was there to translate. I didn't speak a single word of English – neither did our parents. The club did offer to help out but because we had Laura I felt that would be enough, and it was, because she was brilliant.

It was four months before I was back in training – that was in early December. But I still missed the trip to Japan for the Club World Cup. Like Rafa said, it's such an important competition for us. I remember as a 15-year-old having arguments with friends who were supporters of São Paulo. They were saying their team was the best in the world because they beat Liverpool in the final in 2005. It was a historic moment and one of the most momentous games in their history. Of course, when Manchester United defeated Palmeiras in 1999 when it was still the Intercontinental Cup it was not seen as the greatest result they ever accomplished. In Brazil it means everything.

Rafa had moved into the first team dressing room because he was doing so well. The club were being careful with me so I was being treated as I had been when we first came in January. Training with the first team and being treated by the first team medical staff when they could, and by the reserve team staff when they couldn't. It wasn't an obvious separation, but my brother's progress gave me the determination to do whatever I could while I was out to give myself every advantage when I was fit. I stopped eating the rubbish and worked so hard in the gym. By the time I was ready to play again I would say I was in the best physical shape of my life.

Manchester United are not a normal club. We arrived at a time when they were experiencing one of the best seasons in their history. It is unbelievable to think that in those first few weeks and months the guys we were training with were the best in the world. When we went to Moscow it was like Manchester and London had taken over. So many flights, so many English people.

We were in the Luzhniki Stadium for the Champions League Final and when the first team were warming up we were just taking in the atmosphere. I looked up at the big screen and they were doing the pre-match presentations to build the excitement. They started showing all of the nationalities who had taken part in the competition. It came to the Brazilians: Ronaldinho, Ronaldo, Romário, Cafu,

Roberto Carlos. It showed their skills, their dribbles, their goals. Short clips but long enough to make you dream. When the game went to penalties I remember watching the lads showing the courage to step up and take the kicks and I kept thinking to myself, 'This could be us, one day. This could be us.' We were only six months into our life in Manchester but I promise we felt that emotion just as strongly as anyone. It was so tense. If John Terry scored United lose. The intensity was unreal. The celebration when he missed had the same sort of excitement as scoring a goal. When Edwin van der Sar made the save that won the Cup – we were like every fan. This was our life now.

But Manchester United are not a normal club. You don't do something like win a Champions League and then that's it. As soon as the party is over, you're preparing to win every single competition the next year. And that was the environment I was in when I was getting back to fitness. Sir Alex Ferguson wanted us all to do even better than winning the Premier League and Champions League.

My brother and I are very similar in a lot of ways but here is where we had a completely different experience. He was aggressive and believed in the chance he was going to get. I should have shared that confidence. After all, in all the teams we played together, I was the captain. I scored plenty of goals. But seeing how strong that United team were and knowing how difficult it was going to be for me to get a proper chance, I admit, my confidence dropped for the first time in my life. Before I had been important in every team I'd played in. I'd been one of our best players. This Manchester United team didn't need me. They were champions of their country, of their continent, of the world. This is what time out does to you. I didn't think of the injury. I just thought, 'Look at my brother, he's in that team so quickly, and I am not.' It wasn't really logical.

The funny thing was, as my confidence fell, the times where I felt better were when I was training. Yes, I admit, there was some awe in there. I would look at Cristiano and think – okay, I'm good, but I'm going to need to be very, very good to be at this standard. Then I would look at Patrice. It was not only how good he was. It was how loved he was. He was a part of the club. When we were training, because I love football so much, the idea of not being good enough didn't really cross my mind. But afterwards, I remember talking to my brother and saying to him that now I was fit again maybe I should ask to go out on loan.

'No, no, you're going to play, you're going to play,' he reassured me. He's always like that. He sees the positive side. We had that conversation a few times. In the end I thought, no, I have to be strong. I forced myself to think differently. I admit that I was overawed for a little while. Cristiano was the best player in the world. But there was Rio, Giggs, Scholes, Tevez, Rooney. Six months ago I'd been playing video games in which these guys were in my team. I had never played a game of football as a professional before. Sometimes I would be on the pitch at Carrington and I would think to myself, 'Wow. This is really true. This is really happening.' I'm glad I stayed, not only for the obvious reasons of playing for Manchester United, but also because the education that came from training with these players was probably better than you would get in most competitive matches at other clubs. The level of quality and intensity was unbelievable and most of it came from the players themselves. Sir Alex Ferguson, maybe the greatest coach who has ever lived, didn't need to do anything to keep the competitive level high.

You could say that every game for Manchester United is like a cup final, although some are more important than others. I can remember watching Rafa's first few matches and they were all huge occasions. Let me make this clear: there was not a single moment in my own difficult journey where I didn't feel the most incredible pride for what he was doing. After that video montage in Moscow, my brother became the youngest Brazilian to play in the Champions League in United's first game as holders the following season. I have a broad smile on my face remembering those first few games for him and the moment that remains as a very special time in my life was watching him score his first goal, against Arsenal.

You have read his recollection so let me tell you how the Da Silva family experienced it. My shoulder was still in its protective wrapping so I was watching it at home in Manchester with my parents and family. Arsenal are winning 2-0. Rafa comes on in the second half and I swear my wish for him to do something to change the game was probably even bigger than his own.

In the last minute, he controls the ball and then scores this wonderful goal. Together, the entire family roars and jumps up from the sofa. I looked at our mother. She was so emotional that she couldn't even cry. Our father sat back down. He had his head resting against his fist. He too was overcome. They could not speak. There was a moment that went beyond pride – beyond the normal limits for what you experience in your everyday feelings.

Me? It had felt like a dream. But my attention was caught by the commentator – we had a Brazilian feed so that we could understand. He said, 'Look at the way this guy celebrates. He is going to be a star at Manchester United.' The other guy asks him why. 'Because they are losing the game and he has run straight back to the middle of the pitch to kick off. Not many kids will do that.' I got chills when he said that. And I agreed. He's 18, scores his first goal for Manchester United, that goal is against Arsenal, and it's a brilliant strike, and he still doesn't want to celebrate because his team are losing. It was an attitude I shared but sometimes it's an attitude that only comes out instinctively in such moments. Only then can you really see what someone is made of. That's when people understood what made him a professional – but because we were so similar, I think it was a moment that reflected well on my own attitude as well. People knew our mentality was the same.

My first games were for the reserve team. I saw some guys play at that level after playing in the first team and they didn't care. They didn't want to be there, really. For me, I had to win that game. Our coach was Ole Gunnar Solskjaer and I'm sure he was instantly impressed by that attitude. I was desperate to win. Gerard Piqué, for example. He'd turn up and he'd play the 90 minutes. If we lost, if he played bad – it's Altrincham, so what? Why am I here? It doesn't matter. I would get annoyed if I lost at anything. That was just Gerard's way. It didn't do him any harm – he won everything. Maybe he knew he was good enough to. For me you have to *need* to win. If you don't win it ruins your day.

I did well in the reserves. It could have been a good thing that I didn't understand English then but I was aware enough of what was going on to appreciate that there were high expectation levels. That came with playing for Manchester

United anyway. It came from my own reputation as a captain of my national team, as a goalscoring defender. It came because of how well Rafa was doing. And then I started scoring goals for the reserve team. Even then, though, I knew that didn't necessarily mean I would be considered for the first team. It was easy to look at that and say, there's a guy who loves to go forward and attack, but he doesn't care about defence. He has a lot to learn. And that would have been fair. I did have a lot to learn about becoming a full-back in England. Even going back to the very early days, if we were playing two-on-two games in training in Boa Esperança, I would be the attacker and my brother would be the defender in our two-man team. He always had that natural ability to tackle. I started learning those defensive skills in England.

I think that if I had not been injured, Sir Alex would have given me a chance in the Champions League because that would have been an easier introduction for me. I think he knew my style was different. Much better to play in games where the emphasis was on playing football and not against a team like Bolton, for example, where elbows will be flying. But when I was back from my first injury, there were no European games, so my debut came against Tottenham in the FA Cup. I remember feeling so anxious before the match. I was desperate to do well. I couldn't really relax and I think that's part of the reason why I had to come off with cramp just after half-time. I remember Sir Alex saying afterwards that 'the boy did brilliant' – I know I gave a decent performance, but I also know it could have been better. It's difficult when you are in a situation where you have this chance in such a big game, and you want to impress so much but you still know that even if you do, through no fault of your own, one of the world's great players is going to come back into the team.

Tottenham were a good team for me to make my debut against because they like to play. I was able to express myself at times. I can remember trying some skills and the crowd responding well. I can also remember being conscious of my brother's qualities and trying to imitate him. Not so much in what he had done since playing for United – but back in Brazil, where he was committed to defending. He was telling me before the game to be aggressive.

I have to be honest, I had the advantage of playing for a team where everyone looked out for each other. I had Nemanja playing to the side of me. In front of me was Cristiano. Before the game he came to me and said, 'Fabio, I have to tell you. Behind the halfway line, don't try to dribble. Don't try to run with the ball. Don't lose the ball. I'm fast, but won't have the time to get back for you. In our offensive half, you can do whatever you want.' This is the best player in the world – officially. He'd just been awarded his first Ballon d'Or. I still get chills thinking about that – the fact that it's United, my debut, with the best in the world. Some people would think he's saying that because he doesn't want to defend. But it was sensible advice from his experience. It might even sound like common sense now. It does to me, with all of these games behind me at my age. Of course I won't dribble in front of my own box. But I was 18 – and that was probably the way I tried to play in training, as Cristiano knew. He'd probably done the same.

Cristiano played everywhere up front so he was never really a direct opponent in training. Most mornings I remember I faced Nani or Park Ji-sung. Back to those days of video games, some players were more established than others. Nani was a player I didn't know of before I came to Manchester. Oh my God. What a player he could be. He had everything. He could do anything. I felt Nani was desperate to follow Cristiano, and that sometimes the pressure was too much. I can understand why. It must have been difficult. I just wish he'd realised that being Nani was a good thing. He was such a fantastic talent. He had so much skill. And this is one observation to make about how good that Manchester United team was – so Nani wasn't Cristiano Ronaldo. But Cristiano was the best. It didn't make Nani less good. He had an exceptional career on his own merit and made a contribution to United that he should be proud of.

People can say what they want and they did at the time. I can remember some supporters saying Nani was inconsistent. But this was compared against the standards of a team who were the best in the world with some of the best individual talents that – let's be honest – have ever played the game. Some players are only appreciated after time has passed and I'm sure that there are plenty of United fans who would have been happy for Nani to have been playing in their team for the last few years. It was so competitive that even the 'substitute team' at the time could be expected to win most games.

The cramp against Spurs was a setback. I think it told Sir Alex that it was a little too soon for me, that I was still a little fragile to be in the first team so quickly after a serious injury. And this wasn't a time to take chances. Not many teams could expect to win the Premier League and Champions League and do better in the following season but that's what it looked like for a long time. Every match was so intense. So I spent a little more time in the reserves where I could train with the group and know I would be playing in the games. I had a strong routine that helped my rehabilitation and I benefitted from that. So did my form.

We had such a big squad that Sir Alex regularly rewarded good performances in the reserve team with a place in the matchday squad and on the bench. Some weeks, some seriously big names would be rested altogether, and we would feel like we were more included as part of the squad because of that. Even being on the bench and not getting on the pitch helped to make us feel close to the team. My form for the reserves was really good – I was not only playing well, but scoring goals, and these chances to be in the squad helped me feel like it was working.

Ole Gunnar Solskjaer was doing great things with the reserve team and he was impressing a lot of people. This was his second year in charge after he retired as a player. He seemed very keen to put across all of the things he must have learned from that time with Sir Alex, but he was also his own man. He was so good at helping players improve. I can remember the enthusiastic and passionate way he spoke to some of the players – how he would talk in detail to Danny Drinkwater and Tom Cleverley about how much he believed in them and how he thought they would be brilliant in the first team. Danny Welbeck was getting a few chances and he was always trying to build his confidence as well. He was always encouraging the players because it was clear that if they were needed at this stage of the season, their confidence would need to be high if they wanted to make a genuine impact.

Some players were closer to the first team than others. I remain very good friends with Kiko Macheda. He was a special kid. His talent was amazing. I've never seen a player who was so good at finishing at this level. I can remember Ole was on at him all the time. He saw so much talent in him. But Kiko was so laid back – he was so good at that level that he maybe didn't understand how far he still had to go to fulfil his potential. If he'd the drive, I'm not exaggerating when I say that on natural ability he had all the talent to be one of the top strikers in European football. And he was so confident – I'm sure that's why he was able to do what he did when he was called into the team in an emergency situation against Aston Villa. Because his contribution was ultimately a short-lived one over the space of a football career, people might consider that moment a fluke. It wasn't. That was what Kiko could do and he should have done it for longer.

Look at how he played for those 20 minutes against Aston Villa. But then ask yourself, if you had the opportunity to play for Manchester United how are you going to play? Or, if you don't support United, the team you do follow? You have 20 minutes to play. You're going to give it everything just like Kiko did. And for those 20 minutes he looked like he belonged. The problem was that it wasn't his natural style – and you need that intensity for 90 minutes of every game when you're playing for United. And in his appearances after that he wasn't that intense. Kiko knows that. I'm sure he probably looks back and regrets it in a certain way now. But at the same time, he'd probably just shrug his shoulders and get on with life. One thing that can't be taken away from him is his contribution at such an important time that season. A moment in history. His family nearly got on the pitch!

My brother has talked about the game against Everton in the FA Cup. It felt good that after the Spurs game, I was trusted to play in such a big occasion. And there were so many of us young boys in the team. But I had exactly the same problem as I did on my debut – I was so anxious to do everything and be everywhere on the pitch, to basically be one of the best players as I had been for my other teams, that I got cramp again and had to come off. And when I say I was anxious, I mean it made my entire body tense. Afterwards I had long conversations with some of the coaches at the club who tried to calm me down. It's something I couldn't control because of how young I was and I understand it so much better now. But it was a natural thing – I had this chance after not being in the first team for three months and I didn't know when my next one would come. I was desperate to show the fans I could do well. I knew they had expectations for me to do so. Physically I'd completely recovered from my injury and I had no problem playing 90 minutes even on the Wembley pitch. I was 18 – I could have easily played for two hours. Maybe even three! Well, okay, maybe not that long, but you get where I'm coming from. The problem wasn't my endurance. It was the nervousness and anxiety to do well and to excite the supporters.

It is incredible to think that even, as my brother said, with this being so close to a landmark (and maybe it was anyway) in United's history, Sir Alex looked at the FA Cup semi-final and put so many of us in. And we almost did it. We deserved to win it but we lost on penalties. He's the incredible one – no nerves! And he says before the game, 'Enjoy yourself, win the game!' He named that team and felt 100 per cent that we could win it. He was right because we were the better team and lost on the lottery of penalties.

The Champions League Final of 2009 was not a lottery. The journey to get there for a second year in a row was not lucky – getting to the final was fully deserved and led by Cristiano. I had the best seat in the ground for all of the great moments he had that year, watching as he scored from so far out against Porto and Arsenal. He had become a friend and a team-mate. He was doing extraordinary things. It was easy to forget, for a moment, that your friend was the best player in the world; one of the best who has ever lived.

And the Manchester United team you were playing in was having one of the club's best-ever seasons. The confidence was so high. Everyone was playing so well. Like my brother, I strongly believe our team was better than Barcelona's then. We were hurt by the early goal – and we weren't a team that conceded many. We were used to keeping it tight. It upset our rhythm.

We lost, and Cristiano, who had accomplished everything in England, now wanted to do something new. He wanted to go to Real Madrid, a club he loved, and see if he could become their best-ever player and win the European Cup with them too. There was never any doubt that he had the ability to fulfil that destiny. At United we had our own challenges – to get back to the Champions League Final and to win the league again. We'd have to face them without the best player in the world.

We'd also have to do it without Carlos Tevez, but I share my brother's opinion on him. People were sad to see Cristiano go but I wasn't disappointed that Tevez didn't sign permanently. One of the things I loved at United was the family atmosphere. The way our own actual family were made to feel part of the club, for example. It made you appreciate the roles everyone had, and you looked at the manager and thought he'd done so much good work to create that environment. I don't think Tevez contributed to that in a positive way. I don't think he wanted to.

It was strange going into the following season that the exact same situation as before struck me and my brother, but the other way around. He had a shoulder injury and I was in the team at right-back. This time I could compete in a more straightforward way but it was obvious that there was no definite first choice in that position. I played on the opening day of the season against Birmingham City – my league debut – and felt I did okay. I wasn't as anxious as I had been in the first two games, and yet, I don't think I played as well as I did in those matches. After that Gary, Wes and John all played in that position. It was the League Cup game against Wolves a month later when I next started, but I wasn't on the pitch for long.

Just before the half-hour, Michael Kightly, their winger, was through on goal. Someone had lost the ball in the middle and I was the last man. He was clear – and probably going to score. I brought him down and knew I was getting sent off. At half-time, the gaffer patted me on the head. 'It's not your fault, son,' he said. I got away with that. But the suspension meant another month out of the team. And next time I played – against CSKA Moscow – I came off with cramp again. To be fair to myself, I played almost the entire match and I know I did well in a 1-0 win on a plastic pitch. The gaffer was really happy with me and I know I had a chance of playing against Liverpool at Anfield in the following game. I was on the bench – but I was sent to warm up and Jonny Evans came up to me and said I was going to come on. We were losing 1-0. The game is coming to the end, but before I can get on, Nemanja gets sent off. Everything goes crazy – they get a player sent off as well. We lose 2-0. It's always a mad atmosphere at Anfield but this was even worse than usual because we had signed Michael Owen, their former striker.

Owen had already had a great moment for us – scoring the winner against Manchester City in that famous game that ended 4-3. It was just my impression but I felt he was not really into football by the time he came to United. He seemed more interested in his horses. I can remember being very young when he emerged as a star and people expected so much from him in his career. Unfortunately he suffered many injuries and he wasn't quite the same. Because of the level he'd once been at, it seemed like he felt he was still a superstar capable of doing the things he once did. His goalscoring instincts were still pretty good, but physically he was completely different to the lightning-fast striker he had been as a teenager.

There was a big spotlight on Owen's transfer because he had played for Liverpool and that took some of the attention away from Antonio Valencia. This was a player who came from Wigan so it didn't feel like much was expected from him. Man, he was *so* fast. *So* strong. His physicality more than compensated for any criticism someone would have of his technical skill, and for me this was another reason why Sir Alex was such a great manager. He was able to find a player who was completely different to Cristiano but who could still offer so much to the team in a different way. Antonio's professionalism was up there with the best I've known and I can tell you this guy was a nightmare to play against in training. He was horrible to play against. He never lets you do anything. He's there in your face, stopping you play. If you get away from him and attack he's got the pace to recover and get in front of you. He was horrible to play against – but playing against someone as physical and aggressive as he was in training was definitely a huge step up for me in my own game. I became very close with him in the years that followed. Antonio settled into life at United from the start, setting up lots of goals for Wayne Rooney and even scoring in Europe in both games against Moscow.

CSKA's visit to Old Trafford for the return match was easily the worst I ever played for the club. In the first game I felt my good performance had been a really good push for momentum but this absolutely killed all that. The gaffer had told me a couple of days before that I would be starting. I told Anderson because I was so excited. On the bus to the game Anderson is joking with Patrice. 'Pat, you going to play today?' Patrice just says yes, of course. Anderson is winding him up. He knows Patrice hates it – he absolutely hates being on the bench. Ando looks at me, raises his eyebrows and asks him again. 'Yes, of course!' In the end, the boss walks to the back of the bus, gives Patrice a tap on the shoulder and says, 'You're on the bench today, son.' He was so upset! He jumped up and down in his seat and crossed his arms. He didn't need to worry. I played so badly his position as first choice wasn't in doubt, and I think the gaffer thought afterwards, 'We'll wait for a bit with Fabio.'

In between the Liverpool and CSKA games we played at Barnsley in the League Cup, the scene of one of the funniest moments of my career. Rafa and I are used to getting mistaken for each other. It's funny because both of us can have moments where we think, 'Really? I don't look like *him*,' even when we're sitting face to face! As we've grown older we've changed a little bit – different hairstyles, too – but back then we were constantly being mistaken, every single day. And we'd joke about it all the time. Rafa would put my wedding ring on to confuse the lads. We'd do it with the fitness coaches, the physios, the players. They got wise to it. I'd come in and plead with them, 'No, I'm Rafa, I'm Rafa! Remember when I told you that thing.' And many times they'd fall for it all over again.

Barnsley was Rafa's first match back after his injury, so only the second time we'd played together in the first team. He committed a foul on one of their players – Gary Neville had been sent off, so there was a tense atmosphere and players were getting at the referee. I was still surprised when he showed me a yellow card for the foul! We complained at the time but in the dressing room afterwards everyone was laughing about it. Even the manager saw the funny side. We were joking about it in training for the next few days – and I was able to smile about it when the club got the yellow card taken off my record.

Moments like that were a nice relief from the incredible intensity at the time. It was good to know that we could be relaxed and friendly even if the occasion called for us to be serious. Because we were twins, we were able to contribute to lightening the mood. The number of times the gaffer would get on at one of us, 'Rafa, why did you do that?!' I'd plead my innocence and he would get angrier for a second before he realised the entire dressing room was quiet because I was telling the truth. 'Oh, fucking hell!' he would say, and then everyone would just burst out laughing. Him too.

I think we had the perfect spirit in the dressing room. Each and every one of us knew – language barrier or not – what it meant for Manchester United to win every single game. The gaffer had a group of personalities who mostly shared that desire. We also had the ability to have light relief and not lose control or our own discipline. At United, you can't afford to have a lapse, because each moment in a Premier League title race is crucial. We had lost the goals of Cristiano but Wayne Rooney stepped up. I came on for the last few minutes of the game where he scored all four goals against Hull – just another moment where he proved himself as one of the great players in the world. It's not an easy thing to do, to take that responsibility on. I would not say he was in the shadow of Cristiano – Wayne was the star in many games where they played together – but the point is that they always had each other if the other wasn't doing it. Now he had to do it mostly by himself. He was fantastic that year.

Unfortunately it wasn't enough for us. We won the League Cup – and my brother, who was injured the previous year, got the medal he missed out on – but we fell short in the other competitions. The worst of those for me was against Leeds at Old Trafford in the FA Cup. It was a derby and we just did not get started. It was a horrible game. Because it had been a while since the teams had played each other, they sent their strongest team out, and we played a rotated side. I've tried to forget it – and I'll be happy to again now I've relived it here.

Our season turned for the worse in our Champions League tie against Bayern Munich. Towards the end of the first leg Wayne picked up an ankle injury. We weren't sure if he would be fit for the second leg but the gaffer decided to make some changes anyway – all of the press was about whether Rooney would play, so making a few changes would hopefully catch them out. Rafa played and so did Darron Gibson. They were brilliant. Darron scored after three minutes. After 41 minutes we were 3-0 up. My brother was unbelievable. He was up against Franck Ribéry. Ribéry couldn't breathe and Rafa was all over him. He was having the game of his life. But two minutes before half-time, they scored. It killed us.

My brother had been booked for a foul quite early. Five minutes into the second half everything went wrong. Ribéry went at him. Rafa wasn't the type of player to just allow someone to get past him. Even if he was, he wasn't mature enough yet in his development to think it might have been worth it to stay on. The only thought he had was to stop the player getting past him. Ribéry went past him – my brother made slight contact. The German players, all of them, go around the referee. 'Yellow, yellow, yellow!' It wasn't a yellow. I doubt the referee would have given it if there hadn't been that pressure. Rafa was sent off. We did well but Wayne had to come off with his injury. We were against ten men for half an hour and Bayern scored a great goal through Robben. Only one – but one was enough to knock us out on away goals.

Afterwards, the gaffer steams into the dressing room, 'Where's Rafa? Where's Rafa?' and he tore into my brother. No case of mistaken identity this time. Rafa was devastated. He spent a full week at home. I don't think he left the sofa. It's sad even for me looking back and remembering the way he was. The newspapers were full of criticism for a boy of 19 who made a mistake. A veteran professional was able to make the most out of a situation and get a player booked. It happens in almost every game but because he was sent off he was getting all of the blame. There was so much that happened in that tie – we were behind and on the night we were 3-0 up. But all the blame got placed on the shoulders of my brother and he found that very difficult.

There was another refereeing decision that had us fuming before the end of the season. We played against Chelsea and Didier Drogba scored a goal from a few yards offside. It was one of the most unbelievable decisions. And Chelsea won the league that season! To be honest, that was a great Chelsea side, very different to the José Mourinho team. Carlo Ancelotti had them scoring so many goals – over 100 – but the one that mattered shouldn't have counted.

Another medal I missed out on then. At the time I didn't let it concern me too much. I was patient. Too patient, maybe. I was 19. I would have liked to have picked up a winner's medal from the four major trophies United had won since I arrived. But it was because we'd won four and I wasn't even 20, I thought, well – there are plenty more to come.

Rafa – Reunions

AFTER WE had been in England for around 18 months it became easier to understand the language. Much easier to understand it than to speak it, anyway. And there was a period of a year or two when, because we couldn't speak it fluently, sometimes it was beneficial to either pretend you didn't understand, or at least take the time to listen instead of speaking.

You might say that those observation skills had a part to play in me deciding to get married – I had seen my brothers do that, and they were very happy. Fabio, always the calmer one, was even more so and seemed to really enjoy that increased sense of a family life. Maybe it could do the same for me. Well, the intention was there anyway – I still needed a little time to mature! The main reason I married, of course, is because I was in love and it was just as good for me as it was for my brothers. We had settled into our own way of life in

Manchester. To relax I liked to play poker but I didn't really go out; I wasn't one to hit the nightclubs or pubs. We'd go out with the lads if there was a team thing but other than that we would mainly just stay with our family.

So, some things were just the same as they'd ever been – it was no surprise that I would have a similar experience to my brother because we see life in the same way. But our first year as professional footballers in Manchester had seen us take different paths and see some things a little differently. For example, I think I took Cristiano's departure a little harder than Fabio did. I learned so much from Cristiano, but the biggest thing was probably self-confidence. He had every reason to be. He was the best player in the world. The way he could read the game and the way he was able to influence the team … these qualities had improved. He had matured even in the time we were there, to the extent that it was easy to tell that he wasn't just one of the great players of the time. He was destined to be one of the best to ever play the game. That sort of confidence goes through the team. He's a great player but he's one of 11. And for a while, I was one of the 11 too. It was an attitude that he carried with him but also one I saw in other players in the team. People might call that arrogance, even. But I think if you're playing for Manchester United and you are challenging for the top trophies, you need that in your team.

I have had two tremendous sadnesses in my footballing career. One was Sir Alex Ferguson retiring – that will come in this story in due course – and the other was Cristiano leaving for Real Madrid. We were losing not only a great player, but a great presence in the dressing room, and another of the Portuguese speakers. Carlos Queiroz, our coach, had left to take over the Portugal national team around the same time that we were able to start playing again. Nani and Anderson were still there, but Anderson didn't speak much English, so now we were reliant only on Nani if we couldn't understand something.

Playing with Ronaldo was easy. You can develop certain qualities through the clubs you go to, the players you play with, and the coaches who give you advice, but when you are born with the sort of drive that Cristiano has, it makes you almost destined for the sort of greatness he has achieved. He believed he could be the best. Sometimes that mentality can be the most important thing. But this is not new – anyone reading this will know this about Cristiano. It almost makes it sound easy. It is not. His work ethic was incredible and it is difficult for anyone to reach and maintain the standards he set. He did the extraordinary things and because it helped us win games, and we gained our own confidence from that, it elevated our own feelings of influence. I can only speak for myself but I always believed playing with him – if only for that one year – was an experience where I felt really positive about my performances, and, honestly, there was a part of me wondering if I felt I'd played as well as I did because of what Ronaldo did, if that makes sense. Could I be the same player now he was gone? Could we be the same team?

We didn't have another individual like him in the team, but the man leading us had all of the same mental qualities as Cristiano. Sir Alex had standards just as high. He would not allow anyone to work less than what he saw from Ronaldo. You had some rare exceptions – I'm not saying Dimitar Berbatov didn't work, he worked harder than many gave him credit for, but it was easy to see he was a different kind of player. And because he could do something different, the manager was able to make some concessions. But take, for example, Kiko Macheda, a player both my brother and I have already talked about. He had made this early impression and was given a chance because of the different quality he had. His ability to score goals was maybe as good as anyone we had at the club. And so, for a while, Sir Alex kept him around, and hoped that over time he might develop that same sort of hunger that Cristiano had. But, just as Cristiano was born with it, Kiko was not.

Manchester United was a club filled with players who had so much talent but couldn't get a chance in the first team. Zoran Tošić was one. It was during a pre-season training tussle with him that I came off worse and dislocated my shoulder. Exactly the same injury as my brother. If that wasn't strange enough, I later dislocated the other, this time swimming – exactly the same way Fabio did it! I counted my blessing that my injury was at the start of pre-season and not right at the start of, or in the middle of, the season.

Another blessing – my brother got the chance to play at right-back while I was out. Patrice Evra, who played 48 games when we won the double, played another 48 in our first season. In this campaign he would play 51. He was not slowing down.

My first game back from injury was at Barnsley where Fabio and I were mistaken for each other. Maybe the manager confused us for real when he played me at left-back against Beşiktaş at Old Trafford. It didn't go well – we lost. Their fans were crazy, but even crazier when we played in Turkey. I remember thinking that if you play for one of those clubs, it might be a great experience – one of my friends played there and won league titles so he was treated like a God – but when you are against those fans, you can feel the hate coming off the stands. A few years later, I experienced football in Turkey myself, though it came in very different circumstances.

Back at Old Trafford, now I was in the team, I was finding my best form again. One of my most special memories was a win against Wigan over the Christmas period of 2009.

I set up the first goal for Rooney and then scored my first at Old Trafford just before half-time. December is a very special time for our family, as it is for most Brazilian families. We really enjoy having our family and friends around and they were all at the game, so I had an extra motivation to put on a strong performance. I don't speak often about my religion but I thank God for being on my side that evening because it made it a really special one. The goal was for my brother – as I'm sure you could tell from my celebration, when I ran across the entire pitch to celebrate with him.

Old acquaintances were renewed again in January, but there was a different mood this time around. We played against Manchester City in the League Cup semi-final. It was a different Manchester City than United fans were used to now. They were spending a lot of money on players, and giving a lot of money to players to convince them to sign. One of those was Carlos Tevez. I'm not judging him for that, by the way. Each to their own. I'm not here to say what's right or what's wrong. As I said before, Tevez was no friend of mine. So I was quite relieved when he left. I personally would not have left United to sign for a rival club but that was his decision, and it certainly added some extra tension to a game which didn't really need it. It was a Manchester derby in a semi-final. I had all the motivation to play and I was definitely fired up.

The game was tight and the intensity was high. On this occasion, there were a few extra elements to make it even worse. Number one: Carlos Tevez. Number two: referee Mike Dean. This was the start of a not-so-beautiful friendship between Dean and me where I always seemed to get some major decision given against me. He's from Liverpool, so maybe that explains why he doesn't seem to like me. In this game he gives a penalty against me. It's just before half-time – we're playing well, Giggsy has given us the lead. But I am chasing Craig Bellamy outside the box, I pull at his shirt a little bit, and then when he gets into the box he falls down. Shouldn't be a penalty, but it is, and who else but Carlos Tevez scores it. Tevez then scores again and they win the first leg.

It's a learning curve. You have to take responsibility for the things you do. That much remains true even when you're in difficult situations – if the atmosphere is crazy, if you think the referee is against you. It's a thing I'm still learning, even now, as I write this, more than ten years on. You get lost in the moment. And you have to remember all of the things that can go against you. There's another side to that, as well: you have to accept you can't control certain things. For me it wasn't a penalty. I look back now and I still don't think it's a penalty. If I react, I am in trouble – but that is also part of my personality, and I think that fire and passion is a positive element of my footballing style. Because it is complicated, that is why it takes a long time. And some would say that it has never left me. But I would rather be that way and play that way. If I was the type of player to become too conscious of this then the next time I might not go for the tackle at all because I'm afraid of what the referee will do. Playing in France, people are more sensitive to the aggressive challenges. 'Why do you tackle like this?!' they ask. It's the way I play! If I change the way I play, I would probably lose my enjoyment of the game. Even if people see a fault with it, I think it's better to be that way than to be someone else.

Our revenge against City came a couple of weeks later in the second leg. It was a special night at Old Trafford. We put in a great performance, and in the last minute, Wayne Rooney scored the goal that made it 3-1, giving us the aggregate win that took us to the final. They must have been sick of Old Trafford. They'd also suffered an injury-time defeat to us in September, in the league, when Michael Owen scored. I didn't even play in that one – but if I ever see the videos pop up on social media, I always stop what I'm doing to enjoy those moments again.

City were spending so much money that everyone thought they would instantly become like United, playing brilliant football and winning all the trophies. It added some fire to the games. Even when I arrived, nobody talked about City. They talked about Liverpool, Chelsea and Arsenal. Now, two years in, City were buying all these players, and they were being taken seriously. Last-minute winners are always special. But in this case, it was extra sweet.

We weren't ready to be overtaken at the top just yet. Even without Cristiano, we stayed at the top of the league and we kept playing good football. Antonio Valencia came in – a very different type of player, but someone I quickly built up a good partnership with on the pitch. Rooney took on the goalscoring responsibility.

And Nani finally started to come out of his shell and show everyone how good he could be. We played at Arsenal and won 3-1, scoring an almost identical goal to the one Ronaldo had scored against them a few months earlier. But the best goal in that game was scored by Nani – he did this incredible trick where he went through two players and then he flicked it over the goalkeeper.

It is like my brother said – Nani, wanting to be Cristiano, was not half the player Nani being Nani was. There was a lot of pressure from different people for him to be and to follow Cristiano. I think you could say, because of that, it made it difficult for the real Nani to arrive at United. But there were times when he looked like he would. And the times he played his best, he was just being Nani. Against Arsenal, his contribution must have given him so much confidence, because he was fantastic that year.

Even with my injury, I could say that life in Manchester had been close to perfect. I was playing well, being picked regularly, and even when something went wrong – the penalty against City, or the booking against Barnsley – there was something else which meant I didn't really take much criticism from the manager.

That changed in Europe. We came up against AC Milan in the San Siro. It was a night I felt a few nerves. There were many Brazilians in the Italian side, such as Dida in goal, Thiago Silva in defence and Alexandre Pato in attack. But lining up against me was my hero, Ronaldinho. He was part of the World Cup-winning team in 2002. He was, for a time, the best player in the world. And then he moved to Barcelona when we were at Fluminense. For every game, at 4.30pm, everybody at the training ground stopped to watch him play for Barcelona. Okay, I was up against the 2010 version, not 2002 or 2006, but he was still capable of brilliant things, as I found out. It wasn't exactly an error, but I wasn't close to him when he gave Milan the lead after just three minutes. By half-time we'd equalised and the manager told me to keep my concentration. We went 3-1 up, but with about five minutes left I made an error and Milan scored another goal.

Afterwards, the manager was really cross. 'You cannot do that, you must learn from your mistakes,' he yelled at me. I understood, and I took it seriously – but we won the game.

It's the best way to make a mistake. I know I didn't play well – but I put that down to meeting my idol. It's strange to be starstruck and then you have to play well against that same star! United had their own reunion with a familiar face as David Beckham was on loan at Milan. Of course, I knew who Beckham was, he was known around the world. The best way I can explain it is that Beckham was a face we had seen on television, but Ronaldinho was like family. And there was one key difference: I always want my family to play well! I was happy Ronaldinho's influence on the second leg wasn't as great as it was on the first. I'm not often jealous or envious of my brother for many things. But I definitely am jealous that he played with Ronaldinho for Brazil. I tell him so all the time.

Things seemed to be going so well that even my disappointment of the previous year – missing the League Cup Final – was put right when I played against Aston Villa at Wembley and we won that season's League Cup. I had mixed results at Wembley, but it was definitely one of my favourite places to play. It means much more when you win. You love to play there – but you love to win more, especially in a cup final. Michael Owen scored – and my brother has already talked about him. I share his thoughts, but one story Fabio didn't tell was of one of Owen's first training sessions at the club. Fabio challenged him and didn't hold back. It was a strong tackle. Owen was furious. 'You're crazy!' he screams at him. He took it personally. Then he went through the rest of training and saw my brother doing the same to everyone. In the changing room at the end, he was big enough to apologise. He might not have been the most popular signing but he got on with most people at the club. It is true, though, that he seemed more interested in his horses than football. Every morning he'd be reading about them in the newspaper. That was how I discovered what horse racing was!

We hit a great run of form. The win over Villa was the second of seven in a row that also included three points against Liverpool. We won the second leg against Milan to set up a quarter-final in the Champions League with Bayern Munich. The aim for us all is to win the league and get to the Champions League Final for the third year in a row. But then we have a couple of bumps. Rooney scores but is injured in the first leg against Bayern. Without him, we lose against Chelsea (our title rivals) with the Drogba goal my brother spoke about. The referee is Mike Dean – this guy is a legend for Liverpool!

But when it comes to April, the games come very fast, and every one is massive for United. We can't afford to let our heads drop. Wayne is back for the second leg against Bayern and our first-half performance is fantastic. I'm having one of my best games for the club. It might even be my best. I'm defending well. I'm everywhere on the pitch. I even came close to scoring, but I became afraid at the last minute and messed it up. I was not afraid of my challenge against Franck Ribéry, one of the world's greatest wingers. I loved every second of that competition against him.

And then the second half had only just begun when I was given a second yellow card for bringing down Ribéry. He's clever. I'm young. But, as I said before, if that's my excuse, I can only say that I could easily be guilty of the same thing if I went out on to a pitch to play today. It's the way I am. Maybe I am more mature than I was then and there is less of a chance. It is not impossible. Sometimes you can only play your part, and you have your opponents who will do whatever they can to gain an advantage. Maybe I fell into a trap and that was my mistake. It only takes one clever fall and all the players around the referee. I still take responsibility for it. I think I was stupid. I shouldn't have done it. This time there's no turnaround like there was in the San Siro. No second leg like there was against City. Bayern score and they're through on away goals.

The manager came into the dressing room afterwards and was angry with me. To be fair, though, not as angry as he could have been. I was in tears. I was devastated that I had contributed to us going out. I felt responsible. 'You shouldn't have done that, you know you made a mistake!' he shouted; I think he did that because he felt he had to. He's not only a very good manager, he's a very good human being. He was angry, but almost apologetic that he had to shout. He knew that I knew. I took myself into training but I couldn't face him for a couple of weeks after that. I really felt like I let him down.

Chelsea won the league, thanks in no small part to that Drogba goal. But this was a great Chelsea team. Always very hard to beat under José Mourinho and now, under Carlo Ancelotti, scoring a lot of goals. Most of them from onside.

Rafa – Comeback

IT DIDN'T matter who the opponent was: Liverpool, Chelsea, Arsenal, Manchester City. For Manchester United, the challenge at the start of the season was to win the league. And, for the first few years we were there, it seemed like it was also expected for us to get to the final of the Champions League every year. These things seem normal when you're in it and it is only the passing of time that makes you realise what a different achievement it was. We had been in Moscow and I had been on the bench in Rome – that's two of the four finals United had played at that stage in their history. And here we were again, expected to come back from the disappointment of the 2009/10 season and win everything.

Mentality, as I've said, can be so important. It can be the defining factor. Confidence boosts are always welcome and they don't come any higher for a Brazilian than being called up into the national team. That's what happened to me at the start of the following season. We had lost in the quarter-finals in the 2010 World Cup in South Africa and it was time for a new generation of players to come in. Pato, Neymar, Robinho, Ganso – a lot of young players. And, apparently, I was part of that group. I didn't get to play against the USA in New Jersey but to just be in the squad and to be considered close to selection was a wonderful experience and made me very positive about the season ahead.

At United, we knew as a squad we would have to be better too. We could not use the excuse of losing Cristiano. Wayne Rooney and Nani had improved but we all had to if we wanted to win the league again. This was nothing new. Even with Cristiano it was a team effort and he would say the same. Our 2010/11 success featured many players playing some of their best football and included some very special memories. And some strange times.

Wayne had experienced a difficult World Cup with England and the press were not happy with him. As the highest-profile player he was always in the newspaper in the first few months of the season. Sometimes I thought the tabloids would pay people to try and catch players out. It was mad. At Carrington, none of what was going on came into the dressing room. You treat people how they treat you, and my relationship with him was very good. He was a very helpful guy. He's not someone who will trust easily – and you can understand that, because of what he was put through by the press – so I appreciated the fact that he was friendly with us. It meant a lot. When you are friends with him, he is the nicest guy, so generous with his time, and he can't do enough to help. These are the sort of team-mates you want around you.

It was also a strange time because of how influential social media was becoming. I didn't join Instagram until around 2012 and I moved to France before I was on Twitter, but even though I wasn't on them it was obvious they were having an impact. Darron Gibson joined Twitter and closed his account in less than a day because he was getting abuse, even from some United fans. Well, that's what they say, anyway. I think half of these people aren't even real. If they are real they just want to spread hate. Some of them apparently weren't happy with Gibson. Here is a player who did a job and scored some important and good goals for United. And these people were angry! How can you be angry about a player scoring goals for your team? I don't understand. I definitely didn't understand how that could be the case at Old Trafford in this season because of how well everyone played and the history that we made together. It was a team effort.

The first of them I want to mention is Fletch. He had continued to play brilliant football. Everyone knew how important he was to us when he missed the 2009 Champions

League Final but he had continued to get even better and was one of our most consistent performers. I think, because he had twins, he liked me and my brother more! But we did have a special relationship with him.

He was close to Rooney as well. But when Wayne put in a transfer request in the early part of the season, even we were surprised. We were still not completely fluent in English so it wasn't easy to fully understand what was going on. We didn't know the conversations between him and the gaffer. I remember some of the lads asking him why he wanted to leave. There was a sadness about that with the players.

It was sorted very quickly and we were all delighted that Wayne signed a new contract. For us it was the story of the week. Manchester United are the biggest club so every week it's a different controversy and it's the end of the world. Everyone is talking about it. Everyone is desperate for some controversy with United and they try to create it. When something genuinely happens it's like the world stops. It was something normal in football. A player was unhappy and the problem was resolved. But this was another part of what Sir Alex was so good at. He was able to use that as a turning point for our season. Wayne was out injured at the time but when he came back he was brilliant.

And, as soon as he came back and played brilliant – people compared him to Messi and Ronaldo! Everything was so over the top. And I say this in praise of Wayne. Let them play like who they are. Wayne never played like Messi and Ronaldo at any time in his career and they never played like him. They had their own qualities. They're not the same player. You wouldn't want them to be. But he was so good for us this season – world class.

While he was out, other players stepped up. We signed Javier Hernández, a different kind of goalscorer. I loved Chicharito as a player and as a person. If one day I become a coach, I would love a player like him in my team. He quickly settled in at United, scoring plenty of goals. But Dimitar Berbatov was probably our best player in the first half of the season. He was scoring so many goals – a hat-trick against Liverpool with one of the best goals you'll ever see. He scored five goals in a game against Blackburn, a match that felt like the easiest of my career; it was the only time I've ever played as a professional when a player has scored five, I'm sure.

Anderson also had a great run of form at this time. I will say something about Anderson – if he had been a professional football player he could have been the best in the world. I'm saying this with all seriousness. I don't know if he ever took anything seriously. He just lived his life in such an easy and casual way. In some ways that was a quality. It was what made him so popular and one of the most popular players at the club. But he just took life as it came. He would eat whatever was in front of him. We could be on the team coach and pass the services on the motorway and he would jump up impulsively and yell, 'McDonald's! McDonald's!' We would ask him what the hell he was talking about and he would respond, 'I just love McDonald's!' The guy was crazy, but I loved him. Give him a football and he would just play with freedom and sometimes, if he got a good run of games, he could play as well as the best players in the league. Not only that. When he was playing well, we were playing brilliant football.

He picked up a lot of big injuries and then the problems with eating that way would start to affect him. Eventually it caught up with him. It is no coincidence that his best form came when he had a lot of games because that's when he couldn't eat so much. Then he'd get some bad luck and would get injured again. But, especially in this period, he was so good for us. You might ask how a player like that can last for so long at United but from the inside it was easy. The manager just loved him. He knew how valuable Ando could be in big games. There were so many of those occasions where he would be the best player, or he'd make such a difference. Sir Alex trusted him so much. I think by this time, he had been at the club for over three years, and even though the pattern was usually the same – good form, injury, eating too much – the positives of having him around were so strong.

An example of why he could be trusted – the guy came on in a Champions League Final. He was brought on to take a penalty and he took the best of them all, looking like he felt the least pressure. He was not fearful of any occasion. He had the biggest heart and was such a fun guy to be around. He was just Ando, and you couldn't change him. I wouldn't want to.

There was a great team spirit at the club and I am sure that was a big part of why we started the season so well. We qualified for the knockout stages of the Champions League and were unbeaten in the Premier League going into the new year. But we still had to travel to the big clubs – Spurs, Chelsea, Liverpool and Arsenal.

The first of those games was a trip to White Hart Lane. I was running alongside Benoît Assou-Ekotto and he stumbled over. It was a coming together. I stopped my run because he was coming across me. But my old friend Mike Dean pulled out a red card. It was never a sending off. I couldn't believe it. I was so angry I kicked the microphone on the side of the pitch! The gaffer was angry with him but couldn't say anything because he'd been in trouble for the many times Dean had given decisions against us in the past. But even Harry Redknapp, the Spurs manager, admitted I was trying to get out of the way.

I think I had matured since what happened against Bayern Munich. We had played against City in November at the Etihad. Just before half-time Tevez and me went for the ball. It was a competitive challenge. We gave as good as we got, and I'd be lying if I said I wasn't fired up especially because it was him. At Old Trafford I'd been a little too young, a little too naive to really stand my ground when he hissed in my direction if I misplaced a pass. But now I was a regular for Manchester United and he was playing for the enemy. There was a moment when all of that frustration about his arrogance, and my annoyance about our last trip there, came out and even though I was still inexperienced I was not going to back down from him when he got in my face. In the end we had to be separated, but not before I had the chance to tell him what I thought of him. Usually in those situations it's the heat of the moment and you forget it. But this had been building up in me for more than two years. It had to come out. I don't regret it.

So, two red cards in a year, but the Spurs one wasn't as bad as the Bayern incident. We drew 0-0 at Spurs in a tough game (just as we did at City), the manager understood I didn't do anything wrong and I was back after my suspension to play at Blackpool. It was a very dramatic game – we were 2-0 down, not for the last time that season. We came back, also not for the last time! At 2-2 I competed for the ball with Blackpool's Luke Varney and suffered a concussion. It was pretty bad. I have no memory of it happening other than the pictures I saw afterwards of the incident and my brother looking so worried about me. In fact he would have been the obvious player to come on for me, but the gaffer saw how concerned Fabio was so he told him to go with me to the hospital.

People take concussions much more seriously these days and I can understand why. It's better to be safe than sorry. It's a tough job for the doctors. After a minute or so the player is telling them they're fine to play. I'm sure I was the same. Just let me get back on the pitch! You have all this adrenalin still pumping through your body. It's a really difficult call for the doctors to make. Immediately when you see a challenge and someone going down with their head people say it's a concussion. It's such a serious thing that you don't want to make the wrong call. The other side of it is, if a player isn't concussed and the result is in the balance, they will be so frustrated if they are forced to be taken off for no reason. All I can say is that with me they made the right call and I think they treated me very well. It ended well for us as we won 3-2.

We then had a dip in form, losing at Wolves and then Chelsea. Without Rio and Nemanja, we went to Anfield. This was a place where we were hated all of the time anyway but there was a little extra in this game because we were competing for the club's 19th league title. Liverpool were nowhere near it, so this was their best chance of beating us. The atmosphere was as you would expect. They're up for it and score two first-half goals. The intensity, as it always does, comes down from the stands on to the pitch. You don't just go there thinking the fans hate you. Everyone detests you if you play for Manchester United. Their players detest you. It runs deep. Wayne Rooney told us that Steven Gerrard hated us. He said that Gerrard told him on international duty, 'Those twins, they are pricks!' We never did anything to him but wear a different shade of red. I guess that's all it takes. And to be honest, I understood what he meant. The feeling was mutual.

Just before half-time, Jamie Carragher goes in on Nani with one of the worst tackles you've ever seen on a pitch. It's disgraceful. You can see the bone in his shin, the blood pouring from his leg. I didn't see the tackle at the time but I saw the aftermath. And he's not even sent off. Unbelievable. You look for retribution in that situation, you need to get your frustration out, and I flew into a tackle on Lucas Leiva (who became one of my closest friends in football). I'm booked, the same punishment as Carragher! Against Liverpool, you tackle for fun, you tackle for no reason. I love it. In this game it was like the referee was saying we could do what we wanted. So I thought, I'll test it out. Manchester United against Liverpool is like street boxing. You don't have gloves, don't have rules. Go. Fight. It's like that.

In the dressing room at half-time the mood is completely changed by Patrice. 'Nani, why were you crying?!' he is asking, and for a second, some of us didn't know what he meant until they showed the footage again on the television. All of a sudden there's laughter and amazement from some of the lads, Patrice again shouting at him, 'Why are you crying?!' It's like with Patrice can't believe Nani showed a weakness to our biggest rivals. His reaction was funny – not so much for Nani, because that was a crazy tackle. To be fair, at half-time, Nani himself was laughing, partly because he was embarrassed about the way that it looked, him crying and showing the referee where he had been hurt. It was embarrassing, but even more embarrassing that Carragher wasn't sent off.

Liverpool won on the day, but just like when they won at Old Trafford in 2009, it wasn't enough to stop us. Their frustration grew with every trophy we won and every year that passed with them in decline. They would do their best to stop us winning the title that year but they knew sooner or later we would get to 19 before they did.

It was probably the first time when I could truly understand how important it was for us to win the title. It's always important, of course. But in my first year I had played only with the knowledge I was playing for one of the biggest clubs in the world. That has its own pressure, but I knew little of the seriousness of the rivalry with Liverpool and Arsenal.

You're thinking about every game as the biggest you've ever played. It was like that every week in the first year I was a professional. It's not something that comes to mind, that this could be the game where we equal Liverpool's title record. Now, two years later, two years into taking English lessons, I understood the language, and if there was a newspaper at Carrington, or the television was playing, I could understand what they were saying. Three years at the club full-time is more than enough time to fully understand how important this next league title was going to be.

The truth is, I don't know if it's better to know or not know. When you don't know, you can just play. You can turn off everything before the game and after it. It can help you relax and enjoy what you are doing. On the other hand, when you know how important it is, it can improve your motivation. Playing against Liverpool for Manchester United is basically like what it is for everyone else playing against Manchester United. You become so motivated to play and win. For me it was motivation. I could not wait for those games. For some players it can go the other way. I'm not saying that it is a positive or a negative, but that only for me, it's a positive.

The next game is another big one – Arsenal. This time it's in the FA Cup and the manager wants to change the squad around to give other players some time. But in the last round, he did that against Crawley Town, and he was not happy with Bebé and Gabriel Obertan. He had tried them earlier in the season against Wolves, when Owen Hargreaves had to come off early because of his injury problems. This time around he wanted something different.

We're at Carrington the morning before the game. 'Okay, twins. Are you ready to play as wingers?' Of course we are.

So the team is announced and everyone was saying there was seven or eight defenders in the side. They must be mistaken – I was a forward! This was not a José Mourinho team with eight defenders, it was a Sir Alex Ferguson team – sent out to attack and be positive, and to win, most importantly. And we did. As he always did, my brother gave everything. His chances in the team hadn't come as regularly as he would have hoped, so every time he gave so much that he would be exhausted after the game. In this one he had to come off at half-time – he was exhausted! And he'd made the difference, scoring the first goal on 30 minutes. We didn't know what to do – we ran everywhere to celebrate. But I looked at him after that and I thought I could tell in his eyes, 'I want to come off.' He had already done his job. He was so happy that he wished he could just pause time when it was perfect. It was a moment where he did not think it could possibly get any better.

And I saw my brother, and recognised him, and at the same time recognised that I hadn't seen this guy for so long.

He had become so shy, not as confident as he once was and so anxious to do the things that came so naturally to him, so nervous not to ruin it when it was as good as it was. To get this moment, he wanted to relive it again and again. He did come off at half-time – I don't think anyone has been happier to be substituted at the break – and thankfully he went on to enjoy very good times for the rest of the season.

In fact, he took my place in the team at right-back. I was so happy for him. You might think there was a disappointment there but there genuinely wasn't. By now this was a squad that was rotating. It could be the first team, the second team, the third team. Every single game was important for us to win. Fabio played in the first leg in the Champions League semi-final against Schalke. The boss changed almost the entire team for the second leg because we won the first one 2-0. So, I'm in the second team. But that team is still playing a Champions League semi-final at Old Trafford, one of the biggest games in the club's history. You are there because you are trusted.

That 19th title came at Blackburn. I travelled but didn't make it into the squad on the day; Patrice had a rare day off with my brother playing. We were 1-0 down but Wayne scored a late penalty to make it 1-1. A draw would be enough. Before the game had ended, Patrice and Ando started celebrating behind the boss, dancing and waving to the fans.

The celebrations started long before, and continued long after, the final whistle.

I was disappointed, as anyone would be, to miss out on the Champions League Final squad. But I always say my brother is my life, and out of sadness came happiness, because he started the game. For me, I was on the pitch with him.

Fabio – The Beautiful Game

IT WAS a measure of the standards at Manchester United under Sir Alex Ferguson that we could make history and still end the season feeling disappointed. Reflecting helps us appreciate what we did, but even after travelling back to the summer of 2011 and remembering when we became the most successful team in English league history, the disappointment of Wembley in the Champions League Final remains.

The game plan against Barcelona is the first thing everyone asks about. Wayne Rooney said in his column for the *Sunday Times* in 2020 that he thought Sir Alex Ferguson's approach was 'suicidal'. Wayne said, 'I remember Alex Ferguson saying, "We're Man United and we're going to attack, it's in the culture of this football club," and thinking, "I'm not too sure about this."' Wayne's understanding was better than mine, but I can definitely agree that the gaffer said he didn't want to sit back. He felt that in Rome, the team hadn't played aggressively enough or pressed them enough.

You can understand where the manager is coming from. It's a matter of pride on the big occasions and he didn't want it to be as difficult as it had been in 2009. From the outside it looks as if you're not getting close enough. That's the problem when you play against a team who are so capable in possession and have the maturity and experience to be patient. Every time you go to press them, they break the lines. So the idea was to press them early, to be in their faces, even if it would lead to mistakes. Unfortunately, it did.

But here's the thing. We had similar qualities. We had shown them against every other team. Against any other team, our experience, patience and quality was superior and made the difference. In the 2008 semi-final between the sides, United had played a more cautious approach over two legs against Barcelona, and the tactic had been successful. In Rome, in a one-off game, I think the gaffer felt the value of the first goal was enormous. That evening, we did begin with some aggression and it seemed to catch them by surprise. You can understand why he thought it was better to try that again and see if we were lucky enough to get the first goal. But so much depends on doing so.

It was the biggest game of my career. After a couple of difficult years trying to establish myself, I had now become the first-choice right-back in important games at the crucial point of the season. I had never enjoyed a sequence like this before – playing one important match after another. Arsenal at home, Arsenal away, Chelsea at home, Schalke away.

I couldn't sleep on the evening before the Final. It was incredible to be told I was going to play. All my friends and family were in London to see it. The boss had given us the game plan but at the end of the day his advice to me was the same as it had been since I came to the club. 'Son, just go out there, play your game and enjoy yourself.'

The easiest explanation for the game is that Barcelona were too good. This is the best Barcelona side in history and it is no disgrace to lose to them, especially when they're putting in their best-ever performance. But people look at the game and it has been one of those – more than any European Cup Final in the history of Manchester United – where the performance and reason for the performance and the defeat have been analysed so much. Why were we beaten so heavily? Was it as comprehensive as it looked? How did it feel to play against this side? Do you feel in awe? The truth is that we still felt as if we were as good as them. We didn't have Cristiano but we didn't start the game thinking we were doomed to lose. In the end, the manager was right – the first goal was the crucial one, because it allowed Barcelona to dictate the pace. This is what they can do with all that experience and a player like Lionel Messi.

The frustration of playing against a team that plays tiki-taka is that in essence it is a negative tactic. It is not necessarily a dangerous tactic. The purpose of it is to wear the opposition down, and to make them lose the feeling of controlling the ball. So, not only are you tired from trying to win the ball back but when you do you might be in an unfamiliar area to begin an attack. More often than not, your frustration at not having the ball for so long has a big impact on your decision-making, so you are more rash and impulsive, and therefore much more likely to give the ball away. And, when you do, you've fallen into their trap, and if you have just one player out of position they are able to manipulate their positioning and open you up to create a chance. The most important qualities are patience and composure, but it's very difficult to remember that when you are in the heat of a cup final and you don't have the ball for long periods.

The degree of success of any tactic depends on the quality of the players and Barcelona not only had Messi, they had Xavi and Andres Iniesta who are two of the best midfielders of all time and two of the most patient. They're happy to pass the ball to each other 200 times in a game. When they score first, as they did at Wembley, it increases the frustration in the opponent and it increases the likelihood of them making an impulsive mistake as they have to take a chance to get back into the game. Barcelona, meanwhile, continue to play the same way, and their patience would usually win out because of the quality of their stars. Look at any number of their goals and the most impressive quality is the simplicity that comes with the composure. But Messi only played for Barcelona and Xavi and Iniesta finally retired. If they didn't have Messi, how many goals do you think that Barcelona team could score? They would be a nice team to watch but with little direction to the goal.

You can take Manchester City for example. Already expensively assembled with hundreds of millions of pounds spent, in the first year under Pep Guardiola, they were average. Average! So they spend another £500m to boost the squad around two of the best players in the league, Raheem Sterling and Kevin De Bruyne. It's not the standard of Messi and Xavi but in comparison to the strength of the rest of the Premier League it is. And it looks good, because the players are fantastic, but the tactic itself has, for me, revealed itself to have many flaws. As good as Sterling and De Bruyne are, they aren't Messi, and teams with strong defensive skills can prepare to face City and not necessarily feel doomed from the kick-off.

I want to make it clear that I could not be more complimentary about Messi. He is the best player I've ever played against (you will understand that I like Cristiano more, and even Paul Scholes). His ball control was incredible. I think tackling is one of my strong points. I can tackle strong, fast and with purpose – I can control the ball after winning it. Messi does things that most can't do. I went in for tackles where I was 100 per cent sure I was winning the ball. At the very last second – a fraction of a second – he is able to touch it away from you. It makes you look as if you were miles away. You can look a fool. His ball control is so close, his manipulation is at such an expert level, that it could make a fool of anyone in the world. He is a genius, but I have wondered how good that team would have been without him. Would they have been good enough to get to the final, like we did without Cristiano?

It showed how hard it was for Barcelona to win another Champions League – only once since 2011 – and we have also seen that teams who are patient and have the speed to counter-attack can expose that tactic.

In a way, it was possibly the worst thing we could have done to equalise in the manner we did. Rooney scored a brilliant goal but maybe that gave a false sense of confidence that we were going about things the right way. We get into half-time, it's 1-1, and we go out to play the same way in the second half. But we were already tired. They scored early in the second half and it was very difficult to get that same kind of momentum to come back into the game.

The Barcelona style is nice on the eye and it is effective. We were not the only good team they defeated. But, honestly,

I do find it a little boring to just keep the ball. My preference is for a game plan with more excitement, more tackling. More *fun*. The principle purpose for keeping the ball in that approach is that by you having it, you are preventing the opposition from scoring. That isn't what football is supposed to be about for me.

I am convinced that if we'd scored the first goal at Wembley – and in Rome, for that matter – we would have beaten them. If Wayne's goal had been the first goal of the game. *If.* I don't think they would have been able to score past us if we had played in that sort of compact way we did in the 2008 semi-final.

The season had started with Wayne's transfer request. I don't know if that affected his relationship with the boss, but I never thought they were the closest. They had a very strong respect for each other, of that I am certain. The boss had an affection with some of the lads. Cristiano, when he was there, for example. You might even say my brother and me. I don't know why Wayne wanted to leave, but I am sure that his respect for the manager was a big reason for him staying. We were all glad that he did. And he showed how good he was with the performances that helped us win the title and get to the Champions League Final. He played some of his best football. He was so physically strong and such a good striker that he was a big part of our team – and, as such, a big character and also a big part of the squad.

Wayne's first start after the injury was at Rangers, where he scored the match-winning penalty in the last few minutes. It had been awarded for a foul on me – a typically aggressive challenge. I loved the atmosphere at Ibrox. I remember some of the older lads talking us through what to expect before the game – that the supporters could be crazy. You needed to get through that first 15 minutes, show the quality, show your composure, and calm them down. In those first few minutes, don't be afraid to mix it up, hit the ball long for the forwards to get it so they can hold it up and you can press up the field and control possession. Tactical flexibility.

The boss trusted me to play in those European games anyway but I wanted more. I felt brave enough to knock on the door of his office myself. I was training very well. I said to him, 'I want a chance. I've been playing well when I get games, but I would like to play more. I think I deserve my chance. I feel like it's now or never.' I felt like that left a positive impression. Maybe he had not been sure about me before, but on seeing how confident I was to go and ask him, he wanted to give me that chance to see what I could do.

Just one problem. Patrice! This guy had played every league game in the previous season. He wasn't going anywhere. I came on as a substitute at West Brom for Gary Neville – I didn't know it at the time, but this was my chance. Gary was very disappointed with his performance in that game and decided to retire in the middle of the season. It was a big surprise to everyone outside the club but not to us. He would always complain about being tired in training. I want to give credit to his professionalism because it takes a commendable level of honesty to call time on your career in the middle of the season, especially when your team who you have played for all of your career and supported all of your life are on the verge of winning a league title. He had won many, but this one would be special. However, Gary's game was very physical, and he had very high standards. It seemed as if he hadn't enjoyed any of the season and that was understandable. He was having to push himself harder than ever before and the competition was greater in his position that it had been for years. Maybe, having to do that in training, left him too tired to be able to do what he was used to doing on the pitch.

When my brother and I first arrived the lads had joked that Rafa would retire Gary. But he was nearly 36 when he retired, and he had a lot of injuries, so he had a fantastic career which was not cut short by anybody but himself when he decided those high standards he had set for all of us to follow were not standards he could reach himself any more. He really liked me and Rafa. He liked our attitude and the way we played. I think he was happy to see that we could follow in his footsteps.

Even though I had stated my case to the gaffer, it was natural that Rafa would be first in line to get his chance. And he did. He played well at Stoke, and at Spurs despite getting sent off, and then against Blackpool before he was forced off with concussion. I should have come on for him but I didn't even think about football – I'm sure Rafa was wanting to get back on the pitch, and I was probably even more concerned than he was! I went straight to the tunnel. The manager didn't even think about asking me to play. He saw how worried I was. At United, you have to sometimes be cold and calculated and seize every chance you get, but even with that at stake, my brother had to come first.

We both played at full-back against Crawley in the FA Cup, and we both came off in the second half. I don't think that was anything we did wrong – it was not a great game and the boss wanted more from the attack. We won just 1-0 and Gabriel Obertan, who had signed in the summer of 2009, wouldn't play for the club again after that. Neither did Bebé. They were talented lads, but the stage of Old Trafford has been too big for players more talented than them, with all due respect. So my brother and I are the wingers for the game against Arsenal in the next round.

What followed was one of my most memorable nights in football. I have a picture from the game hanging in my house but to be honest the memory will be forever imprinted in my mind. There was so much about the tie which made it stand out as a special occasion. It's a cup match, against a big rival, at Old Trafford in the evening. Normally, every time, United will be favourites, but on this evening, with the seven or eight defenders named in the team, everybody has questioned the gaffer and expects us to get knocked out. When they see him name a team like that they think he's saying the FA Cup isn't important, that we can lose this and we will be fresher for the league and Champions League.

That wasn't the message in the dressing room. He impressed on us that he had selected us as wingers because he felt that was the best chance we had of winning the game. He made us believe it. He loved that we would not allow Arsenal to settle into a rhythm of pass-pass-pass. We didn't.

It wasn't just scoring that was special; it was being involved in the build-up, winning the ball, the combination with Wayne and Chicharito. But, more than that, it was playing the ball to my brother and him being involved in the goal. Me and him. It was like being on the streets back at home, playing football with freedom, my brother showing his skill and me scoring the goals. Two boys from Petrópolis, playing the way we always had, thousands of miles away in Salford for the biggest club in the world.

We won 2-0 but even with many people saying the boss should try it again, we knew it was a one-off. We appreciated that. The best I could hope for was that I had shown enough to be given a chance at full-back, and I was.

A couple of weeks later I was in the team from the start against West Ham. They were 2-0 up in 25 minutes with two penalties. At half-time the manager gave us a couple of minutes where he saw us feeling sorry for ourselves and then he killed everyone. He gave us a lot of home truths. This is where the weight of expectation of playing for Manchester United really comes into play – and the challenge and reality of whether you're good enough. This was a ground where United had lost titles before. We should not put him through that again.

We were a different team in the second half and the only explanation was that Sir Alex's words had made the difference. The turnaround of games, particularly towards the end of the season, really presents an incredible challenge for Manchester United players. You have to make every single one your priority, you have to put in maximum effort. The next time you step on to the pitch you are playing against a team who have probably been saving themselves for you, or, they're going to give that little extra. Every single time. You can't afford to start a little slow, be a little out of concentration or focus. You can't afford for the tiredness of the last game – or, in this case, the rustiness of the first match after the international break which has interrupted your rhythm – to have an impact, or you'll find yourself 2-0 down at West Ham with a mountain to climb.

But, just as history had given West Ham some moments of their own against United, United also had climbed these mountains so many times that a team could be 2-0 up against us and still play with the fear that just one goal can transform the mood of the entire occasion. They're playing against the fear of the reputation that the teams before you have built over the generations and the team you are playing has lived up to. It's not just Roy Keane at Juventus and Ole Gunnar against Bayern Munich in 1999. It's us against Aston Villa and against Spurs just a couple of years ago. It's us against Blackpool just a few weeks earlier.

You know the feeling that can come from scoring that first goal in a comeback and you are striving to do so as quickly as possible. It takes us 20 minutes. Berba comes on at half-time; Chicharito in the 64th minute. You can sense the dread on the stands – you can feel it in your body. Within a minute we get a free kick and Rooney scores. The adrenalin rushes through your body – your energy levels are replenished at the same rate as the opponent starts to feel drained. Your belief of winning increases as you can literally see the fans and the opponents feel that little bit deflated. It's West Ham today, but it could be anybody. They know we're going to come back and win. We don't disappoint them. Rooney scores, and scores again. We've already won the game but Chicha gets a fourth just to make sure.

I want to emphasise just how real it is that opponents are giving that little bit extra playing against United. This was my first experience as a professional footballer so I didn't know any different. But I played for three more clubs in the Premier League and I played against so many of the same players. Many of them, I couldn't recognise. When I was at Old Trafford, these same players were so much quicker, so much more aggressive, so much more committed. They gave more than everything. The way he – and when I say he, I could be talking about anybody – tackles me, he wants to hurt me, and now I'm not in a United shirt, it's like he wants to be my friend!

Our eyes were on prizes bigger than just one victory against a specific opponent. Our FA Cup run came to an end in the semi-final against Manchester City – I came on for the last few minutes, but we were down to ten men and chasing the game. My next start was against Everton. It was an early kick-off and I remember being especially keen to impress because the Champions League semi-final was coming up.

I didn't always deal very well with the early games. I have a sensitive stomach, and I don't really eat much before a game because of the natural nervousness that I had about playing well. So, maybe the nerves played a part, but I felt unwell in the first half and I put that down to not eating very much. You compensate by drinking a lot of caffeine and trying to get as much energy as you can from other drinks. It didn't work well for me, although I wasn't playing poorly.

At half-time, I went straight to the toilet and I was sick. I mean, I was properly throwing up. The manager came in to the toilets; I was trying not to make a noise. I know he saw me, and heard me, but I also know he was trying to make sure that I didn't know.

He knew by now of my anxiety and nerves before and during games. He knew how desperate I was to impress and he also knew, because I had told him directly, that I just wanted that chance to play games. He never told me, but I am sure that when he found me he thought I was being sick because I was anxious, and, having considered it, he decided he would put his faith in me and let me see the game out. I am certain he saw that as a sign of how much I wanted it. With about six minutes left, we scored a crucial winner through Chicharito.

We then travelled to Germany for the Champions League semi-final first leg against Schalke. In training the day before, it was obvious from the way we had set up that my brother was going to play. There was an animated discussion between Sir Alex, Mick Phelan and other coaches on the side of the pitch that was loud enough to catch our attention. I was called over and told to switch sides with my brother for the crossing drills. As Rafa passed me, he said, 'You're going to play tomorrow!' It was a strange feeling, because I realised he was right. He seemed just as buzzing as he knew I would be. He had just come back from an injury so he actually felt I was physically more prepared.

I had a tremendous confidence boost from this and I felt I played one of my best games. Rio Ferdinand helped me so much. He'd been in so many semi-finals and was encouraging me to just feel comfortable, to not worry as he would be there to cover me. It says a lot about Rio as a guy that the advice he was giving this 20-year-old was to be natural. My natural game, as I've said, was more suited to Europe than the Premier League, and maybe the opposite could have been said for my brother, who was still learning with his temperament. One player who didn't need any help with that was Ryan Giggs. He was almost 38 and put on a masterclass of a performance, scoring our first goal. It was an incredible thing to see someone of that experience and age playing at such a high level. It was a freak, it's the only way I could describe it. Gary Neville was younger and his retirement was understandable. It was natural. Giggs was supernatural. He shouldn't have been capable of the things he was doing – we were so grateful that he still was. He didn't just play. He played fantastically well and made the difference.

We won 2-0 – a strong enough performance and result to convince the gaffer to change the entire team for the second leg. It's still a Champions League semi-final, so it is not an easy game, but it was a better environment for my brother to play such an occasion at that time, and I was as delighted for him playing as he was for me.

The next game was Chelsea at home and I was back in the team. It wasn't the mathematical title decider but a win would make it almost certain that we'd be champions. We scored in the first minute – Chicharito with one of his deadly strikes – and it was 2-0 pretty early on as Nemanja got the goal that ultimately won the game. The confidence flowed through the team and I was feeling as good as I ever had in a red shirt. I got the ball near our box and started to dribble; I did well and passed the ball to Antonio.

Half-time comes and the manager picked me out. 'Are you crazy? What are you doing?' It was a reminder that you still need to do your job. There was no Cristiano to tell me not to do it! It was funny – I had started to really feel comfortable in the team, and, after winning that big game against Chelsea, we then went to Blackburn, knowing a point would win the title. It seemed like all of the lads had that uncertain feeling I was all too familiar with.

I wouldn't say we were complacent but I'm not even sure a word exists, in English or Portuguese, to describe the feeling we had going to Ewood Park. United had won league titles. This squad had won many. Sir Alex and Ryan Giggs had won all of theirs together and this was a new feeling even for them. If we got the right result we were going to be champions of England and this would be our 19th title. It would take us past Liverpool, and make us the most successful club in English football history, something we did not fully appreciate when we arrived but know all too well now.

So the feeling was different. Perhaps even a little nostalgic, especially for those older players, the gaffer and some of the coaches. I don't even know if the boss thought it would have been possible when he took over at the club. But he had nonetheless created this incredible journey which had been a privilege to be a part of. I'm sure there are plenty of players, especially in more recent years, who could explain how heavy the Manchester United shirt can be. We were lucky. It didn't feel like that very often for us but this was perhaps one of those days. Sir Alex would always say to play the game and not the occasion. Sometimes the occasion is so big that you can't help it.

Of course, we would win the league with a good result but Blackburn were playing as if they would get the trophy if they won. They score early on and the manager showed how serious he was taking the game when he took me off for Scholesy and put Antonio to right-back. I can't say I was happy to come off, but if it was for anyone, I'm glad it was Scholesy who got to take part in such a historic game.

We won a penalty. Rooney – brilliant all season since he came back into the team – scored it.

We kept the ball for almost the entire last ten minutes. The most fun I've ever had watching tiki-taka. A little time out on the bench alongside my brother to fully take in what's happening.

In this moment I'm thinking about my experiences around the world – being in Asia and seeing thousands of fans who are crazy about the badge on your chest. Going back home to Brazil and feeling the different way people see you now you are a Manchester United player. Being away from home and seeing fans surround the bus, not because they want to touch you or harass you, but because they just want to be able to see you. Watching these supporters in the away end at Ewood Park celebrate in the way they are.

What is difficulty, really, when you're playing for Manchester United? It's all relative to what you know and have experienced. At the time, difficulty was the big disappointment of getting injured in those first months after arriving permanently and to not win the league in the second year. So, of course, playing a part in this league success, getting a medal, and feeling as though I had made a strong contribution – I was able to experience this and really take it in as the greatest accomplishment of my career – at the time, maybe even the best day of my life. I can remember every moment of the day when a draw for Manchester United was finally good enough.

We didn't know what the future held. For some of us we still felt as though we were young enough to experience many more days like this. It was made even more special by the unity within the squad. There were many different nationalities but just as many strong friendships. You could call them unlikely. We were close with Wayne. With Fletch – I can say we love this guy like family. People judge players by their personalities and they like them to be extravagant. Fletch was not like that. He kept it simple. United had so many players like that – imagine, having so many players who had the capability to be a leader, to be so good, and yet to play the game as simply as Fletch did. People do not appreciate how difficult it is to do that. Because we were not raised in England, and we didn't speak the language at first, our friends were the ones we made in the dressing room and at the club, and some of them became very close.

Fletch was one of the best midfielders in the country and played one of his best seasons that year. Like Park Ji-sung, like Antonio. Sometimes, with the goals of a Rooney or Berbatov, the hard work of these players goes unappreciated by the media. Not by us as players. We had so many players like that. Unfortunately, a few of them left us that summer, and although I was sad to see them go, I was happy that they had remained at the club long enough to experience and contribute to our historic achievement.

Edwin van der Sar was one – for a few years he had been signing one-year contracts and every time we felt it might be the last one. He finally retired in 2011 and I don't think I'm alone in feeling he maybe even had one or two years left where he could have played for us. Edwin's catalogue of saves was impressive and crucial but not spectacular. That was because his positioning was so good he was rarely caught out. He made goalkeeping look so easy. He was a calming influence from the back. He was the same age as our dad! Whenever he gave advice, you were sure to listen, in just the same way as you would to a parent. I'm sure, if the boss did not have David de Gea ready to sign, Edwin could have easily played at that level for some time.

Scholesy also retired, and I've already put on record the esteem I hold him in. Even at the age when he retired he still had the ability to make himself free for a pass. The ability to find space on a football pitch is one of the ultimate signs of intelligence in the sport and Scholes had that. The way he was able to make the team work around him despite not running everywhere. How he was able to dictate the pace of a game despite not running from box to box at that stage of his career.

How he could hit a pass 40 or 50 yards and get it on your chest. There was no extravagance to his game but he made it look that way. People sometimes think I'm crazy to say he was the best I ever played with. He's been in the media for a few years now so everyone knows he has plenty to say, but one of the things I especially loved about playing with him was that you would have all of his peers in the press. Xavi and Iniesta would be happy to talk. In England it was the same with Lampard and Gerrard, who were also happy to talk. Scholes just let his football do the talking. He trained, ate, and went home. He presented the same image to us on and off the pitch. And his standard of performance on it made you feel that the standard he set off it was also one to follow. Just the same as the Barcelona players who were desperate for his shirt after the final at Wembley, even in victory.

Rafa – Interpretation

THERE WAS a lot of change in the summer of 2011 as many players left and many came in. The first big change was David de Gea, who replaced Edwin van der Sar. It was hard for David in the beginning. First of all, he was so young, and he seemed too skinny to be a goalkeeper in England, so there was an obvious concern that he might not get the protection from referees. The Premier League is more physical than other European leagues, and David had no time to get used to it before he was expected to play not only at a high standard, but to match the standard set before him by Edwin.

In that regard it became a difficult transition for all of us. Communication is one of the biggest factors in good goalkeeping. The keeper is the one telling you to go right or left, to go or to hold your position, and you need to have trust in him. When that goalkeeper is not only half the age but has not even five per cent of the playing experience of the one before him, and when he speaks a completely different language, you have to roll with that change and deal with it the best way possible.

One thing that is impossible is using it as an excuse for your own poor form. It's a normal football problem, especially in the modern era, as players in key positions could speak a different language and have a different experience in their history to each other. This is part of your personal growth – you have to take that responsibility to understand the difficulty of your team-mate. This is also the time when you have to show the benefit of your experience of working with someone like Edwin. He was such a patient guy, and a supremely effective communicator. It helps you as a player and you have to pass that experience on so that it helps others. David is David, not Edwin, but now it was our time to pass on our experience. And, at the same time, I'm sure the coaches at the club were expressing how Edwin was with us, how we responded to playing with him. De Gea had so much natural talent as a goalkeeper but he also had a lot to learn, and to give credit to him, he did learn, and very quickly.

Ashley Young was a player the manager was clearly very keen to sign and it was easy to see why when he came to the club. He had talent as a winger, yes, but he also worked tremendously hard. He had a great efficiency to his style. He gave everything for the team and showed that when he was asked to play in a variety of positions and always gave a proper shift when he was there. It is an ambition of mine that I'll one day be a manager, and, if and when that day comes, a player like Ashley Young would be the perfect example of one I would want in my team. He was a scorer, a creator, and someone who understood match stamina and the fact you needed to be working all the time.

That was an attitude we were all going to need to deal with Manchester City. They had already spent a lot of money on the likes of Mario Balotelli, James Milner, Yaya Touré and David Silva and then added to that with Gaël Clichy, Samir Nasri and Sergio Agüero.

Competition was nothing new for me, but I did have new competition. Wes and John had gone, Gary had retired, but the gaffer had already brought in Chris Smalling who sometimes played at right-back. Obviously, Chris and I were very different in that position. He was a defensive defender, maybe not as natural going forward as I was. But he was tall, and good at the back, and I knew, depending on the game we played, he would be preferred – he was stronger, taller, maybe better to play against a team like Stoke City. I don't think I played many times against them!

Then there was Phil Jones. He came from Blackburn for a big transfer fee and so it was clear he was going to be given a chance. And he was fantastic when he first arrived.

He was the talk of the club. It was obvious that he had so much talent. Now he has played most of his career at United and he has suffered many injury problems, and people haven't always been fair to him. It was suggested back then that he could be one of the best players in the club's history. You have to remember that was due to how good his form was when he first arrived. He was brilliant. So when Chris and Phil came to the club it was a very big challenge for me; they started very well and I knew I would have to be on the top of my own game. Everyone said that they were going to eventually take over Rio and Vida, but those guys weren't finished yet, and so that right-back spot became the one we would all compete for. I wasn't exactly worried – but it was a reminder that I needed to work more, that the position wasn't mine.

It was a good thing that it happened when it did, though, and not earlier in my time there. I could see a little bit of what my brother felt with Patrice; that Phil was going to start as first choice. If this had happened in 2009 or 2010 it might have affected my confidence. However, like I said, by now, the challenge for my position was not new, even if the challengers were. It was not difficult to remind myself that I had fought my way to play many games and enjoy some very good times when Gary Neville, Wes Brown and John O'Shea were there, and those guys were three of the most consistent players in United's history. And how could I forget my brother, who had been the first choice in the last months of the last season, and had played the best football of his career?

The start of 2011/12 was one of the strangest times in my entire career. I was watching most of it from the bench, waiting for my chance, while we scored so many goals. Spurs are beaten 3-0. Arsenal come to Old Trafford, and we've had some easy times against them in the past but nothing like this day when we win 8-2. We're scoring so many goals, creating so many chances, and yet at the other end we were allowing far too many shots at our goal. I don't know what I put that down to – maybe the enthusiasm of our new players? I do remember that after that Arsenal game the gaffer was trying to get the message across. 'Guys, it's great that we scored eight, but they also had eight shots on our goal! That's too many.' How does that message get home? Sometimes players have to learn the hard way, and there was no harder way than against Manchester City when we lost 6-1 at home a few weeks later. Look, I was not ever happy to miss a game for United, but I think I could make an exception for that. Too many shots. Not enough defensive discipline. What am I talking about? That game never happened. Well, it's vanished from my memory, anyway.

The events at Anfield a week earlier are harder to forget. I wasn't on the pitch when Luis Suárez racially abused Patrice but there was nowhere to hide from that story for the next few months. My brother and I have already spoken in this book about how long it took us to understand and speak English, and how that became such an important part of how we understood football, and the culture and history of Manchester United. Experience can only help your understanding. But there are some things that just don't make any sense, and the idea that Suárez's words should have been taken in a friendly way was ridiculous. It was an insult and would have been taken that way on any football pitch, or any street, in the world. One defence was that he said it in Spanish. Well, Patrice spoke Spanish – did he just presume he could only speak French and English? Of course the entire thing was much more difficult because it was Liverpool and Manchester United, the biggest rivalry in England and one of the most hostile. The truth is it shouldn't happen in any game.

Everyone has different views on how racism should be tackled. First of all, it's a life problem, not a football problem. It's an archaic attitude. It should be in the past. We should stop treating people as if we are different. We are the same. There should not be a discussion about what is wrong or right to say. That is for the past. It is an attitude clearly wrong and if someone is guilty of it, punish them. There is no need for a political conversation about it. Don't defend it, don't argue somebody's right to say something racist. We are in a progressive culture. Everybody should be treated equally.

I wasn't having my best season, to put it bluntly. Before the end of 2011 I played against Crystal Palace in the League Cup, when we lost, and also against Blackburn where we lost again, both at Old Trafford. There was a FA Youth Cup-winning team at the club that year and it had several very highly-rated players in midfield, including Ravel Morrison, Ryan Tunnicliffe and Paul Pogba. Ravel and Paul played against Palace, but we had a midfield injury crisis against Blackburn and I guess some people might have expected Paul to play in that game. I know that many people have said that because he didn't, and I did, that was what caused him to decide to leave the club the first time around. I don't think that's the case. There was speculation about his future because his contract was expiring that summer. That was the case before that game, and the case afterwards, and he definitely played for the first team after that.

There was a lot of talent in that group. Ravel might have even been the best of all of them. But they were crazy guys and when I say crazy, I mean, when it came to having the professional discipline to last at Manchester United. In each case, maybe a loan away would have helped, but they all eventually left. Paul, of course, came back some time later but I think it showed just how the manager felt that I was selected in front of them. Playing on the wing with my brother was an out-of-position experience I cherish. This one, not so much. I'm not suited to playing in the middle. You're constantly having to look back and play it safe. That didn't work for me.

I was glad it didn't count against me. Maybe it was my experience, and the fact we had a lot of big games in a short space of time, but I was playing a lot after Christmas. We won at Arsenal, then we went back to Liverpool in the FA Cup where the atmosphere was horrible. We lost, but a couple of weeks later they came to Old Trafford for the return league game. It also happened to be the first match Suárez was playing in after his suspension. There was a lot of talk about what might happen but the gaffer, as usual, tried to play it as calm as he could. Any discussion about Suárez was done with Patrice privately and not with the rest of us. Patrice had decided to take a big stand, to let his pride take a back seat, to be the bigger man and offer the handshake as the Liverpool team walked past us before kick-off. When Suárez did what he did and declined the shake, Patrice was so angry. He didn't show it so obviously, but we knew him, we knew how that made him feel. I can't speak for everyone else, just for myself, as a friend and team-mate of Patrice – I was angry too. I was furious. How could Suárez do that? It was shocking.

The intensity of those games, as I've said, could usually be felt from the stands – it was probably worse than ever, but on that day, I didn't feel it, because of everything that was on the pitch. It felt like a war. There was anger coming from every one of the players. Winning against Liverpool was always special, but let's just say that that day was more special than most. It was an ugly, ugly game. I'm not speaking of it as a spectacle – I can't say about that. But to play in, horrible. Street boxing once again.

Winning was the name of the game, as it always is for Manchester United. We scored a lot of goals in games against Wolves and Aston Villa and people were talking about how goal difference might be a big factor. The boss never did – not this season, anyway, but he was definitely taking City's goalscoring power on board as something to think about. He wasn't a manager to have many regrets but I think he might have felt he could have urged us to score more at certain times. The league title was decided by eight goals; you could even say that defensive indiscipline at the start of the season was now coming to hurt us.

It wasn't as if we weren't scoring a lot – Danny Welbeck had developed into a first-team player and had a great relationship with Wayne up front. Danny was someone I'd grown up with in the team and here was the greatest example of a player who had learned from going away on loan and then coming back. He was brilliant for us this season. I don't think people realise just how good he was. He had this high technical level which made him a very compatible member of the team, scoring goals but also making a lot. He was 21 or 22 and already playing with composure, which – as Federico Macheda found out – was not so easy that you can take it for granted.

There were many small things that went against us at the crucial moments. We can say that offensively we did well, and defensively we didn't always let a lot of goals in, but we had our moments, like against Everton at home in April when Danny was the best player – scoring a great goal and setting up two. That wasn't one of my better games – defensively, anyway, because I thought I played well going forward. Three of Everton's goals came from my side and it was difficult to deal with. I thought about what I did wrong and I carried it forward with me. It is true what is said about adversity making you stronger; here are a couple of examples that had a huge positive influence in my career.

The first is this game against Everton, where I now felt an extra responsibility for my defensive discipline. I'm not saying that I didn't feel that way before – but it was clear that I needed to concentrate more in order to improve, and those Everton goals were on my mind like a nightmare for the next year. I was able to put that to a positive use. You don't want to repeat the bad things that happened.

The gaffer was furious after that match. Every game United don't win is a catastrophe and this one was described as the one that cost us the title. From the way the manager was shouting at us, it was obvious that he was feeling that that could be true. When you have the experience he has, I guess you develop this intuition for when things begin to turn. It is within him and it is within this entire system at Manchester United that he has created over the years. It is why he is such a winner. He has won everything the game has to offer. Most of us in the dressing room had won trophies with the club and there was a hunger and desire to keep winning. When you are in the heat of a title race, you're trying to win every game anyway, so the true weight of the deeper message needs a little more time to sink in. Maybe it even needs the defeat to help it sink in. So the Everton game was costly. But we were still within ten seconds of winning the Premier League.

We went into the final day of the season – our game was at Sunderland and City were at home to Queens Park Rangers. Realistically, although we were only separated by six goals, our best chance was of them dropping points. We scored very early through Wazza and that was it, 1-0 for the match. From that point on we're all waiting to hear what is happening in the other game. On the bench we're up to date. I can't imagine what it's like to be on the field. We find out early in the second half that QPR have scored, and then they score again. For 25 minutes we are seeing the game out as champions. In the last three or four minutes the mood on the bench is a little like it had been at Blackburn. Everyone is excited because we are

Making a sacrifice. As boys we had to be away from home to chase our dream of becoming footballers.

Brazilian boys, promotional image after signing for United

Rafael scores his first goal for United against Arsenal

'I attack, you defend'. Cristiano giving some advice on Fabio's debut

The First Time – Rafael lifts his first Premier League title in 2009

Champions of the world – The Club World Cup is an important title and Rafael's first major trophy at Old Trafford

Fabio netting against Wigan in February 2011

One of the greatest moments of our lives, playing as wingers and celebrating Fabio's goal against Arsenal in the FA Cup in March 2011

Rafael fulfilling a dream competing against Ronaldinho

Size of the fight in the dog – you could never back down at Anfield

It was an honour to play for Manchester United in a Champions League final at Wembley even if the result was one to forget

Celebrating United's 19th league title in 2011, a landmark moment in British football history

Thanking the tremendous away fans at Ewood Park after claiming United's 19th title

On a pre-season trip to New Jersey

Rafael celebrating scoring against Fulham in August 2012

Primal Scream – Rafael celebrates his favourite United goal with the supporters at Anfield

going to be champions. The players are asking about the other game and the message gets through. The final whistle blew in our game and we were 100 per cent sure we were champions. As our game ended, we are unaware that City have equalised. Ten seconds later – it cannot have been longer than that – we start to see the Sunderland supporters celebrating.

I've experienced many difficult crowds but I was surprised to see a club that had no real rivalry with us celebrating our sadness in such a way. There was a numbness and devastation in the dressing room afterwards. A strange silence. Nobody even dared to speak.

A couple of minutes later the manager came in. 'Guys, look around. Look at each other. Remember those Sunderland fans and how they celebrated. Don't ever forget it. Every single game next season I want you to remember this day and what happened here. You are good enough. You are going to be champions next season.'

We were still processing the weight of that extraordinary defeat and the manager had produced a motivational speech for the ages. He said all the right words that struck all the right notes. How did he do it? You can't prepare to win in such a fashion, so how do you react to defeat like that?

That message, that feeling, is something I will always talk about. I am 100 per cent sure that it influenced how we were the following year. I know that I personally thought about it all the time. Because it wasn't just that the manager was right – we did win the league – but that we won it so early. Our consistency was fantastic and we won 27 games from our first 34. That was the message. Win, win, win.

I'm not sure that you have the same result if you don't have the adversity to go through first. So maybe you could call me lucky, say that I had a little extra motivation. 2011/12 wasn't my best season, that's for sure. I did wonder if the gaffer had lost a little trust in me. But I was called into the Brazil squad for the Olympic Games, another mixed experience with mostly positives and a very difficult end. In fact, I'd say up until the final, it was one of the best experiences in my life. Playing for my country, at the Olympics in England? It was like inviting my entire family around to my new house!

There were so many highlights. Playing for my country at all was one of the best things I ever accomplished. It was a dream – you are brought up in a country where everyone dreams of the same thing, and you know how rare it is to get that opportunity. To be one of the lucky few is a feeling that you can't describe. And to score? Even better! My first goal for my country, against Egypt, was similar to my first for United; a good shot with my left foot. Maybe that's my natural side! I think I called everyone in my family afterwards to talk about it.

I was lucky enough to play in the Maracana when I was in the under-17s. But it was just as special, if not more so, to play for my country at Old Trafford in the Olympic semi-final. It was a comfortable victory as well, against South Korea. I was playing well in the tournament and I especially felt confident in this game – that's why, whenever I look back at this time, I think it really helped me to grow. And it's why, despite what happened next, my thoughts are mostly positive.

In the first minute of the final, against Mexico at Wembley, I lost the ball. Mexico scored from the attack. I don't think there's been a moment in my life where I haven't held my hands up and admitted that I was accountable for a mistake. I am always happy to do that if I did wrong. I made a mistake in this game; but was I to blame for the goal? There were a couple of phases of play before the ball was the net. I'm not blaming anyone else; I just think that I was not the only one responsible. Of course I could do better. So should the midfield. So should the other defenders. So should the goalkeeper. It's not just me.

Many Brazilian journalists did not see it that way. This was in the first minute; Mexico scored another goal, we scored one and we lost, but the blame was all put on me. Unbelievable. But what can you do other than take how it is and move on?

This was the culmination of a few years of issues with some reporters back home. Because we had moved at such an early age, we were often seen as English and not Brazilian; we were accused of not wanting to play for our country. An already difficult path to the national team is made that much more tough if you have never played professionally in Brazil. They look at you differently.

After the final I think they wanted something from me that I couldn't give. They wanted me to cry on the pitch. I'm not that guy. Tears in the dressing room – yes, of course. There I will show my sadness. If you could see how I was crying in the dressing room, how inconsolable I was in the moment, then you would understand how much it means to me. I cried for fun. My team-mates saw it. Was I judged because I didn't cry in public? That wasn't me. I wasn't going to fall apart on the pitch. That was the way I was raised; I'd seen that my father always kept his emotions close. As we became adults he was more open with us, much more emotional, much more free to cry in front of us, but not when we were growing up, and I feel that shaped the way that I am, too. That's nothing to apologise for. I don't need to cry to show people I'm crying.

This was a time when the Brazilian team was being rebuilt to plan for the 2014 World Cup, which would be held at home. Every single player wanted to be involved in that and I was no different. It did not matter how badly it eventually ended. There was no relief that I wasn't part of the squad that lost 7-1 against Germany. It had been my goal to earn selection for that tournament and for sure, between the Olympics and the World Cup, I played the best football of my life. I didn't get one call-up for the national team. I spoke to journalists over this time and I was always asked if I wanted to go. I never said it in so many words. I think what people wanted from me was an apology. I couldn't give that. I wasn't going to beg. I don't know if they thought that it meant I did not care; I did care, but, after the way I was treated following the Olympics, I had to turn my thoughts towards something that I could be positive about – and that was playing for Manchester United, and trying to win our title back.

Growing Up, Apart

Fabio: I ended the 2010/11 season as first-choice right-back, so I felt the impact of the new arrivals just as much as my brother. I was used to being preferred for European games but it seemed like at the start of the following season, that's what I was being kept for. Chris Smalling and Phil Jones were more physical and better in the air. Antonio Valencia also started to play at right-back sometimes – so maybe it's just as well Gary Neville, Wes Brown and John O'Shea all left! Despite this, I maintain that some of my best friendships in football were formed with the players most people would say were rivals for my position. That much is definitely true with Antonio, whom I'd developed a very good relationship with on the pitch, too, in the previous season.

I wish I had a straightforward explanation for what happened to us in Europe in 2011/12. We came from the final carrying that disappointment but that was no excuse. If I had to give a reason I would say that it is possible we took the group stage for granted. This team got to the final in 2008, 2009, and 2011, and the semi-finals in 2007. One thing we were used to in England – teams raising their game to face us – started to happen in Europe more frequently. Opponents would give their usual 150 per cent and so if we weren't at our maximum, we could be punished. I'm not saying we weren't prepared, but maybe we didn't have the motivation or concentration in those group games. It was a lesson for us.

Overall I can't complain because 2011 was arguably the best calendar year of my career. I ended it by playing for Brazil – making my debut against Costa Rica and then playing from the start against Gabon. This was very special, it is a pinnacle of any player's career, but, as someone who has already confessed to being anxious on these occasions, I admit again that nerves undermined my performances in these games. I was not happy with the way I played. I spent so long fighting for my place at Manchester United, which is as difficult as it comes at club level, and now it was a new challenge to prove myself for my country. The difference is you don't get weeks and months to show what you can do.

Football is the most important thing in Brazil. It had become this way in my family because of our careers. So of course playing for the country was special for that reason, even if I felt unable to play my best. I ask myself every day why I felt so nervous. I was too young then to understand that it's not something you can really control. I'm not a person to carry many regrets but I do feel some regret for feeling that way – I know that I shouldn't have, because as I said this was the best spell I'd enjoyed in my career. Why should I be nervous to play a friendly game for Brazil when I'd already played so many important games for Manchester United? It's something you can't rationalise. I sometimes wish I could go back and relive it so I could deal with it differently.

Rafa: The funny thing was that when we both got our chances for the national team, we both played at right-back, so even there we ended up competing with each other. I had the first call-up and even though I don't normally feel nerves, I did when playing for Brazil, especially the first few times. People tell you to relax and have fun but your head is the boss and you have to just work with it the best way you can. And if I felt that way, I was sure my brother would too, so I tried everything I could to encourage him from a distance, in the same way he did for me.

Fabio: Sometimes you worry for nothing. And then you see what happened to my brother at the Olympics, and how he was crucified. They don't care about your age, they don't care about you as a person, they don't care about starting a campaign where they are inviting abuse on social media. You might think that is what worried me, and that is true, but never on a personal level. I can handle personal criticism. But the thought of my brother being the subject of it hurt me. My own concern was how criticism of me would affect my family. I knew that my brother would become stronger as a result of what he went through. I had been so proud of how fantastic he had played in the tournament and then I saw all this criticism. I missed the game, and only saw it afterwards. So I watched it and it was a normal mistake. I knew he would be devastated and I was, too, for him. I also knew that once the dust had settled, he would look back on the whole tournament and be as proud of what he achieved as we were.

The reason I missed that game was because I was playing in a friendly for QPR in Germany after joining them on loan. Towards the end of the previous season I felt courageous enough to tell Sir Alex again that I needed to play football. I talked about it with my brother before I approached the manager. I told him I wasn't going to be happy playing 12 or 15 games. I wanted to play in an environment where I was needed every week, and I was going to ask to go out on loan.

I was confident in my own ability to play well but you have to be realistic when looking at the competition for places. It was great that I was trusted for European football – and playing for Manchester United in Europe was an incredible privilege – but I wanted to prove that I was good enough to play every game. I watched how well Danny Welbeck had done on loan at Sunderland and then he came back to play many matches in the first team. He made the position his own for a while. I felt the best way I was going to make my own case was to do it away from the club.

The manager agreed with me. It wasn't that he didn't trust me – I played in some important games. It could be that he liked me too much and didn't want me to make any mistakes. He didn't want to put me in a match where my confidence might dip. But I needed to get away to prove that he didn't have to worry about that. And I do think it was the right decision, even though QPR were relegated, because I matured so much that year, off and on the pitch.

Rafa: I had always remembered the words of our parents who told us we couldn't play for the same club for all of our lives. So I knew one day that it would happen. My brother is a very intelligent guy and he made the decision to do it at the time that was good for both of us. Honestly, there were times when I wondered if a loan move might be right for me, too. But Fabio made the decision first and it was the right thing, because it was the first time we were out of the comfort zone. That might sound strange – Manchester United isn't a comfort zone – but we always had each other for support. The reality is that that would never change, but the time was right for both of us, after the time we'd had, to become our own people.

I know my brother better than anybody but there was still a little piece of me surprised and in admiration of his strength to approach the manager and say that he needed to go. I learned from that. It was the action of a man and it made me think I was capable of the same. For the first time we would be seen as Rafael and Fabio as individuals and not as a pair. I have to thank my brother for that because he made that decision and it benefitted me. It was good for both of us.

Fabio: Of all the clubs I would go to, it was ironic that it was QPR, considering how big a role they played in United not winning the title in 2012. My memories of that day are similar to my brother. We won the league for ten seconds and then it was gone. We were on the pitch as a squad to thank our fans for the season and we went from heaven to hell in a moment. And I can remember the image of Sir Alex Ferguson, the most successful manager of all time, a manager who won 12 Premier League titles, carrying the devastation of a man who had never won a single medal. He was affected by the nature of City's win and the sight of the Sunderland fans celebrating as if they had won.

I had already decided that I would be going away; I'd already asked. But I had never thought that that would be my last experience of working with Sir Alex Ferguson. He looked so fresh, and he'd been there for so long that we just didn't even contemplate the idea of him leaving. It was Sir Alex! He was surely going to be there for another five or ten years. I can guarantee that there was not a single player at the club who thought there was even the slightest chance that the manager was going to retire. I was sure that when I came back in a year, I would be returning to fight for my place under the gaffer. If I had known it would have been his last year, I think I would have stayed.

Instead, I went to London, and I was encouraged to go to QPR because Mark Hughes was the manager and he and Sir Alex knew each other well. It seemed like the best idea. There was the option of going abroad and maybe my style would have worked well there, considering I normally played well in Europe. When I asked to go on loan, I did expect that I would probably have to go overseas, but I preferred to stay in England, first to be close to my brother and also to remain in the vision of United.

I moved to west London. It wasn't the best place for me to live; London is fantastic, but busy. I prefer the country. But I had some familiarity down in England's capital with Park Ji-sung, who had recently moved to Loftus Road, and so naturally he was my best friend from the beginning. Park had moved there on a permanent contract – it seemed that there was an ambitious project taking shape and it looked as if it would be exciting to be a part of it. Júlio César, José Bosingwa, Ryan Nelsen, Andy Johnson, Junior Hoilett and Esteban Granero all joined in the summer. They also had Adel Taarabt, who was an incredible talent.

On paper it looked as if it could be a great team. But football isn't played on paper and it was obvious to me very early on that this was a collection of individuals and, when you looked at how they all came together, I honestly thought it would be impossible that they could ever combine to win a single game. There was a lot of selfishness.

I didn't blame the manager for that. I didn't think it was Mark Hughes's fault at all. I really liked working with him. He was trying to put across a positive message to the players but football management is very complicated. Bringing a lot of egos together, and people who have achieved a lot in other places, doesn't necessarily mean it will be the best sort of solution for a team in QPR's position. You can be a fantastic technical coach, and you can be a fantastic man-manager, but if you are only one and not the other you will struggle to be a great manager. I'm not saying this of Mark Hughes – the truth is that you can have these qualities and still struggle if you're in the situation that QPR were in, with the players they had. You need many factors to go your way.

Nobody talked to us about what had happened on the final day. That suited me. I didn't want to speak about how it was at Manchester United. Some of these players had egos so big you would swear they'd all won Ballon d'Ors, and I didn't want to talk about what it was like at Carrington because I didn't want to come across the same way. I remember Mark asking me and Park to tell the squad what it was like at United, how high the standard was. We were too reluctant. We didn't want to say, and they didn't want to hear. They all thought they were Cristiano Ronaldo. Only one problem – they didn't play like Cristiano.

Before the season started I was one of those guys convinced that the squad on paper would see us do some great things. And then on the opening day we played at home to Swansea – it was completely embarrassing. We were exposed every time they attacked us and we ended up conceding five goals. I couldn't believe what was happening but I quickly changed my opinion about our prospects and realised it was going to be a very tough year.

Rafa: We lost our first game of the season, too, at Everton. I didn't play. In training a couple of days later, the gaffer came to me and says, 'Raf – are you mature now? Can you do a season for us? I think we're going to need you this year, but I need to know that you're mature.' I told him I was ready. I would have said that anyway – you always have to say yes. But I knew that I meant it. My brother was away fighting for his own future in the game and I had to be my own man too.

So I played against Fulham in the first home game. A couple of minutes in, I slip – they get a free kick, and score. Again, maybe it's not my mistake, but I think if I do better, they don't score. Everton and Mexico flash in my mind. Sunderland. No, I say to myself. This cannot happen with me again. From that minute I played one of my best games. Focus and concentration. That's how I approached every match from that point. There are always moments over the 90 minutes where you have a reason to internally question your own decisions. If you make a mistake, it might hurt your confidence. But I remembered everything, and, above all, Sir Alex trusting in me to take this next step; I had a stronger conviction in myself. You can get a sense of how I played – I had one goal disallowed and scored what turned out to be the winning goal with my head. So I was literally using it!

When you have twin brothers, one is more intelligent than the other and I have to return to my very intelligent brother Fabio's comment about the genius of managers at the very top level. We lost the title on goal difference – eight goals. We'd scored 89 goals. So what does Sir Alex do? He goes and gets the most in-form striker in the league. I scored the winner against Fulham but the game was most remembered because Robin van Persie, who had just arrived from Arsenal, got his first goal for the club.

Robin was only about goals, and he scored them for fun that year. In the next game we played at Southampton – we were 2-1 down with three minutes left and won, with Robin getting a hat-trick. He missed a penalty as well! We had Danny Welbeck and Chicharito who were both capable of scoring goals but Robin was more selfish than either, and in a good way. He was ruthless. Danny would be more involved in the build-up play. Robin would, too, but we knew he was mostly bothered about scoring. An example of this was when we played against Arsenal in November. The game had only just started, I sent in a cross, the defender made a mistake and Robin was there like a killer to put the ball away. He scored before most people realised there was even a chance.

Robin was a special guy. He was a star and he liked to be treated that way – he took playing for Manchester United very seriously, and also his own contribution. That wasn't a bad thing. We also signed Shinji Kagawa – it didn't work out as well for Shinji as it did for Robin. But Shinji was a solid player, you knew he was safe with the ball and that he wouldn't make mistakes.

I've jumped ahead. There was the small matter of a trip to Anfield where Robin and I both scored. We came from behind to win in that game, something we did about ten times over the course of that season. It wasn't my best game against Liverpool but it's a memory that I will look back fondly on for the rest of my life. In fact, it wasn't our best performance as a team, but sometimes the result is all that matters and this was so important for us in setting the tone for the season. As with every match against them it was a battle on the pitch – Jonjo Shelvey was sent off for this crazy tackle on Jonny Evans. Then Gerrard scored early in the second half and the atmosphere then became even crazier. We were their biggest game of the season; it will probably always be that way because of what the clubs have achieved. There was the venom of the previous season but there was also the simple historical tension that comes from these teams playing against each other. There could be nothing riding on the game and still the atmosphere would be like a cup final. You have to be able to control that energy.

Getting a goal back quickly helps. I ran forward and Shinji chested a ball down in the box. It looked inviting so I made up my mind to shoot. It was on my left-hand side, but that didn't bother me as my best goals had come on my left foot. But somebody wasn't convinced. As I went to shoot, I could hear Rio screaming, 'No, no! Don't shoot!' It was too late to take his advice. The connection was good, the ball curled and went into the net off the far post. Our fans were behind the goal so it was great to run to them to celebrate; I was fortunate to score some special goals in some special places but against Liverpool at Anfield has to be my favourite. It helps that we won – Antonio won a penalty late in the game and Robin scored. On the bus home, Rio came up to me. 'Sorry Rafa. I didn't think you should have shot, but I was wrong.' Of course – we won!

Fabio: Our tone was set by the early results, too. Playing at Loftus Road is a completely different experience to playing at Old Trafford. Yes, the stadium is smaller, but the pitch is also more claustrophobic. It's not an excuse. You can turn that to your advantage, but in order to do that you have to have the right attitude. So you need to be committed to the cause. That's easily found in some players. Clint Hill, Jamie Mackie and Shaun Derry – these guys give everything to the club.

Many of players we brought in, or were there already, were veterans. Shaun Wright-Phillips and Bobby Zamora contributed positive things, but it was difficult for players like Kieron Dyer and Andy Johnson, who picked up injuries right away. Other players who came in on high salaries had to play from the start but they were taking the place of a player like Derry. It inevitably led to a lot of resentment within the dressing room between the players who had been there for a longer time and the newer players.

Polemic – that's a good word to describe the squad relations. They were personified best by Djibril Cissé, a player with so much experience, and yet he was one of the few players I've seen who could be genuinely annoyed if his team scored but the opportunity was there to pass to him to score instead. It happened on more than one occasion. The team would celebrate but he would not. He'd be as upset as he should be if we missed the chance.

I had something to prove. I had a reason for my performance to be good. But just a few games into the season I came off with a hamstring injury against Chelsea. I had actually been playing with a pain in my back for all the games down there. I didn't realise I'd suffered a stress fracture to my back and that's what had caused the hamstring. I was keen to get back on to the pitch as soon as possible but the doctors were very serious and stressed that if I rushed, I could suffer a problem later in my life. So I had to spend two full months out, watching as we lost nine and won none of the first 13 games; our fate was almost as certain as that of Mark Hughes, who was sacked in November.

Rafa: The season was going really well for us. I was playing every game – in Europe as well as the league – and then we came up against Reading in a crazy match. They scored from two corners in the first 25 minutes and the gaffer brought me off for Chris Smalling, to deal with the height from set pieces. I wasn't playing great but I didn't think I was doing too badly, and the goals weren't down to me; I was so upset to come off, and would have been anyway, but especially because it happened in the first half. I was so upset that I didn't shake the manager's hand. He normally shakes the hand of whoever is coming off, but because I was so angry, I didn't even look at him and walked to the bench. At half-time he explained his decision to me; I understood, but was still upset. We won, but afterwards everyone was talking about the fact I didn't shake hands with Sir Alex; even my brother phoned me to ask what was going on.

The reporters were trying to set fire to the situation afterwards so asked the gaffer about it. 'Rafa has been my best player this season,' he said. 'He came off and he was angry. I didn't see him not shake my hand. Maybe he didn't see me.'

They were showing it on the bus on the way back and all the lads were laughing, trying to make me feel better. Fletch is saying, 'See, he's just said you were the best player this season. Don't be mad.'

It didn't work – I didn't even sleep that night I was so angry. I am like that. If we play in the evening and if something big happens, good or bad, it is impossible to sleep.

In training the boss came to me. 'Look, what happened yesterday?'

'I was angry,' I said. I didn't apologise. 'I never came off the pitch that early before.' 'I understand you. But never do that again.'

Now, *I* apologise! 'Sorry gaffer. I won't do it again.'

We played Manchester City the following weekend. There was speculation all week, people talking shit and criticising. 'Oh, he can't be trusted.' I was so motivated. I even cut my hair as if I was in the army, preparing for battle! We were 2-0 up at half-time; I set up the second for Wayne Rooney. City came back in the second half and made it 2-2. In the last minute, I showed how desperate I was to win by charging into the area. I was fouled by my old friend Carlos Tevez. I'll claim the assist for this goal, too; Robin scored from the free kick to win us the game.

Our form was great after that, and still full of drama – we had a last-minute winner on Boxing Day at Old Trafford as we went unbeaten over the Christmas period. Early in the new year we played against Tottenham at White Hart Lane. It was another chance to go head-to-head with Gareth Bale, who had emerged as one of the best players in the league. Earlier in the season he'd given me a tough game at Old Trafford when he scored in Tottenham's first win there for many years. I had a good game against him in the return as we drew 1-1. I always say, whenever I am asked, that Gareth was my toughest opponent. I had some very good games against him but every single time I would come off the pitch thinking that guy had pushed me to my maximum. He was physically strong and so quick; you really had to make sure you were always concentrating. One thing's for sure – you're ready for a lie down on the sofa after playing against him.

Fabio: Bale would have been fantastic at Old Trafford. He would have been the natural player to succeed Ryan Giggs. His pace on our pitch – it's incredible to think of how good he could have been.

With some other players, though, they can look like they have all the talent in the world and you wonder why they don't go on to a bigger club. But temperament, and so many other factors, come into play. When I was fit enough to return to the QPR side, I came back for our first win of the season. It was Adel Taraabt who got the credit and rightly so because he scored both goals in a 2-1 win over Fulham. His second was brilliant, a dribble and a finish with the outside of his foot from the edge of the box.

So, why didn't he go on to a bigger club? Honestly, I don't think he had the required discipline. Against Fulham it worked, but even in that game, he just wanted the ball for himself for the full 90 minutes. He didn't want to pass to anyone. He was a stubborn guy, so it was impossible to convince him to even try. Adel was good but did not have the technical abilities to ever arrive at the level of a Cristiano or a Giggsy, so, really, these sorts of occasions – a derby against Fulham – were where he made his mark. But Fulham is a game where the elements combined to provide a good platform on which Adel could perform. Clint and Jamie were in the side, it was a local rivalry, we had just changed manager, and Fulham had started the season well enough that they weren't going to get relegated. The brutal fact for QPR was that we couldn't afford to have players who needed everything to be right for them to pick and choose when they wanted to play. In other matches it felt like Adel was playing by himself, trying to nutmeg people in the middle of the field for some personal victory; it added nothing to us trying to win the game.

Harry Redknapp succeeded Mark Hughes as manager. He had done good things in the past and had a good reputation for how he had got Tottenham into the Champions League, but it did not take very long to realise that he and I saw football and life very differently. He was at an age where he'd been in football for so long that he not only projected this idea that his way was the only way, it also felt like he thought he was much more clever than everyone. He knows more than you and he wants to let you know that. In Brazil we would say he was like a *malandro*. Remember, I came from spending so much time with a manager of a similar age – even older than Harry in fact – who never stopped learning, and was never afraid of letting us know he was learning and using those experiences. Even up to my last day with him on a football field at Sunderland at the end of the last season, he had learned something new that he would carry forward. That is an attitude I can share and embrace.

I'm not saying Redknapp didn't have his qualities. I'm not saying I disagreed with everything. But there was something in the manner in which his views were articulated that I found very difficult to appreciate. It wouldn't be 'do this' and an explanation for why. It wouldn't even be 'do this' and no explanation. It would be, 'Do this, because I know what I'm talking about.' It wasn't for me to say he was wrong or right. Even if I disagreed, he had a history of strong achievement. But it seemed to me that the problems at the club only became worse after he took over. For example, we already had a lot of players who had arrived on big salaries and they weren't performing as well as the club had hoped. And then Harry signed Christopher Samba. He was a good defender, but he wasn't good enough to play for Manchester United or Chelsea and he was on a salary that you would expect from one of the best players at those clubs. It was crazy.

We had a temporary boost – he's the sort of manager you could probably work with for six months and then whatever positive impact there is fades away. At least that's how it was for me. We had a handful of good results – we won at

Chelsea and then won back-to-back games in March against Southampton and Sunderland. I actually played well in those matches. But it was obvious that our problems were too big to overcome and we ended the season winning none of our last eight and going down in last place as the worst team in the league. No complaints. Relegation was a terrible experience, but there were positive things to take away. It was nice for me to experience the real life of football away from United. But my brother was my sunshine that year.

Rafa: My focus all year had been on winning the league again with United. After the Olympics I had decided I wasn't going to read any social media; I was going to avoid as much news as possible, good or bad. It wasn't just me who had listened to what the gaffer said at Sunderland. It wasn't just me who remembered that, every game, and every time we were behind. It was not a coincidence that we came back to win so often. Robin's goals were a big reason for our success but this was a squad effort, where every single player could look at their contribution and know that it was important. Jonny Evans was the back-up centre-back for Rio and Nemanja and he scored some crucial goals for us that season. He was brilliant when he played for us.

It felt like a milestone year in more ways than one. I had established my position at right-back; where once I had been a player looking up in awe of Rio, Nemanja and Patrice as the senior defenders, now I could feel like I was one of them. Of course, those guys were still legends in my eyes, and still guys I looked up to – they will be my idols for all of my life – but now they would discuss matters with me instead of simply giving advice. For example, in a game, Rio might ask what kind of runs I would like to make, so that he could either play the right pass or position himself well in defence. In training, when I stayed behind for extra work, Wayne might ask me what I was doing because he wanted to join in.

After the Reading game, I was very happy with my performances through the rest of the season. We played a very important match at Loftus Road – a special day, because I was able to spend time with my brother, who couldn't play because he was on loan from us. We had so many friends at the stadium. The Liverpool goal is still my favourite, but I was very happy with my goal on this day. I struck the ball clean and it flew into the top corner.

Fabio: In training Júlio César insisted that Samba had been standing in front of him and when Rafa scored and had blocked his view. I thought he was joking. 'No, no, I'm serious. If he is not in front of me I catch the ball!' I said, 'Man, you couldn't even *see* the ball!' and I jumped up to touch the crossbar to show him how high it went. He had no chance.

Rafa: That was, actually, my last goal for United. In the same game Giggsy scored his last, too. I discovered that writing this book and it's a stat I'm going to take with me for life. You don't think about it at the time – not only because you think you're going to play forever. I was just grateful for the significance of it. We won 2-0 and took another big stride towards the title. At the end of February we were 12 points clear of Manchester City. But because of what had happened the previous season, we were not taking anything for granted, and each game was treated with the same level of intensity.

We had also made up for the previous year's Champions League mistake and we were through the groups to play against Real Madrid. I wasn't happy with my performance in Spain but I escaped the hairdryer this time. We went 1-0 up with an early goal from Welbeck but then Cristiano scored a header before half-time. He was like Superman, flying more than two metres in the air (or at least that's how it seemed) – Patrice Evra didn't have a chance. That wasn't how the boss saw it at the break. He yells at Patrice, 'What the fuck are you doing, letting him get the header in?!' Patrice is stunned. 'But boss, he jumped three metres!'

One day later, when Sir Alex has seen the video, 'Sorry Pat.' What could he have done? Cristiano was almost superhuman all the time at this point. Goals every game. No more tricks, just direct, in the box, looking to score. It wasn't that he couldn't do those tricks anymore. I just think he didn't want to. All he wanted to do was score. We all knew what he could do. When he was in direct competition, in the same spotlight, as Lionel Messi, it seemed to change his focus. Messi was scoring all these goals and Cristiano wanted to prove that he could, too. They saw each other break records and pushed each other to do better.

He also scored in the second leg but in my opinion it would have never got to that if the referee had not sent off Nani. We were in front and defending very well. The crowd were really behind us and it felt as if we were destined to win. The referee then decided that Nani's foot was too high and gave him the red card. It was ridiculous; a terrible decision. He was going for the ball and Arbeloa went down as if he'd been struck by a sniper from the stands. I felt for Nani; I'd been there. Maybe I was young and stupid – but Nani definitely didn't deserve what happened to him. Then Luka Modrić and Cristiano scored quickly and we were unable to get going again. We lost the game but I still get chills remembering the roar of the Old Trafford crowd on that evening. I want to take this opportunity to thank every single one of the fans who created that atmosphere for us. If you were there – thank you. I'm just sorry that the evening was ruined. I hate to blame the referee but for sure that was a game where a bad decision determined the result.

I don't remember Sir Alex speaking after that game. I remember his feeling of devastation, similar in some ways to what I'd seen from him at Sunderland. But I don't remember what he said, if anything – it would not have been much, but, at the time, as players we did not appreciate the significance of that defeat in the same way that he did. I know he didn't speak to the press afterwards. But we were all so sorry for ourselves that no one in particular stood out.

It did not affect our league form. We lost at home to Manchester City but we still had the opportunity to seal the title well before the end of the season. When Aston Villa came to Old Trafford, all we needed was a victory. I was convinced that we would win that day. All day long I was thinking about Everton, and about Sunderland. This was a chance to celebrate a great season, to put in a strong performance and enjoy every minute of it. I had just one sadness – that I had a chance to score, and missed by a few inches. It was still a perfect day to become a champion, and we did that when Robin got a brilliant hat-trick.

This was my third title, and although the other two were special – you can't ever beat the first time, and the second was overtaking Liverpool – there was something significant about the 2013 win because of how involved I was. The first, I played quite often, but this time I felt like I was the first choice. Maybe now, because Liverpool won the league in

2020, getting to the 20th makes it even more significant. I hope that United can add to that before they are overtaken.

Rafa – The Hardest Goodbye

AT MANCHESTER United it was very rare that you would feel relaxation when it came to competing. The closest you would get was those few games if we'd won the title early, but even then there was no room for complacency, because there was usually something else to play for.

There were four games left to play after winning the Premier League in 2013 and two of them would usually be the most high-profile. The first was at Arsenal, where we were given a guard of honour. It must have hurt the Arsenal fans to see their team do that for Robin. They would have been more annoyed when he scored to get us a point. Even though the intensity wasn't the same for us, it was for our opponent, and that stirred us to perform. It was a flat game against Chelsea, too. It was going all the way to a 0-0 and then Juan Mata scored for them with three minutes to go. Straight after that, I went into a tackle with David Luiz. He over-reacted – he always did – and I was sent off. I don't hold it against him. We play for the badge on our chest. Lucas Leiva is one of the best friends I have in football but once he had that Liverpool badge on his shirt I always saw him as an opponent to tackle with everything I had. You're not friends on the pitch. Outside the pitch, yes. That's how I think; it's football. I'm sure they say they same. So we lost the game and in the dressing room afterwards I got the hairdryer.

'What the fuck were you doing?' the gaffer yells.

'Ah, this prick, he's always doing this,' I reply. I'm just as annoyed in the moment.

'Yeah, that's true,' Sir Alex says back to me, a little less angry now, not quite seeing the funny side, but definitely a little bit more relaxed.

And I didn't even think anything of that. More relaxed but there was no hint of what was to come that week.

We had a couple of days off ahead of the game against Swansea, the last home game of the season and the day the trophy would be presented. But celebrating was the last thing we felt like doing when the news began to break that Sir Alex was going to retire. I wasn't big on using social media at that time but when a story like that comes out in a country like England where football is everywhere you find out about it right away. You can't escape it even if you wanted to. Especially something like this – one of the biggest football stories of all time. Because it was so big it felt more real. At Manchester United you're used to everything being a story and a lot of it is not true. But you can't just 'make up' a story like Sir Alex retiring and so there was a strange feeling when I was heading to Carrington the next morning.

He stood in front of us all and told us the news was true. I could tell from the way he was talking to us that it was a hard thing for him to do. It was better for him to tell us all as a group. I can't imagine having to tell everyone individually. We were all still very surprised because it felt like a different experience, something you never expected to happen. We, like the fans, expected him to go on forever. I remember having to remind myself in the moment that life is like this. You want your parents to live forever, you wish for everyone you love to live forever, but they don't. That is the natural passage of life, it happens beyond our choice. A decision to retire is a choice and so you hope, in the case of Sir Alex, that it is never made.

At the same time you have to accept and respect that life is a cycle and he had given so much of his life to football that he deserved some time without it. And his family deserved some time with him. He mentioned that his wife and family were the main reason for his decision and at that moment, as difficult as it was for me to deal with, I understood him perfectly. The decision was a surprise but the reason wasn't. It takes it away from football. No footballing reason would ever take him away from the job, in my opinion. He was so passionate about the game and about the club. Because he had been there for so long people naturally wondered if there was more to it, some extra reason, and I must admit that even I – for a while afterwards – thought that might be the case. But I kept returning to the simplicity of the decision. Family. It was the right one. He would never have left otherwise.

He was my father within football. He was all I knew as a manager from the moment I became a professional player. For every day up until the day he announced he was retiring, I thought he would stay forever. You are living and sharing these days with a man everyone is saying is the best coach who ever existed. You are creating your legacy with him. It is an honour and privilege to share that journey, especially to be there in the last few years of it. I was his last right-back. It's a very special feeling.

Perhaps it was not an obvious path to affection. A Scottish man in his 70s and a couple of 22-year-olds from Brazil don't make a natural fit. But that's football; it unifies in a way that other walks of life don't. Even within that I don't know how. He loved Brazilian players but didn't have the greatest of track records with South Americans before 2007. But I know he loved Anderson, he absolutely loved him. I think because Anderson, my brother and I helped to win these trophies in this period; we helped to prove that theory wrong. Other than that, it's difficult to put words into the mouths of other people. I can tell you I felt that affection from him but I can't speak for him why he felt that way.

In one game – I can't remember against who, but it was quite early into my time at the club – he gave some instructions from the bench in my direction. I gave a thumbs up to show that I understood. I didn't think anything more of it until we were next in training. Fletch came up to me and said, 'Just to let you know, the gaffer doesn't like it when you do that.' For me I thought it was a good thing. I was showing I understood. I was showing that I was listening to his advice. So I was surprised that I had upset the boss.

I went straight to him – I was so young that I was fearless enough to do so – and told him what Fletch had said. I said it like this, 'Boss, Fletch said you didn't like it when I did this. Look, you should speak with me, because I meant it positive. It is a good thing. It was not disrespectful. I come here to say sorry if you took it as a sign of disrespect but also to tell you that it was the opposite. I wanted to let you know I was listening. I won't do it again because I know you don't like it. But I come here as a man to say if I have upset you, please come to me and tell me. It is not the same culture, I'm in England now, if you don't say to me that I have upset you and I find it out from other players, this is how I find out what you like and don't like.' Sometimes even I find it hard to believe I did that but I am absolutely certain that he respected me more as a person and as a man because I did.

I also thank Fletch, although I don't think he expected me to go straight to the gaffer! Every opportunity I get to mention what a good guy Fletch is, I will. I can't speak highly enough of him. At the first sign of what he thought might be trouble, he was trying to smooth it out. He was the person who did that – he stepped in. How many take the time to do something like that? I'm sure that he was instrumental in my brother getting a new contract. Yes, maybe the club and the gaffer would have done it anyway, but I know that it was Fletch who reminded him that there was a year and a half on my brother's contract. We call Sir Alex our father in football, and it follows that Fletch is our brother in football. He was an example on and off the pitch.

That family atmosphere makes you feel things in a more deep and meaningful way. I admit for a while afterwards that I thought about my red card against Chelsea. That was my last involvement under Sir Alex; that was the way it was it going to end. It took some time for me to come to terms with it and accept that the journey was a full one and not just about the way it ended. I prefer to say that it ended with winning the Premier League.

It was strange to experience this time in Manchester without my brother but we continued to see each other often.

After we won the league I went down to London to spend time with him and celebrate the title, and also celebrate the fact he was doing well – even if it wasn't going well for QPR. It was a different feeling for us both, but we knew that things were going to be different to the few years of stability we had experienced. We had been lucky to have the stability for as long as we did.

I wasn't going to let my lack of involvement in the final games stop my right to celebrate. It was a party in the Manchester rain as we beat Swansea with a late goal from Rio. We had scored so many late goals that season – and under Sir Alex it was Fergie time – that it was right that the last home game was won in that fashion. It was a very emotional day. The other titles had meant a lot to me and I did feel like I contributed but I had such an extra sense of pride in the fact I'd been the first choice all year. I felt important. To have a celebration of that on one day, and knowing that it is the end of one era – as Sir Alex spoke to the crowd to say goodbye but to also remind them of the standard of Manchester United, it was a reminder to me, too. He was giving the same message he always gave to us at the end of a season if we had won trophies or if we had not. After winning the European Cup. After winning the 19th title. After Sunderland. He wouldn't be a part of the next chapter – he wouldn't be with us – but the expectation was for us to continue to win titles.

By now we knew the next part of that story would be led by David Moyes, the Everton manager. I swear that I was so wrapped up in my sadness about Sir Alex going that I hadn't even thought about who would follow before it was announced.

After such a journey your thought about who comes next already has a negative attached to it. This wasn't something expressed by the players in the dressing room, or even to each other, but I know they felt it like I felt it. If you follow the best ever it is only natural that you will not be good enough. It's bad for a professional to think that way – it was bad for us to think that way – because you're expecting to be disappointed. And you know you will be, because Sir Alex was the best for a reason. Again, it is a natural reaction, maybe unavoidable for all of us involved. It's unfair on whoever follows. You just have to hope that the difference in quality isn't so big, that it isn't so obvious. But how can you follow when the first thing that is hoped is, 'I hope he keeps things the same, I hope nothing is different to when Sir Alex was in charge.' In that thought, you're almost undermining how good Sir Alex was because you're expecting the next man to be as good as him. And yet I stress that it is natural, it's there for players just as it was for fans. It wasn't fair on Moyes. He wasn't Ferguson. It wasn't an honest way to treat him and that was true of everyone, right from us as players to the press.

The squad was criticised. Of course we all heard those comments. But we didn't just win the title – we won it by 11 points. So to go from there to finishing in seventh, 22 points behind the next champions? You can't say that is all down to the players. We know Sir Alex was so good, the best ever, and definitely a good enough manager to make a difference, but to say such a thing is to pretend that players don't matter. The truth was that many things went wrong and everyone shared responsibility for that.

I hope that what I have already said shows that I have a lot of respect for David Moyes. He did a great job at Everton. He was there for a long time and if you're at a club in England for a long time that is an important achievement in itself. Who knows how good they could have been if Chelsea and Manchester City hadn't had the takeovers in that period? He did well and we always knew it would be a tough game against one of his teams.

As it turned out, David wasn't the right man for Manchester United, but everything looked much worse because none of the major decisions went in his favour, and sometimes you need a little luck in that regard. He had none. It must have been a nightmare for him. We have seen some of the biggest names in world football attempt to coach Manchester United since Sir Alex retired and we can see that it is not easy – so imagine being the one who followed him, knowing that every mistake that is made will be judged even harder. You can't win. Even when you win, you can't. Even when you play well, you're not playing as well as you did under the last manager. The only way he would have been a success was to win, win, win, every single game of football, and that has never happened in history. I'm not saying David was the right man. What I am saying, I think, is that nobody was the right man.

I also think when he came to United you could say he made decisions that many managers would make at a new club, but every single one of them turned out to be a mistake. Everything seemed to be wrong. The first player he signed was Marouane Fellaini. He was criticised for that because Fellaini was from his old club. Before Sir Alex retired, every time we played against Everton, Fellaini was great. There were plenty of rumours that Sir Alex wanted to bring him to United. Nobody was complaining then! But then Moyes brings him in, and immediately, everyone was saying how he had to go back to his old team and how the style of everything was going to change to be like it was at Everton. Cross, cross, cross. But when Sir Alex was interested, everyone spoke of Fellaini's positive qualities. Now, apparently, he wasn't a Manchester United player.

The truth is that some of it was true. Fellaini wasn't a bad player but he was a different player. Having him in the team meant we would have to cross more if we wanted to really get the best out of him. For me at right-back it would mean playing the ball into him so he could control and hold it up. I wasn't used to playing like that. Fellaini wasn't a player who is going to play the one-twos and be part of a fluid attack the way the previous seasons had seen us play. I know Robin van Persie felt that it wasn't his style of football. He was there to play that passing style. So was I. I'm just saying that I could understand why Fellaini was signed. David knew him and trusted him. He also knew his value to a team. That value had been emphasised on the tighter Goodison pitch where everything was a battle.

He also brought his own trusted staff with him. You see that with almost every manager as well. Steve Round and Jimmy Lumsden came in. Phil Neville was known to a few of the lads because he won so many trophies with United.

I don't know the reason why, but David didn't talk to me about my position at the club. He didn't sit down with me and talk about his plans and what he thought about my future. You need to be honest with players. You need to speak with them. How can you build a relationship with anyone in any walk of life if you don't talk to them? I don't know if it was because he was the manager and he thought he didn't need to. But we were all dealing with a lot of change. In a period like that it is best if the things that you can control, you keep as normal as possible.

David wasn't a person who came across as scared or afraid but for whatever reason he just chose not to speak to some of us. Maybe it was nerves? He was stepping up to manage Manchester United and there were some big players who had won lots of things. I was confident enough to approach David and ask him what was happening when I didn't feature in a couple of games at the start of his reign. He told me my time would come if I was patient. Even though I had enjoyed my best season, I understood that I didn't have a divine right to be selected and that the new man wanted to see the entire squad. And he was good to his word – I can't complain that he didn't give me a fair chance.

David has complained that he wasn't given a fair chance himself. I'm inclined to agree, but I have to add the thought that I still didn't think he would have been the right man to manage Manchester United over a longer period. He didn't have a lot of time. He had a very difficult job to do. Of course I am sympathetic but you also have to be realistic. His Everton team were not renowned for playing beautiful football. He went to Sunderland and West Ham after Old Trafford and has not had a reputation for attractive, passing football in those places. I wouldn't say he was defensive, but his attacking style was very old-fashioned and typically British with the big strikers and the crosses and long balls. That's been his way for most of his career and it doesn't look like he is going to change now. That style wasn't compatible with United. It isn't natural. It impacted performances and results. Very early, it seemed like things were going wrong, and David needed something to turn it around.

My first league appearance under him came in October when we won at Sunderland in a game that was already being described as crucial. That match is remembered for Adnan Januzaj coming into the side and scoring twice. He was a very good player, Adnan. He had a lot of talent. But he was a teenager, and – this is just my opinion – he didn't yet have the footballing intelligence or maturity in his decision-making to take on such responsibility as a regular player at United. He was only a kid and maybe it didn't do him any favours to put that pressure on him. It projected the wrong idea about Manchester United and fed this strange feeling that a team who had won the title six months earlier were now relying on a rookie to get results.

I'm sure that as a squad – well, I'm sure I personally can say this – there was a genuine expectation to be challenging for the title. We were fighting and trying to win but it wasn't working. Although I described David as unafraid in his personality, I do think that very early on he became fearful of losing games as manager of Manchester United, and the conservatism that comes with that feeling is very different to not wanting to lose. Nobody wants to lose. But when you are fearful of losing because of everything that comes with it – the self-doubt from within, the criticism from outside – it impacts on all your decisions. And when you're manager of a football club, that is felt by the players, too. You second-guess yourself. You make decisions you might not usually make. And, when you are confronted and have to be safe, you retreat to the things you are familiar with and hope it works. There is no room to retreat at Manchester United. Every minute of every day you are the public face of the club and you cannot afford to show vulnerability. If you show that you are, you're a dead man walking in the job.

The decisions he made just in the first few months back that up. Januzaj was one. Then he admitted he was afraid to bring off Robin in a game because he knew the press would criticise him. Before that match, against Newcastle, he spoke about making it difficult as though we were the underdogs – and they won. The fallback option was Fellaini as a target man and plenty of crosses. We weren't used to it. It didn't work.

Wayne Rooney started very well under David. It was easy to see that towards the end of Sir Alex's time in charge their relationship hadn't been great, so Wayne seemed to have a new enthusiasm. He had a strong motivation and had a really positive influence. He worked hard and proved that he still had a lot to give.

He was given a new contract, which surprised a lot of people. Maybe Wayne had considered leaving but once it was clear he was staying you would never question his commitment to the team or the cause. He was one of the better performers under David – but because he was past his peak, many people questioned the wisdom of giving him such a long contract on such high wages.

Many blamed David for that but I'm not sure that's fair. Decisions like that are made above the manager. It wasn't just David who was new in the role. Ed Woodward was there. There had been a transfer chase for Gareth Bale but they couldn't get him to Manchester. Of course they weren't going to lose Rooney so it was a case of doing whatever it took to make him stay. Wayne was part of that group of local players who really helped us settle into life in Manchester, so it was great for me that he was staying. I also think that my brother and I had values and a way of looking at life that those players appreciated and respected. It went a long way towards making a strong relationship.

Rooney scored a great goal at West Ham around the time of the new contract. From the halfway line. I was right behind it – it was one of the most special goals I've ever been on a pitch to see. Not many players could score a goal like that. Not many had his intelligence of playing the game. He understood how to play in different roles, as he was doing under David. I'm sure he could have played centre-back well if he'd wanted to.

I admit that they weren't pleasant days. My brother was back with us and fighting for his place but he was like a different animal for those few months back at the club. He had grown in confidence from his loan spell and felt as though he deserved more chances to play. David saw it differently. Fabio was arguing with everyone. He was deeply unhappy. He wasn't even getting proper game time in the League Cup. The anger and the unhappiness changed him. I remember one big argument he had with Ryan Giggs, of all people. In training he had completely changed. He was like me, normally, all over the place, running all the time. Now he was walking. No energy. I'm sure he questioned how everything was going: why should he run if he wasn't going to play? Giggs was angry with him and Fabio exploded back at Giggsy, all of the frustration coming out. The next training session they made it up. Fabio didn't apologise but explained why he was so unhappy. He spoke about those three or four months of running and running every single day, and how he thought he had proved himself already. And he wasn't even getting on the bench sometimes. Alex Büttner had been brought in as back-up for Patrice when Fabio went on loan, but now he was back, and Büttner was ahead of him and playing when Patrice had a rest. So what was the point? It wasn't the best thing to do – you can't just stop running in training, even if you are that unhappy.

I understood where he was coming from. Of course I did. Enough was enough and he had to move. I think he had to go when he did because he would not have grown like he has if he stayed and suffered. He made a good decision for him; even though I was, naturally, sad to see him go, I was also proud of him.

Things continued to go wrong for us at United and sometimes spectacularly. We got to the semi-final of the League Cup and the second leg against Sunderland went to extra time. In the last minute Phil Bardsley scored and it looked as though they were through – then Chicharito scored and we went to penalties. I don't think I've ever seen a worse set of penalty kicks, and I was, too. Five kicks each and they won 2-1. Four misses – mine was the last. I've never watched it back. I don't even know why I took one; I never did. It was shit. It was an ugly game – one of many.

Then there was Fulham at home. René Meulensteen had become their manager after being one of the guys who had to leave when David came in with his own staff. We drew 2-2. There was no Fellaini in this game but plenty of crosses. Cross, cross, cross; 81 in total. We were breaking records but not positive ones. That was the way we trained then; we'd become a team that just did crossing drills. You have Fellaini in your team and after some time you just get used to crossing the ball. You're doing it all the time. When you're keen to get a result you do things in desperation. You cross the ball and hope for the header or the knock-down.

Despite everything, we had done well in the Champions League group stages and got through to play against Olympiakos in the second round. We went to Greece and I learned I wasn't playing. Not only that, I wasn't even on the bench. I couldn't believe it, but you accept it – what else can you do? Chris Smalling started at right-back. I understood when Chris played because of height at set pieces. But to go from being the starting player to now not even in the squad for the biggest game of the season so far? Olympiakos won 2-0. Suddenly, David's position at the club became a target of speculation in the press.

The season had run away from us, and him. By February we were more than ten points behind the top four – it doesn't even seem real to say that – and games were running out to qualify for the Champions League. Being eliminated by Olympiakos was an embarrassment he might not have survived.

I didn't take it personally. I also had other things to worry about – my wife was due to give birth and did so the day before we played against Liverpool. I was with her in the hospital through the night until early morning. I then got a phone call from David telling me that he wanted me to play, even though it was an early kick-off. There was no way I should have played but I wasn't going to say no. Maybe today I would. It wasn't my best game, I know. Maybe you could say the result would have been different if I wasn't playing. I was booked – I went in on my best friend Steven Gerrard – and then gave a penalty away for handball. I wasn't alone, and the referee gave two more penalties for Liverpool. At Old Trafford! Would you ever see that at Anfield for United?

We were losing 2-0. Everyone knew we were going to lose the game. Everyone knew in their heart and in their head that the end for David Moyes was near. There can't have been many who thought he would turn it around. And still I have to say that last 20 minutes inside Old Trafford on that day were incredible. To anyone who ever criticises the noise, I tell them to watch that last part of the game. Watch a team losing against their biggest rivals, knowing their manager is going to be sacked, and hear the crowd sing in support of him and the team at the level they did at the end of the game. In a funny way it was a nice reminder of why Manchester United are so special.

We let another goal in. There was a brief pause – and then the chanting got even louder.

I can honestly say that I never took for granted the opportunity and privilege to play for that great club. But a reminder never hurts, even knowing we couldn't get a result for them on the day.

I was in for the return game against Olympiakos and we won 3-0 with Robin getting a hat-trick, a rare moment that felt like the old days. Again, the stadium was rocking. Rio and Ryan played after a few months away from the first-team picture. We were through to the next round against Bayern Munich.

The reality of our situation hit again when we lost against Manchester City at home. They scored early and late to win 3-0 but again there was no getting away from the size of the defeat. Afterwards, David said we should want to be like Manchester City. Everyone knew what he meant, and of course we wanted to be challenging for the title, but there are things you just cannot say and unfortunately when he was under pressure he made these comments which made everything look and feel even worse than it was. It seemed like he didn't know how to express himself and the problem was that at Manchester United that never changed.

I was sympathetic to what he was experiencing. But there is a simple fact: when a manager is admitting publicly that he isn't sure about the decisions he is making and when he is speaking in a manner that does the opposite of inspiring confidence for the present and the future, it does not inspire confidence in you as a player that the direction you are getting is the right one to follow. You're not even sure if it's the one he wants you to follow, or the direction he thinks he should give you, because you're not sure how confident he is in himself to give that instruction. It might not have been his natural way. Unfortunately, football is unforgiving in that respect.

A few days later we played Aston Villa at Old Trafford. The pressure was high. We all saw in the press that there was going to be a banner flown over the stadium insisting that Moyes should be sacked. It's not the sort of story you can avoid. It's in your head that it's happening but you can't let it affect your performance. The fans in the stadium showed their support and we won 4-1.

I came off injured and missed the rest of the season. David didn't make it to the end either. Bayern eliminated us from the Champions League – we had brief hope in Germany when Patrice scored a brilliant goal, but it wasn't enough. We went to Everton knowing we needed to win all our remaining matches to have a mathematical chance of qualifying for the Champions League, but we lost 2-0, and it was symbolic that even David's old club were now above us in the table.

A year earlier we had experienced the news of Sir Alex's retirement. His announcement still felt like a huge shock to us all. After losing at Goodison it was speculated that David was going to lose his job and it was not a feeling of surprise when he told us at Carrington that he would indeed be leaving. The only thing that might have caught the players off guard was the timing, coming so close to the end of the season and yet not at the every end.

David wasn't the 'Chosen One' after all. He didn't speak very much. He basically said he wouldn't be here any more and that it was just how football went. He was up front and honest, acknowledging that the results had not been good and that it was, after all, a results business.

I remember Felli being the most emotional, as you would expect. He'd known David for a long time and David had brought him to the club. For the rest of us, we were sad, but I think we were all ready for another change.

There was another signing David made. He broke the club's transfer record to sign Juan Mata from Chelsea in January. Juan is an exceptional footballer but he is an even better human being. I say this with sincerity and I hope that it comes across as I mean it. He is one of the best people I have met in my life. When I speak about Juan as a player I cannot say it fairly because the fondness I have for him is so great that it is always more favourable and biased. He is an example to us all and I love him, just as we all did.

How has he contributed to United? Well, he is a player to build around. Everyone knows his qualities and his skillset. No, maybe he does not have the quickest pace, but he can *set* the pace for the entire team, and that's more important.

His intelligence as a player is on another level. He is not a player off the shelf that you can just put into a team and ask him to fulfil a job. He'll do it, because he's a consummate professional, but to truly get the best out of him you need to build around him and not just fit him in. It's just my opinion – United have played some of their best football in recent years when that has been understood. Of course there is a conflicting argument because United have been used to pace and power and this is different. But football is about embracing difference – Moyes had definitely brought two different styles in the players he signed.

You could say that Mata and Fellaini didn't suit each other – you might even say they represented opposites in football – and they were also both different to the way we were used to playing. All of those are fair comments. It showed the confusion and the contradiction with how David was trying to set up his version of Manchester United and is probably the biggest obvious example of why it always felt doomed to fail.

Ryan Giggs was given the caretaker job and, although I didn't play, I felt that positive attitude return to the club. The familiar feeling that we were Manchester United again. I honestly feel that if he had been given the job for a full season then he'd still be there today. Maybe I would too. Instead, another man was brought in, and our sense of losing what we were as a squad was about to be taken to a whole other level.

213

Fabio – The Hardest Goodbyes

IT WAS strange when my brother and I started to have these different life experiences, even though we knew it would happen. He played in the Olympics and became a father. I went away to live in London and prove myself. Of course we could not share these experiences physically. Another in this line was of Sir Alex retiring. I heard about it on the news, and my brother confirmed it when he found out. I echo everything he said about Sir Alex being a father in football to us. This is the perfect description.

Everyone had their own relationship with Sir Alex. It wasn't just the manager and the players – he took the time to get to know us personally. You might have thought that with me and Rafa being twins, he would treat us as though we were the same, but he took the time to get to know the little differences in our personalities. My brother would get the hairdryer because the gaffer knew it motivated him. He knew that he wouldn't shrink. I'm not saying I would shrink, but I'm quieter. If I got criticism like that then I would take it to heart and it would affect me. I'd be disappointed in myself. I had grown in my time away, so maybe it would have been a different story if the gaffer had still been in charge when I went back to United, but it was not to be.

I also want to pay a different compliment to Sir Alex. He was a man who made my dreams come true. That happening is special and I never for a second took it for granted. Everyone has their own path in life and many are not as fortunate to meet somebody who can do that for them. When you do, you want to repay them with everything you can give, and that is on and off the pitch. So we gave everything that was asked of us. And the man who gave us that dream just happened to be the best manager in the history of football. Maybe in a couple of centuries someone will beat him but it won't be in my lifetime. For people to still comment on the special relationship we had with him is a big honour for me. I know that for the rest of my life, I'm going to make sure that I tell my own children and my nieces and nephews how a man like Sir Alex conducted himself.

But, in the manner he would have wanted, we all started life under David Moyes with the intention of business as usual. I was under no illusions about my own place. QPR had been relegated – so even though I was happy with making the choice, and I still am because I think it was the right one, I can see that it didn't look like the best move. But I used the confidence I had to treat everything as a fresh start. If David was looking at my past then he would surely see that I'd also played in a Champions League Final two years earlier. I felt like a different player for the first few weeks and months under David. I was training better, I had more attitude in my performance, I felt much more confident than I did before. I played in the pre-season tour and scored. I hoped for a chance in the first team and it came a few games into the season.

That was against Crystal Palace when I started at right-back. We won and I played well. I'm not going to say I was the man of the match but we won 2-0 and I know I didn't play badly. In my mind I thought it was good enough to at least get another chance. But in the next game in the Champions League against Leverkusen I was on the bench and didn't come on. I didn't even make the bench against Manchester City in the league. In fact, I played five more minutes for United – and in that time, scored a goal and got a red card!

I don't know why David decided not to give me another chance. I didn't think it was completely fair, but he didn't talk to me about it, so I could not know what he was thinking. Results were not going brilliantly and he was making a lot of changes. Because he was doing that, and because results and performances continued to be poor, people criticised the squad. Look, I think you could have put Pep Guardiola in charge of United at that time and he would not have done as well as we did under Sir Alex. The gaffer had a trust and knowledge of his squad, he knew every single player, he knew what they could do and what they could give him – in every single minute, of every single game, against every single opponent. So while I agree that nobody else would have been able to make that squad champions again in the following season, I don't think that it was to do with the quality of the squad. It was the knowledge and familiarity and control and trust of the manager, and the relationship he had with his players. It became its own thing. If Sir Alex trusted you to play right-back or left-back you played with the confidence that you were going to win the game. When he trusted my brother and me to play as wingers against Arsenal was the perfect example. It would have looked ridiculous under any other manager. And maybe under any other manager we might have asked what was going on.

These comments make it sound as if Manchester United was a special problem, and maybe that's true in some ways, but in other ways it was just a normal part of football. People criticised the squad but there were many veterans coming towards the end of their time and this should have been a good opportunity to make those changes without upsetting anyone. Giggsy, Carrick, Rio, Patrice; all these guys were coming towards the end but they would have probably understood if it had been managed well. It went as badly as it could have done.

I don't want to say David didn't take responsibility. But he came from Everton to Manchester United and I think he came with the expectation that he was going to see perfection in every training session. So if the ball left the ground by a few inches, he would shout at us, 'Come on boys, this is meant to be Manchester United!'

It would have the lads laughing.

I'm not a guy to just criticise someone. It was difficult for him. But to come in to the club and tell *us* what the standard was supposed to be, this was just one sign that the job was too big for him. It felt sometimes as if he believed the newspaper descriptions of us and didn't take the time to get to know us. For example, Sir Alex used Rio Ferdinand carefully. David played him every week at the start of the season and then dropped him. Rio! Rio was just one of the players who were – and there's no other way to put it – bigger than him in football. Rio, Giggs, Patrice. I think those guys tried to help him and we tried to follow their lead. But it wasn't easy for the rest of us when we saw David trying to tell Rio how to play, and then he took him out of the team. But it wasn't just Rio, it wasn't just me, it was all of us as a collective. And you have a manager who hasn't won anything who came in and tried to tell a squad with a history of winning, without getting to know them, what their own standard was.

When he tried to put his own influence on it, it didn't really help. He had been working with us and watching us for a couple of months and then signed his old player from Everton, Marouane Fellaini. Like my brother, I have no problem with that – but it was how quickly everything seemed to change that was so confusing. So the results and performances hadn't started the way he wanted, and he thought the best way to do things was to do as he did at Everton. So straight away training changed. It wasn't as if we changed to *just* play long balls, but it was obvious that David felt this was an important quality missing from our game. The instruction to us as full-backs was to hit the long pass into Fellaini. Fellaini can usually control the ball and you start your build-up play from that point, but that's not how my brother plays or how I play. And my brother had made himself first choice. So he was dropped and Phil Jones, who was happy to hit these passes, got the games. As far as I remember, Phil hated playing right-back, but would do it for the game time. He was a good player but had become a defensive full-back after his promising start. And defensive full-backs are good for certain games but for a run of Chelsea and West Brom at home? I'm not sure that's right for Manchester United.

Fellaini had to play which meant you were going to lose either a passing midfielder or one of Robin van Persie and

Wayne Rooney. It made it difficult for us to trust the manager when it felt as though he didn't trust us. I also think it didn't help him when it came to how he was seen by the press – and football can become very hard, very quickly.

That's how it was for David, but, honestly, for all of us too. We didn't just have a new manager, we had new coaches. Remember that Sir Alex wasn't in control all of the time – well, he was, but he wasn't always there. Mike Phelan and René Meulensteen were coaches we trusted. Steve Round and Jimmy Lumsden were good guys and I have no doubt they were good coaches. But when you have a long relationship, and then you lose that bond you have with the coaches who are the bridge to the manager, and you're starting again where you're building that bridge with the coaches, it can be a very difficult time. It felt as if they were keen to establish connections with the senior players. It was almost as if they were in awe of them. It should have been the opposite way. Mike and René looked after the younger lads. The veteran players didn't need their input for motivation; they'd been at the club for so long it was second nature to them. But it was like the coaches were trying to learn that mentality from the veterans. The younger lads understood why Sir Alex had to go but were very sad that Mike and René went too. If they had stayed that might have helped a lot of things.

But the truth was that it was starting to feel like it wasn't Manchester United. Or it was, but in a bad dream. I'm sure that supporters had the same experience because that's what I'm told. I feel bad to mention Fellaini again because it makes it sound like I'm being critical when he was a good guy and a good player, but I speak about him only as a former Everton player who was familiar with David – everyone knew he represented a long ball trying to chase a result in difficult circumstances. It was a plan B for Manchester United but it was used as David's plan A, and very quickly the feeling that there was some panic was something that encouraged our opponents, I'm sure.

Then you had David's comments to the press, which didn't always come across in the best way. When you have been working for Everton for ten years you are experienced in speaking as an Everton manager but at Manchester United, where the pressure is different, and the expectation is to win and to win convincingly no matter who you are playing against. I don't think David changed the way he was. The questions were the same and he answered them the same way he always did. It's only afterwards, when people expressed alarm that a manager of United spoke that way, that he would have realised. As players we knew the standard and level of expectation. The comments didn't bother us but it was easy to see they upset the supporters and made them feel uncertain.

That's what we felt as players. The fans were nervous. We felt it. We could tell that they thought the manager didn't have confidence. We agree. It all feeds into us and became part of those performances.

I didn't play for a while after the Palace game. I came on as a substitute in injury time against Norwich City in the League Cup and still had time to score! It was the last goal in a 4-0 win, normally the perfect time to celebrate, but I couldn't. I put my hands up to the Stretford End, something within myself feeling as though this was a good moment to say goodbye. I didn't know if David would ever pick me again but I did know that three or four games a season wasn't going to be enough for me. I also knew I had to take the opportunity to say goodbye to the fans I loved so much. I didn't know if that time would come again.

But the first time David talked to me about my future, he actually offered me a new contract! He asked to speak with me in his office. I thought we were on the same page – that we were going to discuss a loan or a transfer. 'I want to give you two more years,' he said. 'Sir Alex told me all about how much he appreciates you, the way you are as a man.' I could see it was from Sir Alex and not from him. Maybe I would have signed it for Sir Alex. But he wasn't there any more.

I thought at the time that Palace would have been the opportunity to break in. Tom Cleverley was giving me a lot of praise for how I played and that it was a reward for how good I'd looked since I came back. But I should have taken the call in to the team as a sign of things to come – there was no conversation, no discussion, just the announcement that I was in and somebody else wasn't, and then there was no conversation when I wasn't in the next game. And that's how it was – no more league minutes for Manchester United. I had been so positive about it but afterwards those old frustrations came back. Did I not play as well as I thought I did? What could I do to be better? What did I do wrong? Was I doing something wrong in training?

At the start of 2014, Ole Gunnar Solskjaer was hired as Cardiff City manager and the transfer window opened. There was a lot of speculation about the players he might sign and naturally that included some who he was familiar with at United who weren't getting a game. I was included in that group and the idea of feeling wanted appealed to me.

I thought I was training well and with Swansea City as opponents in the FA Cup at Old Trafford, I expected to finally get a chance. But I didn't. Chris Smalling was right-back and Alex Büttner was left-back. Cardiff made an offer and I agreed to go. David said I was going to be on the bench against Swansea and at first I said I didn't want to, I just wanted to go to Cardiff, but he convinced me.

I came on for Rio with 15 minutes left. Four minutes later I was sent off, my frustration at everything off the pitch spilling on to it. The fans still applauded me as I walked off. I would have preferred the Norwich appearance to have been my last. Unfortunately it was not to be.

That week I told David I wanted to make the move as soon as I could. 'You were this close to starting against Swansea,' he said, pinching his fingers together, urging me to reconsider. I don't know why but that angered me even more. I knew for a fact I had to leave. I wasn't happy any more. This wonderful chapter of my life was sadly over.

People ask if Ole was a big reason why I went to Cardiff. Truthfully he was *the* reason. He made a point of making me his first signing. Before he was even appointed he called me to say he was about to take the job and would like me to be the first player he took to the club. The bookies were still taking odds on who would be manager!

It wasn't just being wanted that convinced me. It was the feeling of being needed and being appreciated. 'I need someone with your mentality and your talent. With you, I'm sure we can keep Cardiff up.' Okay, I was convinced. Because my contract was due to expire I was already free to discuss deals with clubs from other countries. And maybe because I was from Manchester United, a few clubs expressed interest. Leverkusen were the first.

Rafael in the 2012 Olympics team for Brazil, welcoming his international team-mates to his club home of Old Trafford

Rafael celebrates his stunning strike against QPR in 2013 – his last goal for the club

Rafael taking the opportunity to let the world know how grateful he is for Sir Alex Ferguson's influence on his life after the 2013 title success

Legends present and past – Rafael competing with Ronaldo for the ball in 2013

All smiles – but Fabio takes the moment after scoring against Norwich to say goodbye to Old Trafford as he knows his departure is close

Fabio in red again, but for Cardiff City, soon after signing for the club in February 2014

Fabio in action for Middlesbrough against Manchester United at the Riverside Stadium

Manchester is orange – victory at City was always sweet, even for Lyon and Rafael

A team photo from July 2018, soon after Fabio signed for Nantes. There was a true brotherhood at the club including Emiliano Sala who tragically died in 2019

Rafa in action for Lyon against Kylian Mbappe

Some pictures of us with family.

Top row, left: The Botafogo FC love runs strong through our family.

Top row, middle: with our dad and grandma.

Bottom row, right: following in our brother's footsteps.

Fabio feeling good to be back on the pitch in October 2020

Rafael in action for Istanbul Basaksehir

Ole showed persistence, though. It was clear he really wanted me. I looked at the table. Cardiff were bottom. 'Ole, it's not going to be easy,' I told him, but he made me believe that I could help them survive. Of course, a move to Cardiff would mean I wasn't so far away from my brother. It was a big move, the first time we'd be apart permanently, but that decision had to be made sooner rather than later and when I considered everything and talked it over with my wife, Cardiff seemed a sensible choice.

I still believe it was. I don't regret making that move, even though in the end we *did* get relegated. I felt like I settled quickly – maybe because I felt so wanted. And because of that, I felt I developed a very good relationship with the supporters.

Ole is one of the nicest guys in football. But some people take advantage of that attitude. One of my first appearances was a crazy match against Liverpool which summed up our team. We could win games and we could play well but this was Cardiff's first year in the Premier League and the pressure to stay up was something everyone was feeling. The mental exhaustion that comes with this need to concentrate with such intensity for a full match is something that is a big factor in the lowest rungs of England's top league. There is less freedom to be yourself, to be expressive and maybe even make a mistake trying to do something positive. That mistake could cost you the game. That lost game could cost you your place in the division. The economic factors associated with relegation and the impact these defeats have on the supporters – these are all pressures you carry with you. Sometimes it can get away from you. So we played Liverpool and started very well. We led twice but they equalised just before half-time. They scored early in the second half and took control, eventually winning 6-3.

Ole could tell that there was a fatigue in the dressing room. He gave us three days off to recharge. He said to get it out of our head and come back fresh of mind. He told us to go and spend a little time with our families, to take time away and enjoy life.

I know that didn't go down well with some of the players. 'He's too nice – we've just been beaten heavily, what is he thinking?' They thought he didn't understand the pressure of the situation. They didn't realise that what he was saying to them was for their own good and, as a consequence, surely good for the team. Some players who are used to playing in struggling squads expect the manager to demand they go into training on Monday at 8am.

On our time off I was driving back to Manchester all the time to stay with my brother. My wife was heavily pregnant – she wasn't very happy that we were making these drives of two or three hours every time! But although the football decision had been more easy than I'd expected – and by that

I mean leaving David Moyes's Manchester United, not the Manchester United I love – it was much less easy losing that closeness with my brother. I know I didn't lose my best friend but it felt like it.

Eventually my wife talked about how much of a struggle these long drives were and we agreed that once our first baby came along I needed to dedicate my time to being at home in Cardiff. She was right. It made me a better husband and a better father. If we had continued to make those journeys as often as we did, I would have been splitting my attention between my brother and my daughter. I had to realise that I was gaining not losing. I could never lose my bond with my brother. But the extra time before our daughter came along gave my wife and I more time together, for the first time in our life by ourselves, and then when she was born we had a new best friend for life. When I went to London, my brother had gone through a similar experience with his wife and child. He was able to appreciate that I needed this moment too.

Having a baby also gave my brother the opportunity for revenge. Being an uncle was very funny – the tricks we often played on everyone we knew by pretending to be the other – well, of course I had to do the same to my niece. 'Come to papa, come to papa!' I would say. When she was very young she would of course come to me and then when she got to me there would be a questioning look – *are you sure you're my dad.*

She realised pretty quickly. It's funny how she could tell but people who knew us for years couldn't! At one year old she no longer fell for it, and yet Sir Alex Ferguson never learned to tell us apart.

I don't think our chances of survival at Cardiff were ever better than it seemed they could be after my debut. We won against Norwich and I played very well – Kenwyne Jones, who had just signed, scored on his debut. You have a player with his size, strength and skill playing as well as he did on that day, and then you have that natural high of a win where you think if you just play like that for every other game, you're going to win every other game you play. Look, that's unrealistic, but it's one of the biggest buzzes you get in football.

But the next week we lost the derby 3-0 at Swansea and the reality of where we were was there for us all to see. We won just two more games that season.

Joining Kenwyne and me were some more players Ole knew well – Magnus Eikrem and Mats Dæhli who had been at United, and Wilfried Zaha who had just arrived at Old Trafford but wasn't getting any game time. There was a mix in quality in the squad. When new players are learning to become familiar with their new surroundings, sometimes the existing ones can become frustrated if things are not going well. Craig Bellamy is a great example. Here was a player who loved Cardiff. They were his team. But he was frustrated by how things were going and he was always outspoken; sometimes he was critical and said things that I thought didn't necessarily need to be said. I can understand the way he was – he was so passionate. But he was now a veteran, unable to show the explosive pace he had when he was young, and because he was such a committed player, I think sometimes he felt the others didn't share that commitment. We did. We all had something to prove. But there was a gap in quality in the squad and unfortunately we couldn't turn it around.

I would like to think Craig could not find any problem with my commitment to Cardiff. I felt that I connected well with the area, the fans, the club, and the players who clearly felt a lot for the club. There couldn't be a more dedicated servant to Cardiff than Peter Whittingham – a midfielder who had played hundreds of times for Cardiff over the previous seven years. He was fantastic as a player and as a person.

The news of his death a few years later in 2020 shook me to the core. He had a fall and I read on social media that he had died. I was stunned, so quickly sent a text message to Matthew Connolly to ask if it was true. He said the rumour was premature – that Peter was in a coma and that it was complicated. But he did pass away soon after. It was very difficult to come to terms with. This is for later in the book, but the news came soon after the tragedy of Emiliano Sala and added to this heartbreak I was feeling. I could not make sense of life at this time.

I read the tributes to Peter that were posted online and in newspapers. One piece described him as one of the greatest midfielders to play in the Championship. That is a great way to describe him – to play well in that division in midfield you need to have courage and ability. More than that, he was such a nice guy and is very much missed.

As for my own contribution in the relegation season – well, I had a taste of this at QPR, but it was obvious from the start that, because I came from Manchester United, because I had played in a Champions League final, because I was a Brazilian left-back, people thought I was going to be dribbling around everyone and scoring lots of goals. In the end I'm sure it was my work ethic that earned affection from the supporters. Perhaps they were not expecting someone who would compete for everything, but that is the player I am. I shared in that responsibility of us going down and I was keen to take Cardiff back up. I was serious about settling in the area and when my daughter was born that summer it started to really feel like home.

We started the next season in the Championship quite well, but had a bad run of form when we lost in the last minute against Wolves and then Norwich came back from two goals down to win against us. When we lost to Middlesbrough, Ole was sacked – and it was only September.

It was this and not the relegation that started a poor period in my career. I know that there was an issue with my attitude but I was 24 and for the first time I was realising that not everybody saw things in football the same way as I did. I was invested in Ole, I was invested in Cardiff. I thought we were building something. But football can be cruel, short-term and selfish. At United it had felt like things could stay the same forever but even then in the last few months it had been different. Now it was starting to feel that I would have to change and become a little more selfish if I wanted my career to be successful. And yes, for a while there was a part of me that thought of myself as the player who had come from Manchester United and played for the Brazil national team. I thought of myself as above the Championship. But I had only just moved there so instead it was my motivation that was the issue – I focused on my new daughter, which isn't a bad thing, but I lost discipline with my diet and for the first time I am afraid to say that I did coast through games sometimes. I tried, of course, but it wasn't the same level as it had been in my earlier months at the club. I was lost as a person at a time I should be settled. I wasn't enjoying football and was even talking to my wife about wanting to go to Brazil and play football back where I could have fun.

The Championship is a very difficult league. It takes a long time to get used to and you can't afford to have the attitude I had for those months. That's why I pay so much respect to Peter. In the Premier League you know more or less where most teams will finish. You know the top six, you know who will struggle. Yes, there are surprises, but let's say if you pick the top six you're usually at least guaranteed four or five will be right. In the Championship if you do the same I think it's a swing the other way. You might get two – you'll be lucky if you get three. Even if you get the top six, you can't predict the order of the top two. It's crazy how many times you see teams dropping out of the Premier League who then struggle with relegation the next season.

Ole didn't leave us in a position where we were battling for survival. But the club's expectations had changed. Even fifth or sixth in the Championship wasn't enough for them in that moment; they wanted the top three.

I can't emphasise enough how much my mood diminished in this period. I felt like a different person. I wasn't getting any enjoyment from football and I could feel that I had changed. Because of that I felt that the solution was to go back to Brazil and restart my life and career.

It was my wife who convinced me to consider solutions that would see us remain in Europe. She said we should make more of an effort to settle in locally. We should start bringing family to us more often. It was a conversation that lasted for a long time. In the pre-season, after a full year in the Championship, we returned to Brazil to spend some time with our families. Our parents had spent two years in Manchester before returning home, and we would return as often as we could. There, my father had some advice for me personally. He told me how he remembered our love of football from when we were young, that the reason for us going to Europe was because we had determination to succeed and be winners. He told me that I shouldn't forget it. He said I shouldn't react this way to setbacks in my life. These were important conversations because they helped me realise that I had changed because of those disappointments. I wanted to desperately return to the way I was, the way I knew I could be, and the best way I could do that was not to accept defeat and to adapt to these new circumstances. It was to meet the challenge head on and try to succeed. It was the only way I could feel fulfilled.

I was lucky that the mood around the club was also more positive on my return. There was a strong feeling now that Russell Slade, who had spent some time getting used to the squad, had settled in after succeeding Ole.

I was committed – maybe a little too committed, as I ended up being the player with the worst disciplinary record – nine yellow cards and a red card. But I was enjoying myself again and enjoyed my favourite moment in a Cardiff shirt when I scored one of the best goals of my career – a long-range shot against Middlesbrough at the Riverside Stadium. Unfortunately for us they came back to win. And that was a snapshot for how our season ended – we went into the last couple of games with a really good chance of getting into the play-offs, but a defeat at Sheffield Wednesday left us facing another year in the Championship.

Russell was a funny character. When you won, he'd celebrate with the players and sometimes get more drunk than them. He was one of the lads. It was the first time I'd ever experienced this in my career, where a coach was as involved with the players as much as he was. It took me some time to get used to.

Russell was doomed to the same fate as Ole, and Paul Trollope came in as his successor. Our time together was brief but memorable. Paul was making a name for himself as one of the outstanding coaches in the game – he had been part of the coaching staff for Wales at the European Championships that year – and Cardiff gave him a chance as first team manager. I really enjoyed working with him. Wales had played three at the back and that was the system Paul adopted at Cardiff. I loved playing wing-back and I'm sure that Paul was really looking forward to how it would work. And then, in the last week of pre-season, Middlesbrough came in with an offer.

Paul was sad about it. And I was sad to leave Cardiff in the end, because in that final year I had really put my worries behind me and started to enjoy my football again. But when Ole signed me, he had made sure there was a clause in my contract that if the club were relegated, a team in a higher division could sign me if they offered £2m. In a perfect world I would have been back in the Premier League with Cardiff, but when the opportunity came to go back into the top flight, I was excited to test myself again.

Rafa – Standing Up

THERE WERE so many changes at Manchester United in the summer of 2014. Some of them were not unexpected. The way things had gone under David Moyes had changed the perspective of many of the players, but I want to stress that that was not necessarily to do with David personally. It's as much to do with the idea of Sir Alex retiring and now understanding that there was life after him, at Manchester United – or anywhere. For some of the older players who were coming towards the end of their careers, a new challenge could provide some new motivation. The entire defence that I had played with to win our last title had all gone. Rio Ferdinand went back home to London. Nemanja and Patrice had offers from Italy. Those offers might not come again for them.

I was just 24 and invested in the idea of a future with Manchester United – in my future I saw four or five more league titles at Old Trafford.

I had heard everything about Louis van Gaal and Brazilian players. The year after his arrival as the new manager was the hardest of my life and it taught me a lot about reality and perception. It seemed to me that van Gaal came with his ideas of what he wanted to do and he wasn't prepared to come in and allow his preconceptions to be changed. He came in with an idea of the players he wanted and didn't want and set about making those changes instantly. I'm not saying that's the wrong way to do things – it has been very successful for some managers and had been successful for him in the past. I can only speak as a victim of that and say the experience wasn't pleasant.

The second day he was at the club he called me and Ryan Giggs to his office. Ryan had retired but, after his spell as caretaker, was now assistant manager with a view to one day getting the top job. Van Gaal was straight to the point.

'I don't think I'm going to use you a lot this season, so you can go.'

Well, wow. Years of my life, my entire career with Manchester United. Gone in the space of five seconds. That's football. It can be as clinical and as cold, and as cruel, as that.

I put a brave face on it. I didn't argue – what was the point? I was devastated about the idea of leaving but I was far from the only one. In the days after that, Ryan was talking to me, trying to bring me back around. 'Keep going, show him what you can do, show him how good you are, and he will have to play you.' So that was how I decided to play it.

This kind of fight for a player is rarely a positive thing. You're not just fighting to get into the team – so good form and good attitude isn't always enough. You're fighting against the preconceptions. They are formed in numerous ways and I am a big enough man to take responsibility for my role in that. I wasn't Cristiano or Wayne. I wasn't Robin. Forwards naturally get the headlines for their contributions and how they influence things. How often do defenders get the headlines? How often do they get noticed? What was van Gaal's prior experience with me? He was the manager of Bayern Munich when I was sent off in 2010. I hadn't even realised that until I was writing this book and trying to come up with a list of reasons for why he might have had something against me personally before he arrived at the club. This was his direct experience with me. It didn't matter that it was over four years earlier.

So sometimes it doesn't matter how well you do. You're fighting your own fight and then another one where the rules are unpredictable. How do you convince a person as famously stubborn as van Gaal that they are wrong, and that you have changed? You can't do it. It's impossible. So your best is never good enough and every mistake is amplified to be even greater because it serves to vindicate that person's reservations. You're taken off the pitch, dropped, and put in the reserves.

I have to say that at the same time I had a big problem coming to terms with the way he wanted to train and the way he wanted to play his football. Maybe all of this affects the way you see someone personally. You get tired, very quickly, of everything they do. It makes you feel more reluctant. How can you be enthusiastic about this guy? He'd be there after training in the cafeteria, long talks about nothing. It would be boring. You'd want to get away. It had never been like that at United.

He wasn't a bad coach. Of course he wasn't. You don't accomplish the things he did in the game by being a bad coach. It was a matter of compatibility. At Manchester United you're expected to play expansive and expressive football. When van Gaal came in, it felt as if he was teaching us how to play. An example – I could be three metres from the touchline in training. Van Gaal would complain, stop the play and instruct me that I must be two metres. He would tell me exactly where to stand. I would laugh because you would think it is nothing – he would go crazy about it, it was so important to him. It felt like a power play – the manager telling the player that this was his way of doing things and that his way was the right way.

My style of play is my style. I can say I felt I had matured – maybe that's something I'm still working on today. But I know, because it was said so many times, that my instinctive way of playing – right from when I was a young boy through to the time I was playing some of the biggest games in club football for the best club in the world – was a positive thing. It was the reason I was so at home at Old Trafford and I'd like to believe it was one of the reasons I had such a strong relationship with the support. Okay, so maybe I had to learn how to get a stronger balance between playing with the heart and the head, but it seemed like van Gaal wanted no heart and all head.

He wanted to tell you what to do and how to do it, and what he wanted to see on the pitch was a result of that instruction. His preference for players was therefore mostly those who were more likely to be agreeable to carrying out instructions. The problem was that this wasn't the culture at Manchester United. We had a lot of players who had a similar outlook on playing to me. We had been encouraged to be expressive. That was, as far as I was aware, part of the *identity* of Manchester United.

From that perspective, it felt like Ryan was there as a go-between. He was there to ensure van Gaal was aware of the way things worked at United. And, as someone who knew all of us as players, he was there to try and make sure this transition wasn't too difficult. I knew he liked me as a player, so he was keen to bring me around and make me feel more comfortable. I felt reassured by him telling me to just play my natural way, but it became clear quite early on that it wasn't going to be enough.

Because Louis had a stronger track record than David, and because it was, after all, Manchester United, standards and expectations were high. Still, patience was needed. Okay, so Nemanja and Patrice had gone and they were big losses. But this is football – these changes happen. And as everyone knows, it took time and patience for those two to settle, too. They weren't world stars when they arrived but they were two of the best players in the club's history by the time they moved on. They had the right profile and personality to play for the club.

Transfers can be a lottery at the best of times. United made so many that summer that it sometimes felt as if the pursuit of short-term progress overshadowed the sort of stability that had made us so successful. Van Gaal had a three-year contract, and he was telling everyone that that would be it for him, so he had to find success within those three years.

The biggest name of all the players we signed was Ángel Di María. He wasn't wanted by Real Madrid, even after being the man of the match in the Champions League Final that year. He's a good guy, I have nothing against Ángel. He is a player of such talent. But it felt as if he signed for United because it was a boost to his ego at the exact time the club he was playing for didn't want him. *Real Madrid don't want me? I'll show them – the biggest club in the world want me.* Crucially, it wasn't a case of him saying, 'I'm desperate to play for Manchester United.' It seemed a strange move on both sides, because almost straight away it seemed as if van Gaal wasn't going to help him. He wasn't a van Gaal kind of player, he wasn't cold. He played with emotion and fire. It didn't take long for it to be noticeable that Ángel's head wasn't in Manchester any more. Three or four months. It was obvious he was already thinking of his next move and I could sympathise with what he was going through.

There was a lot of talk about who was responsible for signing the players – particularly when Luke Shaw and Ander Herrera, two players David had apparently wanted to sign, arrived before van Gaal. And then Marcos Rojo, a defender with a style of play that definitely didn't seem to be the manager's type, was signed. Rojo played with the heart, and he was crazy sometimes. Sergio Romero made it three Argentinian players that van Gaal signed in his first summer.

Daley Blind was a player van Gaal was more familiar with and definitely had the qualities the manager liked. Here was a cool guy, always consistent, very intelligent. Truthfully, I don't know if that consistency was quite at the level required to be at the biggest club in the world, but with everything else happening the way it was, maybe it's just that the value of that consistency was not as high as it normally would be.

On transfer deadline day Radamel Falcao signed and Danny Welbeck was sold. People were excited about Falcao because of his history. At his best he was one of the top strikers in the world. Again, though, I have to be honest – nobody will be surprised by this – he wasn't ready to play football when he was at United. He was still suffering with his knee injury and I think he'd been rushed back to play in the World Cup that summer. It could have been a completely different person who came to Manchester United because it didn't look like the same guy at all. He was still in the middle of his rehabilitation if we're being completely truthful. But he was brought into a situation where there was a lot of pressure on him to do well immediately. He wasn't allowed the time he needed. How could he impress in the way he wanted to? And he was the nicest guy. I have a lot of respect for him and for what he was going through. He had another year in England after things didn't work out at United – I guess he was desperate to prove himself. But at Chelsea he faced a similar story. Back at Monaco, he looked something like his old self.

People look at this time and say it was the start of something different about United. That is true but I don't agree that signing Ángel and Radamel was the start of players thinking they could go to Old Trafford and just coast along. I need to make a point here because a lot of people paid attention to a comment I made on social media about Alexis Sánchez – by now of course everyone knows that Sánchez signed for the club a few years after I left and didn't last very long at Old Trafford. He apparently told his agent that he wanted the contract to be terminated after his first training session. I commented, 'Maybe he saw a ghost and get scared, that would explain why he played so bad every time.' When Sánchez came all the headlines were about the wage he would be earning – I can't say anything about that, but I do remember the same was said about Ángel and Radamel, and so I can explain how I felt it was at the club at that time.

For Falcao, this was a step up to the biggest club in the world. Di María was moving at a difficult time in his career and was desperate to prove how good he was. Of course, this is only my impression of things but I felt they were both good guys who were there to help United do better and, though they had their own individual reasons for coming to the club, they appreciated the stage and hard work that went with it. I am not able to comment on what happened after I left, but I can say for sure that the reason Di María and Falcao didn't work out with United was not down to a lack of hard work on their part.

But it was a lot of change in a short space of time. Maybe it was difficult that a manager had come in who hadn't lived in Manchester, or England, and neither had any of the players we signed apart from Luke Shaw. That is not a difficulty in itself but when you are replacing all of that experience it has to play a part.

The final part of the issue was that when you sign for Manchester United you're not just signing for the biggest club in the world. You're signing for *Manchester* United and whether you grow to love or hate living in the north-west of England, a period of adaptation is required, and a large percentage of your ability to be successful depends on your capability and even willingness to settle, and the support you have to do so. I am not going to say my wife hates Manchester. She doesn't enjoy the cold and the rain. But she knew I loved playing for Manchester United so much, that it was just one of those things she dealt with in order for us to have a happy life. I'm not quite sure Ángel fully appreciated what the reality would be like – maybe he thought it was a bit of a joke that people exaggerated.

So it seemed like a different way of doing things at United with the transfers we were doing. Van Gaal also had a change of system on the pitch to 3-5-2 with wing-backs, which should have been something I could adapt to comfortably. But I wasn't first choice – that was Antonio Valencia. Like I said, Antonio was one of my best friends at the club and I honestly felt he had the perfect qualities for a role like this. He was very fast, incredibly strong, committed and he concentrated. He could contribute at both ends. It was a change of position for him but he adapted very well.

It was a more natural adjustment for him to play there than for Jesse Lingard and Ashley Young, who started the season in those roles. I wasn't even in the squad on the opening day against Swansea. Jesse got injured so Ashley moved over to the right and Adnan Januzaj came on at left wing-back. We lost. As early as the first game you could see the fit between Louis van Gaal and Manchester United wasn't natural. There were occasions when some of the players would pause and you could almost sense the uncertainty. There was no relaxation in there; the players were thinking, 'What does he want me to do next?' He hated tricks. He hated instinct. Everything had to be done by instruction. It felt like everything positive was being undone in these moments. Under Sir Alex the emphasis had been on moving quickly. If you could go in one touch, go in one touch. Van Gaal hated that. He *hated* it. 'No, no, control the ball.' The difference seems so small but it had an incredible impact on the way we played. It slowed it down so much that it was unrecognisable. If and when my opportunity to coach comes, my style of football will be to use one-touch whenever possible. It makes everything quicker.

We lost against Swansea and drew at Sunderland. And then there was the embarrassment of what happened against MK Dons in the League Cup which people remember to this day. It is difficult enough when your team is in a bad run of form. It's harder still when you're forced to watch it from the sidelines, desperate to get on to the pitch and show you can make a positive difference.

My first chance came after the transfer window and the first international break. We played against QPR and won 4-0. Ángel and Ander scored. It was a false indication of how our season was going to go. The next week we went to Leicester when Ángel scored another great goal and we were two in front.

Then the referee Mark Clattenburg decided that I had fouled Jamie Vardy in the box and gave a penalty. I was furious. It was never a penalty but it changed the game completely, and afterwards nobody spoke about it. Not even the manager. Normally the manager comes out and complains about the decision to defend his player. They do it even when the player is wrong, sometimes. I know Sir Alex would have defended me. Even Moyes. Even if he didn't want to defend me, at least criticise the injustice of the decision – it was never, ever a penalty. They scored it. And then Tyler Blackett, another of our young defenders making his way into the team, was sent off giving away another penalty and they won 5-3. I didn't know what disappointed me more – the decision or the lack of defence. I couldn't believe that nobody was talking about it after the game. It was like it didn't happen at all, but I know it did, because back at the club when we were going over the match, there it was, 'You could be more careful.' What is that? If we'd had VAR then, the penalty would 100 per cent not have been given.

I think if this had been a year earlier then Rio or Vida would have stepped up and said something. But Tyler was a kid. Marcos wasn't going to say anything. I didn't expect Jonny Evans to. The truth was that I didn't expect the manager to be saying what he said.

The media loved it. They wanted to concentrate on the two-goal lead being lost and Leicester winning 5-3. United were in crisis. Everything's a mess. They love it – click, click, click for their websites.

I was determined to put that defeat out of my mind so I was fired up against West Ham. I felt I had one of my better games. I was really pleased with my performance, particularly as I was playing next to Paddy McNair, who was making his debut at centre-half next to me. I helped him and played my natural game, even setting up an early goal for Wayne Rooney, who was later sent off. We saw the match out and won 2-1.

Van Gaal showed us the video on the Monday morning. After five minutes he paused the tape, right when I have the ball, and announced to everyone that my attempt at a cross was 'bad'. Why am I hitting it on the bounce? Why am I not looking where I am crossing? I couldn't believe it. I was looking around the group and thinking, 'What does this guy want?' I know Wayne did well to score. It was a good goal. But van Gaal was making it sound as though my cross was a problem and not a good thing. I'd struck it first time. He did not like that. It wasn't part of his instruction. I quickly learned that this was what he did with players he didn't like – if there was anything he could criticise them for, even if the reason was clear only to him, he'd take the chance to do it.

It was a strange season. Despite the inconsistency, van Gaal insisted that he wanted United to play like Barcelona. He kept on with that even when it was clear it wasn't working. Pass, control. Pass, control. The three-man defence went out of the window for a while and things changed; 4-3-3, a midfield diamond, 4-3-2-1. Then things would turn around for a little while – and as soon as the players started to get confidence, he seemed desperate to get back to that three-man defence and try it again.

I think he thought that as time passed people would just become robots and accept his instructions without discussion, that we'd just nod and say yes to whatever he was telling us to do. But some of us just weren't made like that. Ángel wasn't, so he found himself being used less and less. You could see him losing his motivation.

Life started to feel as if we were at army camp and van Gaal was the captain. After lunch every day there would be long conversations where he would sit talking to us, and I can't even remember what we'd talk about. He would say he wasn't interested in our private lives and then he'd make a comment if someone had been pictured in the press. Talking, talking, talking, all the time.

I had been injured and was then left out of a few games, but came back into the side over Christmas. I was in the team that went to Yeovil in the FA Cup, where I went into a challenge for a header and clashed with one of their players. I had to come off – they had to tell me I was being substituted at half-time, because I wanted to go back on to the pitch. In fact, I had to have surgery. Back at Carrington, a couple of days after the operation, I finished my lunch and was waiting for the rest of the lads to finish while van Gaal was talking. I was still feeling discomfort, so was rubbing my temple and had my head down for a moment.

He walked over and touched me on the shoulder.

'What are you doing?'

'Oh,' I said, not expecting to be challenged on my action. 'I'm just in a bit of pain so I'm rubbing it.'

'When I speak, you need to listen. You need to respect me.'

I went red. My English wasn't the best at this time but I tried to get my message across. 'I don't respect you? I do respect you. I touch my head because I just had an operation,' I said, and then, it all came out. 'I try all the time, you never give me a chance.'

He didn't expect it. He was taken aback.

'You need to look at me,' he said.

'Keep talking. I'm not talking any more,' I responded.

He talked for maybe a couple more minutes and sent us to the dressing room. The rest of the lads had been quiet as we argued but, once we were by ourselves, were laughing that I'd answered back. Fletch came into the dressing room after and said he was happy that I spoke up for myself. Then Antonio followed him and said with straightforward seriousness, 'Rafa, you're never going to play again for Manchester United under van Gaal.'

'Mano [that was our nickname for each other],' I said, 'what was I supposed to do?'

'Mano, you'll never play again.'

He was right.

Well, *technically*, he was wrong. I had two more minutes for the first team, as a substitute in a win over Spurs. That came after I'd played so well for the reserves, scoring, ironically, against Spurs, that he couldn't keep me out. But that was all I got.

My first games for United were some of the biggest you can play in football. I ended my time there playing for the reserve team. I wasn't alone in that – many big names were told they had to play for the reserves. So it wasn't embarrassing for me as much as I think it was done to *try* and make me feel humiliated. Everything felt as though it had gone backwards. I wasn't a kid any more. I'd proved myself and I'd won trophies with United. In terms of the squad we had, I was now one of the most experienced. I'm not saying that I deserved a first-team place because of that, but I felt that I was at least worthy of the respect of having a conversation about how things were.

To get respect you need to show respect. You can't treat someone poorly from day one and expect them to respect you for it. Worse still, van Gaal seemed happy that there was a distance between him and the players. It was never that way under Sir Alex. Maybe it's just different personalities. Maybe it's a result of the time the boss stayed at the club and how comfortable he was having conversations with players, even if we disagreed. They were both managers who liked control but they went about it in a very different way. A great example is this: I can remember many times Sir Alex wanted to play with three at the back. There were so many conversations we had as a group about it. In the end the players never felt comfortable with it they'd explain why, and it very rarely happened. He listened to them. It was a relationship.

At least the last game I played was a win at Old Trafford. It was the start of a little run where van Gaal had changed formation again and we played against some tough teams – Juan Mata scored two great goals at Anfield and then we won against City. Those nine points went a long way towards ensuring we'd qualify for the Champions League, which showed just how much things had changed.

Minor changes are okay, they can help. Against Spurs only Daley and Ander started from the players van Gaal brought in, and we played a formation that had Marouane at number ten. It was effective. But soon afterwards he started trying to go back to the shapes he preferred. We won one of the last six games and in four of those we didn't score a goal. Now it became about specialists for positions. Robots. I was a defender who was at my best when I was trusted to go and play my natural game. It was that way when I was a right-back. It was that way when I was asked to play on the wing against Arsenal. It was a big change but it was not overcomplicated. We were trusted and made to feel like we were. 'Okay, that's where you're playing boys, just go and play your football.'

Van Gaal asked you to control and pass the ball. You had to do it in the way he wanted in the position he wanted. You had to move where he wanted you to. If you did what he asked then he would be happy with you. It wouldn't matter if you won or lost the game. If he could say that a player did what was instructed, he would be happy with them.

I wasn't going to do what he wanted me to do. So he signed a player who would – Matteo Darmian, the Italian international. And even then it made no sense to me. Matteo was a traditional Italian defender – very good defensively but would not contribute much in attack. Why would you sign a player like that when what you really want is to play with wing-backs?! Memphis Depay came in. Van Gaal knew him from the national team and knew his character – he knew Memphis was an individual and still signed him. I only trained with him for a week, and spent much longer with him in France, but it was clear that it was a move that would end in conflict.

Many more players left, including Fletch, Anderson and Nani. Then the summer came and van Persie and Chicharito went. They were all for either nothing or very small fees. You could say for most of these guys that they were coming to the end and needed a new challenge. You can say what you want about where I fitted into things. But I could never understand why Jonny Evans was allowed to leave. He was the best defender left at the club. He was coming into his peak years. Have they had a better defender than him since he left? Both he and I were allowed to go. Jonny went to West Brom and then Leicester and proved how good he is. He could play for any top team in the country.

I was reluctant to go. But when I wasn't part of the pre-season tour it was obvious where I fitted, or didn't fit, into the plans of the manager. I had some offers from different clubs but these were conversations that never really moved into firm negotiations. Lyon came in on deadline day and they were playing in the Champions League. There was a new spotlight on French football, too, with the takeover at

Paris Saint-Germain, who finally managed to get Ángel Di María that summer.

Joining Lyon was the easy part of the decision – they showed that they really wanted me and the idea of playing in the top European competition again was something that appealed. Of course, leaving United after all that time was the difficult part. You never know in football but there was a period in 2013 – after we won the league, and before Sir Alex announced his retirement – where I felt the rest of my career would be in Manchester.

Just two years later I knew all about the uncertainty that comes with the sport. My brother was getting on with his life and career. I had to do the same. What do you do? I was heartbroken to leave this part of my life behind but I didn't want to show van Gaal that I'd been hurt in that way. I decided the best way I could move on was to take all of the positive experiences and lessons I had learned and try and prove my ability. I needed to find enjoyment within football and I had to believe that Lyon would offer me that. As I have said, leaving Old Trafford was a tough decision, but once I knew I had to leave, I'm happy to say that Lyon turned out to be the perfect place for me to rediscover my love for the game.

Rafa – Lyon

IT TOOK a little time for me to settle in France. Because I didn't know the language, I wasn't able to get to know the manager Hubert Fournier very well, although from what I did know he seemed like a nice guy. In those early months I was trying to settle and it was very frustrating – getting used to leaving Manchester and settling in a new town, a new country, a new club.

I was desperate to settle in as quickly as I could. But in my anxiety, when I was trying to understand what people were saying, I was associating it with English and trying to make the right translation. In reality, Portuguese is obviously much closer to the French language, and it would have been much easier to just relax and use that.

I was also picking up a lot of injuries – not serious ones, but niggles, so I'd be out for one or two games which it made it difficult for me to get into any sort of rhythm.

When I did play, I didn't think I was playing well. When you can't speak the language, you want to at least try and communicate through your football and show how committed you are on the pitch so that the fans, and your team-mates, can get to know you. My first chance to do that came against Monaco in a big game. We were 1-0 down late on and had a corner. There was me, a right-back, but for this match a left-back, and in this moment, I was a striker. The ball bounced to me and I was the man furthest forward. I turned and struck it into the net. My celebration was one of relief – getting all of that frustration out. The goal earned us a draw.

I think in those few minutes the Lyon fans were able to see me. They were able to see immediately that I'm a player, and a person, who is fuelled by emotion. I'm motivated by a love of the game and by wanting to win. That's what I'm commited to. Sometimes playing that way gets me into trouble and ends with bad consequences. When you play from the heart and with emotion you can get carried away. But it is never with bad intentions. A couple of weeks later I was booked as we won an important derby with Saint-Étienne to go second in the league; it felt like an important day in establishing that connection with the support.

That match was our last win in Stade de Gerland. Shortly after we moved to the Parc Olympique Lyonnais, by which time we had also changed manager with Hubert being replaced by Bruno Génésio, who had been his assistant. These changes would turn out to be positive in the long term, but as they happened I confess that it was more upheaval that made a difficult first few months a little bit tougher.

Lyon is a club with a rich tradition of Brazilian players, such as Sonny Anderson, Edmílson, Giovane Élber, Cris, and Fred. Possibly the most famous of them all was Juninho Pernambucano, the free-kick expert who was sporting director when I arrived. But there were no other Brazilians in the squad when I signed, so it was a strange time. Juninho helped me a lot (more towards the end of my time than the start) – he is a very nice guy. He is a legend of football. Maybe he didn't play 100 times for Brazil but he is loved at home just like he was in Lyon. His set-piece ability moved him into the arena of players who we adore in a special way. It's the same as Roberto Carlos, or David Beckham. All of them are great players but because they were so good at free kicks – and come on, who doesn't appreciate the art? – then they have this special place in the supporter's hearts.

When you are in a career that involves so much moving around, it helps whenever there is something that can make you feel at home. Lyon is a long way from Petrópolis but being at a club that had a long history of Brazilians – even if I was the only one at the time – helped me to settle.

But yes, the new country, new club, new language, new stadium. All of these things were difficult enough. After the derby win we lost four out of five and Bruno was appointed as the new manager. Bruno is a good guy – I would say that in my years as a professional he is only second to Sir Alex in terms of coaches I worked with. I loved working with him, I agreed very much with the way he wanted to play the game. And sometimes a change can provoke many positive changes. I wasn't going to let the bumpy beginning make me feel as though I'd made the wrong move. And it didn't take much to turn the feeling around.

Moving into a new stadium and playing on a new pitch is something many teams struggle with at first because they have to get used to it. I think with our squad there was such an excitement at being part of a new chapter in the club's history that it really helped us put in some strong performances. Because you're there at the start, it's *your* home. And in that moment, it was a fresh start for the club, the other players and the fans just as it was for me.

The stadium was beautiful and the pitch was fantastic. I feel sure it elevated our performance; it really lifted us. Because the results started so strongly, it really helped our confidence turn around. In our first match there we won 4-1; it was 1-1 in the 71st minute and we scored three goals late on to make our supporters happy. In fact, we won six and drew two of our eight league games there in the first season. The form helped us get second place in the league.

But it was more than luck and a change of circumstances – we had a really good squad that was better than the results before Christmas suggested. Many of the players had been developed by the club, and, as I learned at Manchester United, that in itself is a positive thing. It creates an instant motivation to do well for the club and a greater personal connection. Alexandre Lacazette was a goal machine and as for Nabil Fekir, this guy should have been a superstar. As soon as I arrived he scored a hat-trick at Caen. To me it seemed obvious that his destiny was to follow Karim Benzema at Real Madrid. But then he suffered a terrible ligament injury which really hurt his progression. He missed much of the season but I was excited for when he would get back into the team. Corentin Tolisso was a great midfielder; Mathieu Valbuena too. Samuel Umtiti was a great defender, fantastic to play alongside and a very good guy. For a centre-back he wasn't very tall, but he was so uncomplicated, and because of that he was often unappreciated.

Of all of them, Fekir was the one. He was a machine. He's still a very good footballer, a tremendous player, and it's a shame that injury might mean we don't see the best of him. I'm sure he can still do something special in the game with a bit of luck. But that list of names is impressive enough – they were part of a generation of success for France.

Our rivals for the title were Paris Saint-Germain, who won it comfortably in the end. That's where most of the Brazilians in France were. They had Thiago Silva, Marquinhos, David Luiz and Maxwell in defence. They had Lucas Moura, and then the other big stars that they had been able to acquire in their new regime: Edinson Cavani, Zlatan Ibrahimović, Javier Pastore. And there was Ángel Di María, who had moved to France before I did, to finally get the transfer he seemed to want. They won 23 of their first 27 games. When they finally lost, it was us who ended their unbeaten run.

Coming from England, I was used to facing an opponent like this. At least at United you can try to compete. It's much more difficult to do that in France. The influence the money and transfers on the success of PSG is undeniable. Other clubs have to combat this in the usual way, through a mixture of smart recruitment and a strong youth policy. That's what Lyon did. Monaco were also doing the same – players like Fabinho, Ricardo Carvalho, Bernardo Silva, Tiémoué Bakayoko, Thomas Lemar, plus Kylian Mbappé who was breaking through.

In one-off games we were good enough to take on anyone. We beat PSG, and beat that Monaco team 6-1 in our last home game of the season. Football is like this, filled with beautiful surprises. The reality is that a team such as Paris, with the squad of players they had, should win by four goals in most of the games they play in Ligue 1. They did that more than ten times throughout the season. The only other team to beat them were Monaco.

But it was Monaco who were better prepared for the following season. They also had Benjamin Mendy and Djibril Sidibé – two brilliant full-backs. Mendy was so good and difficult to play against. His engine was unbelievable. They haven't gone on to show their Monaco form for the teams they've moved to, but for this season in particular they were fantastic. They also had Radamel Falcao, who looked like the old Falcao. He had a confident team around him. They had a positive attitude.

When Monaco did what they did there was a certain beauty to it. They upset the system against PSG. Speaking as a football fan you want to see it continue but when teams like that overachieve it is never long before other clubs come in and start to make offers a club like Monaco can't turn down. The players have their own ambition, too, and you can understand it. But it's still sad.

We were in a similar position when you looked at the squad we had. That's why, when I look at my time in France, I appreciate what Monaco did, but I still honestly believe that our Lyon team was better. Some supporters complained that Bruno wasn't the man to lead the team – that a more experienced manager would get more out of our very talented squad. As I've said, I think Bruno was a great coach, so that wasn't the problem for me. We were very inconsistent in my second season there. Maybe it's that the squad wasn't big enough to cope with playing in the Champions League. Sometimes, though, it seemed as if one or two of our players were looking at their next move.

When you're not fully concentrating on your goal as a team, even if it's just one or two per cent, you can lose that collective determination that you need, especially when your consistency needs to be high enough to get over 87 points as PSG did. Monaco did have that – and to be honest, it was brilliant as a neutral to see, even though I was sad it wasn't us. To prove the point, our games against Monaco and PSG were tight. We lost three of them by a single goal but won 3-1 in Monaco. Winning big games didn't seem to be a problem. The eyes of the country were on us and our players could perform. But Guingamp and Lorient at home, to name just two, were both lost. You have to treat those matches just as seriously as you do the games against Monaco. The reward for winning is the same – three points. Everyone has to run and show commitment.

As a professional footballer – as a footballer at any level – trying to find that consistency within a team is a normal problem. I could appreciate that the level of consistency we had at Manchester United was a rare thing, it was *not* normal, but because you have been there, you hope you understand what it takes to get there again. So being in a situation in which we were trying to get that momentum – no problem, that's football, it's universal and there are no surprises. I think it's only ever the situation that can create the surprise.

Take for example the crowd trouble that I experienced, particularly in the second season I spent at Lyon. I come from Brazil – I'm not surprised by crowd trouble, how passionate supporters can be, and how that can sometimes get out of control. But I wasn't expecting it in France, because French football doesn't have that reputation. I didn't know these things happened there.

The first incident was at Metz, in December. The game was abandoned because a firework was thrown on to the pitch near our goalkeeper, Anthony Lopes. It's hard to know what to say about such an event. It was a bad thing, a terrible thing. Honestly, though? I looked at Anthony and thought he was overreacting. You have the initial shock when, to be honest, anything could happen, but once it was obvious he was okay, that should have been it.

Afterwards, you can make a joke about it. 'My friend,' I said, 'fucking hell, I thought you were dead!' That's *after*, I stress. Once you've seen the videos and you know he's okay. In the moment you're with him, it's a team thing. He arrives in the dressing room holding his hand over his ear, looking really sad. Come on, man, that's too much. You're okay. It reminded me of Nani at Liverpool – you've got to make a joke about it.

Of course, look, the moment is truly shocking. Someone threw an actual firework on to the pitch. Anything really could have happened. You make a joke after because you're laughing about it to get through it, and because you know your friend is okay.

It was a little more difficult to make a joke about the events at Bastia later that season. I'll never forget that day. Without exaggeration, there were moments I felt I would be lucky if I got out alive. It was crazy. There was fighting in the stands and the kick-off was delayed, then more fighting as the game started. We get to half-time and some fans get on to the pitch. One confronts Anthony, who pushed back, and suddenly it was a riot. Our players and staff got involved, kicking and hitting back. We got into our locker room as quickly as we could. Bastia fans were outside, banging on the door. They wanted to get in to get us. We were alone – just us, in the dressing room with no help. They were so angry that I was certain if they got in they were going to kill us. It was terrifying. I was genuinely afraid of dying. The biggest mistake they made was fighting back – when it was a few people on the pitch it was like our guys were 'winning' for a minute. But we had a small team of players and staff. We were outnumbered by about 15,000. So we were quick to get to the dressing room – and as soon as security could get us to the team bus, we escaped. There was no way the game was going to continue. Bastia were demoted because of financial problems and luckily we never had to go back.

In January, Memphis Depay arrived from United. He was not a Louis van Gaal guy, and by now José Mourinho was manager at Old Trafford, so clearly Memphis was a player Mourinho felt he could sell. Memphis came to France still with that same individualism. He is a guy who did not care about how others perceived him. He could respond to good leadership as a player, but he was never going to change as a person. I'll be honest, getting to know him was a little difficult because of that. After a little time, once we became more familiar and I was able to understand him more, I could appreciate him more.

You could never doubt his talent. From the first weeks he was fantastic for us and made a great difference on the pitch. A few weeks after he signed, he scored from the halfway line against Toulouse. I wasn't in the squad on the day, so I had a great view of his fantastic goal.

Memphis and I shared a common target – the opportunity to be reunited with Manchester United in the Europa League that season.

Nabil Fekir was brilliant in the knockout rounds. He scored a hat-trick against AZ, and was brilliant against Roma in a great game for us. We had a memorable quarter-final with Beşiktaş where we scored twice in the last few minutes to win the first leg, then it went all the way to penalties in the second leg. We won, to set up a semi-final with Ajax.

This was one of the greatest disappointments of my career. We were enjoying the sort of run where you feel destined to make the final. And, in the other semi-final, Manchester United were playing – they were strong favourites to knock out Celta Vigo to get to the final in Stockholm, Sweden. What an incentive – the opportunity to see everyone again. We threw away the semi-final in 49 minutes of the first leg. Ajax went three goals up and it was just impossible for us to get back into it. We scored, but they scored again, and we knew that a 4-1 defeat was going to be almost impossible to overcome. We gave it a go and in the second leg we missed so many chances, enough to level the score, but we only won 2-1 and so we were out. This was a great Ajax team – Matthijs de Ligt, Frenkie de Jong, Donny van de Beek. It was the team who would go on to do so well in the Champions League in 2019 so losing to them was no disgrace, but it was also no consolation.

I was devastated to miss out on the chance to play against United in the final, though. It's the only thing that would have compared to playing *for* them in a final. That's life. It didn't happen. And life was on my mind in the week of the final when there was a terrorist incident in Manchester which claimed many lives. I was still regularly talking to the guys at United and a couple knew people who had died. I wish I'd had the chance to spend time with my United family that week.

José Mourinho's team won the Europa League, to follow up their League Cup win. Van Gaal had been sacked the day after winning the FA Cup. Could I have stayed on, and outlasted him in the hope of staying at United? A year of your life is a long time to wait. I had no regrets about moving to Lyon. After two years we were settled there – my wife and children loved the city. My son was too young for any real memories of Manchester, but my daughter was a little bit older and she seemed to love France. She seemed to love it more than Manchester, so I was surprised when, after a few years, we decided to sell our house there and my daughter became really upset and said she wanted to go there again!

So Ajax ended my dream for that season – and that team was shortly broken up when some of the better players moved on. We had a similar situation when Lacazette moved to Arsenal. He was scoring goals at such a rate that he was being linked with all the top clubs and in the end chose the Premier League. Tolisso moved to Bayern Munich, a stage he deserved.

Meanwhile, Paris had responded to losing the league to Monaco by signing two goalscorers themselves – Kylian Mbappé from the champions and Neymar from Barcelona.

Neymar moved for €222m, Mbappé for €175m. Just like that. You had to laugh. Everyone knew Mbappé was moving. PSG knew they couldn't sign him because it would have broken the Financial Fair Play rules. So they loaned him, but come on, they bought him. He's signed. Everyone knows. It had the desired effect and Paris won the league by 13 points. They scored more than 100 goals.

I felt the professional frustration, of course I did. A footballer's career is short, you don't get the time back, and there are only so many trophies to go around. But at Lyon we were still strong enough to be competitive and I was up for the challenge. I believed in my team-mates and felt that we could all do something unexpected, as Monaco had. I know that we all believed it – and we proved that when we won against them in January. Who I really felt sorry for were clubs like Bordeaux or Dijon, who might have to be smarter with their resources and pay more modest transfer fees. It wasn't fair on them.

We made the best out of our situation in the 2017/18 season and got more points and scored more goals than before. Memphis and Nabil really stepped up to replace Alexandre's goals. We were great at home, only losing twice. The thought in our mind was to emulate what Monaco did. We finished third, which was an improvement on fourth the previous season, but we didn't do ourselves justice in the cups. At least in the Europa League I had the chance to return to England for the first time, though I didn't play when we faced Everton in the group stages. I had two more Brazilians with me at Lyon – Marcelo and Marçal – but I joked that I was actually English, I was so excited to go back. It's true, to an extent. I love the country and it feels like home.

We had great periods of consistency, but I have to admit that it was demoralising when you were on a good run and every week Paris had scored five goals again. You could say that it might make it easier for a club like Lyon, because there was no real expectation on us to win the league. We couldn't afford to think like that. We had our own standards to maintain and we wanted to take Lyon from being a club that was in the Europa League to one that was always in the Champions League. We could try and use this to move up a level and challenge for Ligue 1, and we were at least one of the few clubs that could put a good effort in.

I'm a motivated person. I am motivated to win every single game of football, so it doesn't matter how unlikely someone thinks success in the bigger picture is. I don't know if you would call it a changing of motivation or a maturing – an understanding and appreciation of what is reasonable. You have to define what is reasonable to call it a success. I think we were successful at Lyon. For a long time before I arrived at the club, Lyon were not as competitive as they wanted to be.

You have to have harmony in your professional and personal life to be happy. So I admit the first year in France was very difficult, for a few reasons – the language, the changes, some personal circumstances which were very difficult. My wife was very ill for a while and naturally my concern was for her. Thankfully, she gradually recovered, and I was so relieved that I think I started to see things differently. I became less worried about the obstacles that made the start of life in the country difficult, and I just felt grateful for having the opportunity; I started to enjoy playing football again. If you take into account the fact that those last months in Manchester had been very difficult, it had been a long time since I enjoyed my game.

After spending three years in France, I was settled, I was happy, I was enjoying myself. Then came the best news ever – Fabio was signing for Nantes. I remember when he called me to tell me he was coming to France. I thought he was lying. I couldn't believe it. It was one of the best feelings. Even though Nantes is far away from Lyon, it would mean we could see each other much more often than before. Even when I couldn't see him I could watch him play, as he was in the same league. Straight away I looked at the calendar – our home game with Nantes was in September.

After all this time, I was so excited to play against him. And then, in the week before the game, Bruno was laughing as he said to me, 'Relax. You don't need to be nervous. We're going to rest you this week because we have a Champions League game we want you to be ready for. Maybe if I need you, I'll use you.' I did come on for the last ten minutes, so I was able to share the pitch with my brother again for a few moments. It was special.

We made a couple of good signings that season. Moussa Dembélé scored goals, and Tanguy Ndombele was a player I hadn't heard much of before we signed him – and after just a couple of months he was so impressive in our midfield that I was compelled to call friends in Manchester to say they should spread the word about getting United to sign him. He had so much talent and was a very good player for us. A little while longer, and I admit my judgement might have been hasty. There were certain things that made me think he wouldn't be right for United – but he was certainly fantastic for Lyon.

In the Champions League we were drawn with Manchester City in the group stage, and our first game was at the Etihad. I was delighted to return to Manchester, but before the game everyone wrote us off. City were Premier League champions under Pep Guardiola. People weren't only saying we were going to lose – they were dismissing us so much that they were talking about new record defeats. It wasn't just me with something to prove. And we did prove ourselves – they were not expecting us to be as good as we were, and we scored twice in the first half. I was against Raheem Sterling, and then Leroy Sané – two of the quickest players in football. When I came off with 14 minutes left, I was exhausted. We held on to win and it was a very special day for me.

It was our only win of the group and we still went through after we drew all the other matches, but that only tells half the story. Against Shakhtar Donetsk we were 2-0 down but drew. In Hoffenheim we were winning in injury time but drew. At home against the same team – 2-0 up, but drew. Still, we qualified, and our next challenge was as difficult as it could be – Barcelona. Almost a decade had passed since I was involved in games with Lionel Messi and Cristiano Ronaldo. Much had changed in football but those two were still the best in the world. It was almost boring. I'm joking, of course. It was a good draw for us in France but Messi was the best player in the return game and they won with a big score. Those are the games you play football for. Even though Messi is so great, you want to share a pitch and you want to have those moments, because it means you are challenging and you're doing something right. Of course it's difficult. The greatest achievements are.

We could beat Manchester City, draw with Barcelona, defeat PSG, win 3-0 against Monaco and still only finish third in the league. The comment from everyone, from journalists to supporters, was always the same – we can beat anyone, but we can't win the league. You have to agree because the facts are there, but it was crazy because I honestly looked around our dressing room every year and felt that on talent alone we had a team good enough to win the league. To win *something*.

But we didn't. I look at us as players for that but the supporters were unhappy with Bruno as manager. They felt he should have achieved more with the squad he had. Because of Bruno's inexperience, because he had been Fournier's assistant, the fans felt that the club needed someone with a track record of winning and a higher status.

I can remember the fans hoping that Arsène Wenger would come in. Meanwhile, Bruno left and went to work in China. What I can say is that he was a popular guy with the players. We always played for him, and for the club, and there is always the danger in football that you get another coach in and things go so badly that people start to appreciate the third-place finishes and the wins over teams such as PSG and Manchester City. Wenger is actually a great example because of what happened to Arsenal before and after he left.

That was the position we were in, during the summer of 2019. We were prepared for change – we just didn't know how much change would occur in the following season.

Fabio – Bluebirds and Canaries

I STILL had ambitions of playing in the Premier League, so that was why we negotiated a release clause into the contract I signed with Cardiff. I discussed with Ole the fact that my contract at United only had six months on it, so I would have been free to go anywhere; I would be lying if I didn't say Cardiff being bottom wasn't a little concerning, so we made sure there was a clause inserted so I could return to the Premier League if a club came in. I stayed at Cardiff in the first place because Ole did – but I have no regrets, because I really began to enjoy myself towards the end.

Towards the end of the summer transfer window in 2016, Middlesbrough made it clear that they wanted to sign me to be part of their effort to stay in the top division after just getting promoted. They talked to me and to Cardiff who, as you could appreciate, wanted the best deal for them. They asked for £5m. It was a strange thing – it was like nobody at the club knew about the clause in my contract, so when I was told what was happening I was confused but reminded everyone.

I talked to the owner and asked him directly – 'Why are you asking for £5m if I can go for £2m?' – and he looked at me with surprise. They knew they could not keep me, and although I'm not sure what the fee actually ended up being, I know it was resolved much more easily than it might have been.

I discussed it with Paul Trollope, too. I was in the last year of my contract. I was on a good salary, especially for a full-back in the Championship. I told him that I didn't expect to be offered a new contract with the same salary and he agreed that would probably be the case. He eventually said that I should do what I needed to do, but admitted that he still really wanted me to stay. I knew opportunities didn't come around every day – I had played for two years in the Championship, and this was my first offer to go back into the Premier League, so I had to take it.

I was leaving a guaranteed place in the team in a good formation for me to enjoy myself, and arriving at a club that made it clear I would be part of a squad and that I would be competing for a place in the team against an established player in George Friend, who had been the best left-back in the Championship in the previous season.

I was feeling really confident about my own form after the last season, and I felt wanted by Aitor Karanka, who was in charge at Middlesbrough. He was a very good coach, who had learned some of his management style from José Mourinho when he was his assistant at Real Madrid. Like most managers, Karanka had spent a lot of money in the summer to try and build a squad that would stay up. There was a big Spanish presence at the club, which he added to with the signings of Victor Valdés, Antonio Barragán – another full-back – and Álvaro Negredo. We also had Daniel Ayala in defence. These seemed like strong additions to a very good squad because you only have to look at the names and think of the quality – Ben Gibson in defence, Gastón Ramírez in midfield, Stewart Downing, too. Up front we had a couple of young stars who would go on to be really good Premier League players. Adama Traoré had so much pace, almost too much. Because he was so young sometimes his decision-making hadn't matured to catch up with how quick he was. There was Patrick Bamford, a striker who had come through the youth system at Chelsea. I could empathise with his journey.

If I'm being honest, the difference in standard of play and training between Cardiff and Middlesbrough was a big jump. There was a much greater intensity, there seemed to be much more quality. I was surprised by the pace. We had shorter sessions. It felt different and positive, and I was sure we'd have a good season.

The problem is, when you're a team who will be fighting for their place in the league, you need quality and you need everything and everyone to come together. It wasn't something that was apparent to me straight away, but after a little while I began to realise how strange it was that Middlesbrough were effectively a Spanish club, with a Spanish manager and Spanish coaches. There is nothing wrong with that – it can work if everyone is pulling in the right direction. When you're a new boy everything feels positive, you don't see people's reservations. Then you begin to see them and wonder why – and then, when things are going wrong, those reservations become big barriers in the dressing room. Spanish was the main language Aitor and the coaches used to communicate, and while that didn't really bother me as someone who didn't speak English as their first language, I can see how it contributed to the problems we had.

Our form seemed to follow the same pattern – we started pretty well, we managed to remain competitive going into the winter, and even though we were never really heavily beaten or embarrassed, all those fine margins you need at that level were not working for us.

I knew that competition for my place would be tough. I knew I would have to wait for my chance. I wasn't involved at all in the first few games, and my first chance came against Fulham in the League Cup. I had been training very well and felt positive, so I was keen for the chance. After eight minutes, I made an assist for David Nugent to put us in front.

Just before it, I had been involved in a challenge – it was an awkward collision with a Fulham player, and I could feel that it had hurt my knee badly. Imagine – six minutes into my first game for my new club.

'No no, I keep going,' I told the physio.

I get the assist, carrying my injury.

A couple of minutes after that I realised how severe the pain was. I couldn't keep going. I'd suffered ligament damage.

After the game, Aitor was very proud, and, even though we lost and I'd only played a short period of time, he made sure to praise me. 'How is Fabio?' he was asked. 'Fabio is better than everyone,' he said. It was nice to be complimented, but the injury meant I would miss almost three months of football.

But football is like this, and it was an injury to George Friend that gave me my chance to return to the team, against Chelsea in late November. We lost 1-0 but I played well. This was the story of the season, really – frustration for the team but some personal satisfaction in my own form. The next game was at Leicester, who, strangely enough, were reigning champions of the Premier League. We were 2-1 up in injury time but they got a penalty with one of the last kicks, and got a draw. I played very well again. I can remember the response around the club at the time – there seemed to be a lot of surprise about my performance.

With games as tight as this we had to make sure we were picking up wins against the lower teams in the division. We won 1-0 against Hull, when I was up against Robert Snodgrass, one of those players who was too good for the Championship, and a danger man for teams like Hull if they are to get shock results. After the game, Ben Gibson – one of Robert's good friends – told me he'd said I was the best defender he'd ever played against. I was feeling very good, confident and aggressive. George was back and ready to play – one of the captains at the club – and everyone was joking that he would find it difficult to get back into the team.

A 3-0 win against Swansea before Christmas put us in 14th, the sort of position that seemed to be a good reflection of how well we were competing. When we went to Old Trafford on the last day of the year I was, naturally, desperate to play. It was just my luck that Aitor chose that game to tell me he was going to give me a rest from the busy Christmas schedule. We had Leicester at home in 48 hours and he wanted to start me in that match, so I was going to be on the bench against my old team.

It was the first time I'd experienced a visit to this ground as an opponent and I can remember it vividly. When United are at their best, any team goes there looking for a draw as a good result. That would have been an amazing result for us, but, when I finally did get on the pitch in the last ten minutes, we were winning 1-0. It was a result that would have done so much for our momentum and confidence. United were throwing everything at the goal and they equalised in the 85th minute. In that moment I felt what I knew other teams must have felt when the United team I played in did the same. The stadium came alive with an energy. The noise of the support was crazy. You almost know, you can feel, that United are going to score another goal. They did.

It was my first time playing against them. 'So *that's* how you feel,' I thought.

There were 75,000 supporters bouncing. I'd felt it plenty when they were on my side. I don't want to say it's not about the players – of course it is, they have a job to do; they played well and won the game. But you're playing against something bigger. It's a sensation that comes from the stands, from the supporters.

It was so familiar, and yet things felt so strange. I remember Michael Carrick – in his last season as a player, and one of the few players left from when I was there – saying how much United needed that win. They were sixth and fighting for a top-four place.

The result was as damaging for our morale as it was uplifting for theirs. We struggled to score. Defensively we weren't bad – I think we kept a high number of clean sheets for a team who were fighting for their safety – but 1-0 defeats and 0-0 draws were really beginning to hurt our chances of survival. I felt sorry for Bamford and Traore because of the pressure on their shoulders. Adama clearly had lots of potential but when he signed for us he had only something like 38 games as a professional, so had the rawness you would expect from a player with that inexperience. Patrick, as I say, I could relate to – he had played for a big club so was carrying this expectation. I'd played for Brazil and in a Champions League final – people expected that level of performance every time you were on the pitch.

I was luckier than Patrick, in a way, because I'd had a couple of years getting used to the fact that not everything in football was designed with the same sort of facilities as Manchester United. I'd grown used to people expecting these things and I'd been able to deal with that pressure in order to be able to play and enjoy myself. You can see the difference in Patrick's confidence in more recent years. That is one of the big hurdles for footballers in our position. You hear the noise from everyone. But the biggest battle is with yourself. You have to overcome those self-confidence struggles and show to yourself, more than anyone, that you can do it. I could say that, despite Middlesbrough's struggle, I had proved to myself that I was good enough to play at this level, and to play well. I won two club player of the month awards that season. It was the most confident I'd felt in a long time.

By the time of the return game against United we'd slipped into the relegation zone, and Aitor Karanka lost his job in the week building up to their visit. If I'm honest, it felt inevitable. The cultural differences between the staff and the players had become a bigger problem as each week passed, and the momentum of the poor results became harder to shake off. When you're in a good position you can almost carry the negative things – it's like the elephant in the room, it seems to be working, so you don't let that side of it into the game. Maybe it's just that Middlesbrough – a club with a strong identity, which can be difficult for some to understand – just didn't suit such a strong Spanish influence. I know, as a Brazilian, that Boro had a rich history of players from Brazil, but it's one thing having a few players from the same country and another thing when the whole management structure is from a country that isn't the one the club is playing in. I liked Aitor, we had a strong relationship, but when he eventually left it seemed inevitable.

Steve Agnew was his replacement as caretaker. His first game in charge was against United. I was picked to start and came up against Antonio Valencia who was now the regular right-back. Antonio is so close to us that he feels like family. I felt the same from him in this game – everyone knows what a physical player he was, but it was almost as if he didn't want to tackle me! He scored, United won 3-1, and we were in further trouble, running out of matches to save ourselves. That proved to be the case when we were relegated a few weeks later.

Under José Mourinho United were struggling to make the top four. This was a time when it seemed as if they were concentrating on the Europa League. I could remember the criticism we received for failing to win the Premier League in 2010. I remembered the headlines when we didn't win the Champions League in 2011. I remembered the feeling, and, having experienced this and also relegations with different clubs, I can say that the level of criticism at United when you lose one game is so much more intense than you receive at another club even when you go down. I could only imagine what the lads were going through, the pressure they were under, fighting for the top four, trying to find this new identity while playing under different managers. Imagine the difference between swimming in a pool and swimming in a river, and then the difference between swimming in the river and swimming in the ocean. It takes courage to swim far in the river. It takes more than that to swim in the sea, knowing to a large extent that you are controlled by the elements. Being relegated is very bad. It's very difficult. But to be in a bad moment with Manchester United is even worse.

It was even harder for them when they were competing with Manchester City, who had all the money in the world and now had Pep Guardiola in charge. Guardiola's first year in Manchester wasn't great. I think that it was clear to see that, since he had been at Barcelona, many coaches around the world had planned how to play against him. They developed tactics to play against his teams. It's true what they say that money doesn't guarantee success but enough money surely does, as at City he was able to overcome those early failures by spending hundreds of millions of pounds on full-backs. Without that investment all over the pitch, I'm not convinced Guardiola's style of play would have ever suited English football, but he eventually bought so many top players that it did. It's just my observation, but you can still see the vulnerabilities of the style of play when it is up against a team that can play an effective counter-attack. The possession has to be faultless; it has to be perfect. Most of the time it is because the players are so much better.

We were beaten by City in the FA Cup but drew with them in the league. My opponents up the pitch in those games were Pablo Zabaleta and Jesús Navas at right-back. Bacary Sagna was on the bench. None of those were deemed good enough so Guardiola bought Kyle Walker. It's the sort of money that's enough to strengthen your team and weaken your rival. I'm reflecting on this in the late stages of the 2020/21 season, a year in which City have been their most solid defensively under Guardiola, and it is obvious that the money that has been spent is the big reason for that.

In the summer after we were relegated, Middlesbrough spent a lot of money, too, hoping to get promoted instantly. Garry Monk was hired as the new permanent manager. Having proved to myself that I could do well in the Premier League I didn't want to have another year in the Championship. On top of that, my family had not settled as well as we would have liked, so I informed Garry I would like a transfer. He said that that was okay, that he wasn't there to stand in my way.

It seemed as though he was preparing for me to leave, as he signed Cyrus Christie to play right-back and had George on the left. I received an offer from Sporting Lisbon, which seemed like a good move for everyone, but the season started without the transfer being completed. It was a difficult start and we lost two and won two of our first two matches, hardly what we wanted. We had a League Cup tie against Scunthorpe and Garry wanted to change the team around so told me I was going to play. Even though I wanted to go, and the plan seemed to be for that to happen, I am a professional and agreed to play.

I played very well. I scored, and had a good partnership with Adama on the wing – he had also told Garry he wanted to leave. In fact, he didn't even want to play. In the pre-match meal three hours before the game, out of nowhere Adama just said, 'No, no, I'm not playing, I'm going to go!' Garry said there was no way that could be the case, as he knew he was starting. Adama eventually backed down and, as I say, played really well.

The next day Garry called us both into his office. 'You're not going to leave,' he told us. You can imagine our responses.

I was arguing and I reminded him about the offer from Sporting. It's all there, ready to go. Adama didn't speak English as well as I did but he seemed even angrier than I was.

'No, no, we're going to offer you new contracts,' Garry said. He talked about how much he liked us as players, how important we would be to his style of play. I told him he couldn't be serious – I had the offer and had to go. I told him that my family wanted to leave. He told us to just wait for the contract offer to arrive.

So we waited and gave him a chance. I thought my wife was going to kill me! The transfer window closed. The new contracts never arrived.

Garry couldn't look me in the eye after that. I was professional, I still played and tried my best when selected. I will say that under his management, from a purely football perspective, I played well and enjoyed being on the pitch. But you can't behave like that and have the full respect of the dressing room. It was probably no surprise that we didn't get any strong consistency in the first months of the season. Win one, lose one. After the spending in the summer I am sure the club expected us to be in the top two but we were struggling to fight for a play-off spot. The owner made a decision that shocked many but clearly one they felt they had to take. Garry lost his job just before Christmas.

His replacement was Tony Pulis – almost the opposite in that he was a more honest and direct guy, but he did not exactly have a strong reputation for playing attractive and expansive football.

I was injured when he arrived – I spent a couple of months on the sidelines – but it was obvious I wasn't his type of player and even when I was fit, he didn't include me in a squad for about six weeks. But I was popular with the Boro fans so they started to make it clear they wanted me back into the team. They were chanting my name in the games, tweeting, phoning the radio, that sort of thing, so Tony was being forced to talk about it in his press conferences and eventually gave me a chance to get back into the squad. I was training really hard and I could tell he respected my professionalism, even though we both knew I wasn't the usual type of player that would be in one of his teams. He was honest and up front about that – but also honest about giving me the chance that I had earned.

We were going for the play-offs and having a bit of a wobble in terms of our form. We went to Sheffield United and were 2-0 down at half-time. Grant Leadbitter had been sent off and Tony realised he would have to do something different, so I came on at the break and played on the wing. We pulled it back to 2-1. I knew I'd played well; I was so keen to show what I could that so I think I went everywhere on the pitch that day looking for the ball. I was desperate to get us a good result. Unfortunately we lost 2-1 – this was a good Sheffield team – but I was kept in the squad for the next game against Bristol City.

Before the match Tony was showing the squad the videos of the previous game. He focused on praising the energy in my performance. 'That's what I want!' he said. The guys were laughing – the performance at Bramall Lane was probably a bit energetic even for me, and now that seemed to be what Tony wanted. But I didn't start that one – I only came on for the last couple of minutes. We'd reached a strange understanding. He would use me when he wanted to put something different into the team. I can jump, I can head the ball. But I'm a passer of the ball. I like to play the game. He wanted the ball up to the forwards so that they could fight for the second ball. He wanted the taller players for set pieces. Even with free kicks in our own half he'd be looking for that long ball to cause problems in the air. There's no problem with that. That was his style, it had been successful for him earlier in his career. He'd been criticised for it but he didn't care.

I was a substitute for three wins in a row, coming on in the last ten minutes to see out the victories that got us into the play-offs. Aston Villa were our opponents – they had a great squad and gave us a tough game. They scored early on and I came on with 25 minutes to go when Daniel Ayala was injured. We had a great end to the game and I remember setting up Adama a few times, but we just couldn't get the ball in the net. It was so frustrating.

So we lost 1-0. Because Ayala would miss the second leg, everyone expected that I would play, with Ryan Shotton moving from right-back to centre-back. Ryan's a great guy but at 6ft 3in he was a more obvious choice to play in the middle. Under Tony, he'd been at right-back.

The day before the game, Tony was handing the bibs out to the players who would be starting. There was one left and even I thought I'd been selected when he called my name. 'Son,' he said. 'You did fantastic in the last 30 minutes but I cannot play you in this game. You'll be on the bench and you'll come on.' Ryan kept his place at right-back and Dael Fry – 6ft 4in, but only 20 and with fewer than 30 professional games under his belt – was chosen to play in the middle. It was the biggest game of Tony's time at Middlesbrough and in the end when he was forced to make a choice between experience in the team and his way of doing things he went for the latter. The other lads couldn't believe it. I must admit it's nice when your team-mates want you to play and think you should be, and I seem to recall that the fans were a bit upset as well when the team was named.

We did well in the second leg and got to the last ten minutes 0-0. Just one goal would level us up on aggregate. Tony called me over and said I was going to come on for Ryan. It was too late to make a difference.

Faced with a full season in the Championship, Tony and I both knew there was little point in me remaining at the club. I'd made no secret of my desire to leave a year earlier and it was obvious I wasn't going to play much. The difficulty was that the club wanted me to stay. After the relegation, my wages had been reduced, and as far as the club were concerned it was a good wage to keep me on. I was frustrated and had some conversations with the club about the situation. As frustrated as I was, I'm not the type of guy who would ever stop training or send letters to the club or to FIFA as some players do. That's embarrassing behaviour. I'd signed the contract and respected the club's position.

You do feel some responsibility as a player when a team is relegated. I did think that I'd shown enough in my own contribution and form to prove I deserved to play in the top division. But I believe in loyalty and professionalism so I spent some years in the Championship trying to get Cardiff and then Middlesbrough back up. I tried my best. I'm not saying I'm above that – I knew what I was signing when I went to the clubs and I discovered how tough a league the Championship was, so my eyes were open about the reality when I went to the Riverside. But it was very frustrating when I wanted to move, and the manager clearly was happy for me to move on, yet the club seemed intent on keeping me. I wasn't going to fight – I respected that I was paid a good salary. I respected that football is a crazy profession for that.

I reported for pre-season. Tony didn't start me in any of the games. An offer came in from Nantes, but it was almost as if the club were pretending it wasn't happening. I spoke to Neil Bausor, the chief executive, who insisted that he wanted me to stay and that it would all be okay.

I ended up sitting in Tony's office, telling him what Neil had said. He actually went and called Neil into the office so all three of us were in there.

'What's happening with Fabio?' Tony asked. 'Why won't you let him go? The boy is doing everything that's asked of him, he's training and working hard every day, so please do what he wants.'

Tony explained that Nantes were offering a deal that made economical sense for all parties. He said how it was a personally important move for me to make to be closer to my brother. Neil couldn't answer. He didn't know what to say. Eventually he relented and said, 'If he wants to go, he can go.'

So things started to move along with the transfer, which was straightforward from that point. After the meeting, Tony came to me and said, 'Honestly, I'd really want you to stay here!' He was laughing when he said it – we both knew I was going to move, and we knew how funny it was that he was saying it. But he was being sincere. He said he wanted different options in the squad and he liked the way that I changed games from the bench. He did say that he was granting me the move because I deserved it.

When I arrived in France one of the first things I read was a newspaper column in which Tony spoke about me. I am quoting his words here – I don't feel comfortable repeating praise about myself, but these were his words after I left: 'Fabio is one of the best pros I've ever worked with. He's a fabulous lad, I enjoyed his company, he was bubbly and he always gave everything. I'm pleased he's got his move. He's only a couple of hours away from his brother now, which was very, very important for him so we are pleased. He goes with my best wishes and everyone at this football club's best wishes because he is a fantastic lad.'

In a strange way, I was as proud of that as anything from my career. To get through a period as difficult as that – well, if you are reading this, you're a football fan, so you know how rare it is in football for a player to endure a period like this and come out of it being praised by a manager.

I left Middlesbrough with a gift – a Tony Pulis pre-season! I'm told these are traditional pre-seasons of Tony's – trips to Austria that are like army boot camps. It's not human. You wake up at 5am, you go to the mountains. You cycle. Honestly, I'm surprised the things on those pre-seasons are expected of footballers. It was the training regime I'd expect from athletes preparing for a triathlon. Three times a day we would train until we were exhausted. I like to work hard – I like that feeling of collapsing on your bed and just wanting to sleep. I know I am blessed to be a footballer, I know that many people envy the money that footballers earn. Even within the football bubble, I know that you can't take for granted the ability to be able to do it, to be able to train rather than have to sit it out injured. So I love that feeling of pushing myself until I am exhausted, because those are the moments where I feel I have earned my wage for that day. I did everything that was expected of me on the pre-season – and, despite the way everything turned out, the pre-season is now a fond memory.

I was delighted to go to Nantes, *Les Canaris*, for many reasons. Of course, being close to my brother again was an obvious one. It was strange to go to a new country and for it to feel like a homecoming but it really did feel that way. All the press were speaking about it, and of course this was helped by how well Rafael had done at Lyon and how popular he had become there. It was a warm feeling.

Miguel Cardoso was the manager and it was the first time I had worked with a head coach who spoke Portuguese. He was very tactical – we spent hours on the training pitch concentrating on tactics. One thing that immediately struck me was how different that was to training in England. There was not the same intensity. It took time to get used to.

Miguel really wanted me. I'd like to say it was because of my quality, but he was really desperate for a right-back, and full-backs were such an integral part of the way he wanted to play. They played like wingers. People talk about Guardiola and the way he wants full-backs to play but it's a lot easier to do that in his position. It's not so easy when you have the resources Nantes has in relation to their rivals (and, by the way, I realise that I have mentioned Guardiola a few times – I have nothing but respect for his incredible ability as a coach). You could call Miguel crazy, when you looked at the way he saw the game, because it was so different – to him, he won the game if you had 70 per cent of possession or higher, especially against the bigger teams. If you could dominate the play against a team like PSG he would see that as a win, regardless of what the score was.

I arrived at the Nantes pre-season camp on Tuesday after signing on Monday. My first day of training was Wednesday – Miguel wanted me to play in a friendly on Friday. So, after that intense time in Austria, I'd had a few days with less intense training, and in the first half of the friendly game I pulled my hamstring – following the tradition I was building of getting injured soon after arriving at a new club. It was a grade three tear and I was out for a couple of months. I used to think that I struggled when speaking English but I used English to communicate with the physios and compared to them my English was fantastic!

I was in the stands for our first game against Monaco. The crowd were great – very loud, lots of noise and lots of support. Monaco at that time had some great players. Cardoso played the same way, high up the pitch. We played well, but it was terrifying to watch. So many times our approach would leave us exposed with three against five at the back. It was like we were losing 1-0 in the last five minutes of a cup final, but it was the first few minutes of a long league season. On every single one of our attacks we seemed to be left wide open.

It is the kind of tactic that needs luck and more often than not needs you to score the first goal to control the pace of the game. We thought we had – but it was disallowed. Then they scored, and were chasing. They scored again. We chased again. They scored again.

The season didn't start well. We lost three and drew two of the first six games. I was finally fit to get on the bench against Nice on 25 September. Cardoso was so keen to get me back in the team that he was arguing with the medical staff. They were cautious and thinking long-term. Cardoso had told me before the game with Nice that I wasn't going to start, but I would definitely start against Lyon four days later because of my brother playing for them.

We lost against Nice. Everyone expected Miguel would be sacked after the Lyon game because the expectation was that we would be defeated heavily – but we played very well. I set up our equaliser to earn us a 1-1 draw. As he's already said, my brother came on with a few minutes to go and it was great to share the pitch with him again. However, I was happy that I was able to get through most of the first game concentrating on my own game and own performance for Nantes without it being about me against him.

We were happy with the result and performance. Miguel was the man who brought me to the club; I'd been through these changes before, so I knew what could happen. I didn't want him to lose his job, but he did in the days after that match and was replaced by Vahid Halilhodžić.

Vahid, well, what to say about this guy? He was a former Nantes player. He had coached at Lille and PSG to name just a couple of clubs, but when he replaced Miguel his reputation was mainly earned as an international coach. He had taken Algeria to their best-ever World Cup performance in 2014 and after that spent a few years with the Japan national team.

He and I didn't have a good relationship but I'm not sure he got on well with many at the club. It was a hostile time. There were a lot of arguments with staff and players and those arguments would usually be centred around Vahid trying to establish authority and reminding everyone that he was the boss. That can work – for a while – if you're just like that with the players. But he was that way with everyone and it can be counter-productive to be that way in a period of time when you're trying to command respect from everyone. I would say that he talked to people as if they were children but if I'm being completely honest I don't think I would ever speak to children in that manner.

That sort of management is perhaps best suited to short periods – such as international level – and, at club level, you can often see that it results in short bursts of form. We had a good start under him but had a really poor run over the winter, before a strong end to the season when we defeated Lyon, PSG and Marseille in a three-week spell.

We finished 12th, but we should have finished higher. Vahid stayed at the club. It seemed as if he was always in conflict with someone – the president, a director. We signed

Marcus Coco and Vahid made it clear publicly that he didn't want to sign him – after he was already training with us! It was no surprise that he left a few days before the start of the following season.

But the biggest story of my first few months in France was nothing to do with what happened on the pitch. Aside from what was happening with the managers, I could not have been happier to arrive in the dressing room. There were many Brazilian players. There was Diego Carlos, a fantastic defender who went on to be brilliant for Sevilla. I knew Lucas Lima because he played for my team, Botafogo, when he was younger. Andrei Girotto became my best friend very quickly. Gabriel Boschilia and Lucas Evangelista came to the club around the same time as me.

After a decade without many Brazilians around me, to have such a large number there incredible. It must be the same for any nationality but Brazilians know each other. We know our lifestyle, our food preferences. Within the first week we were having large barbecues with all of our families present. My house in France was filled with 15 to 20 Brazilians and as much as I loved my time in England that wasn't the case after we left Manchester. To be able to express yourself in your own language with people of your own nationality – normally, when I am injured for long periods, I have a tendency to get sad and even depressed. But because all of this was so new, I was still settling into my new life, I was enjoying going into the club even just to receive treatment. It was fantastic for my family and that made me even happier.

That good mood extended beyond the Brazilian camp. We were all very close to Emiliano Sala. Even though the number of my compatriots made it much easier for me to settle than would usually be the case for a player arriving in a new country, Emiliano still did whatever he could to help me settle in.

What you can find with Brazilians is that we become *too* close. We rely on each other too much and that can lead to potential difficulties in the dressing room. But I think we, as a group, understood that because of where we had all been previously, and whenever it felt like we were getting close to the point of excluding others we made the effort to connect with our other squad members.

I'm writing this and finding it hard to return to the subject of Emiliano. It's been a couple of years now and it's still raw. If I could avoid it, I would, but I'm trying to get everything down on paper to express how I felt at these different times in my career.

Emiliano was a great guy. He was also at the highest point in his career. He had enjoyed a good journey so far. It had led him to Nantes, where he had really found a home. He scored a lot of goals but all of a sudden he seemed to go to another level. His form was incredible. He was one of the best goalscorers in Europe.

When January 2019 came around he became one of those players that European clubs would look at when they are in need of some strike power to elevate their chances of winning the title, qualifying for Europe or, in the case of my old club Cardiff City, staying in the Premier League after being promoted again. He was 27. This was his time, his chance for the big money that is on the table when you go to England.

He wanted to stay at Nantes. It was a reluctant decision to go. Emiliano had a strong connection with the club and the supporters. He hoped that Cardiff's offer would make the owners of the club offer him a new deal to stay. However it was big money on offer for Nantes as well as Emiliano and they had to accept, even though Vahid didn't want to let him go.

I hoped for the best for him. This was the best move of his life and in Argentina they were talking about calling him up to the national team. You had to believe that the exposure of playing in the Premier League would help him achieve that if his form continued. It seemed like every time we played he scored.

Normally when players sign for a new club you say the usual things. Goodbye, we'll stay in touch. But you go, sign the contract, have the medical and things are just moving so fast that you just move on. I can't remember many cases of players signing for a new club and then coming back. I never did it and I remained close with many of my former team-mates. Emiliano had no wife, no girlfriend. He lived by himself. He had no reason to come back. So it says how much he loved being at the club that he returned to say farewell. His best friend at the club was Nicolas Pallois, who had been with him at Bordeaux before they both come to Nantes. But it wasn't just Nicolas – he wanted to say goodbye to all of us. And when I say all of us, I mean everyone at the club. The physios and the coaches, too. It seemed as though he wanted to express his gratitude to the club for giving him this chance, this home. He had nothing at all to do at the club but just came in to have lunch with us. I told him that if he needed anything at all he just had to ask. Just call. Just message. I'd already talked to the boys I knew at Cardiff and told them about what a great guy Emiliano was, and that they had to look after him. I told them that they could expect someone who had the same professional sensibilities as me and my brother. He worked very hard. I spoke with him about my favourite restaurants. I knew he liked Brazilian barbecue so I gave him my recommendations.

He left for Cardiff via private jet. It's not a long flight. One hour or so, maybe less. He said he'd message me when he was settled.

The next morning I arrived for training. The staff were waiting for the players.

'The flight of Sala never arrived.'

'What are you talking about?'

Their look was solemn. I'll never forget it.

Fuck.

They explained how the flight had been lost from the radar. I can't explain the feeling of that morning. Many of us were crying. Vahid was devastated. We tried to eat. We couldn't. Some people tried to raise hope. 'Wait,' they said. 'Maybe there's some way.'

We went to the gym and wanted to stay together as a group. There were about 25 of us sitting in silence. Time passed. No news.

We left to go back to our families. I told my wife. 'This cannot be true,' she said. I was on my phone all day. Still no news. It was very difficult to come to terms with. I'd made, effectively, the same journey in return when I'd signed for the club a few months earlier. That's life as a footballer. Most of the guys in the dressing room had made similar journeys. This type of quick move – a plane to sign somewhere; we all did it at least once. It could have been any of us. My wife and I spoke about this and realised how fragile life is, and how much it should be valued. It was a very difficult moment.

The next few days were a blur. We had a game but that was cancelled. I'm a hopeful guy. I have always tried to be positive, but the reality was more than devastating. You know what it means when a plane disappears. You are bracing yourself for the worst possible news because you know it is coming.

We played against Saint-Étienne on 30 January. In the morning there was news that some wreckage from the plane had been found. The fans were behind this incredibly emotional campaign of 'Pray for Sala'. It felt like they chanted his name for all of the 90 minutes. I don't know how we all got through it and I mean the club collectively.

On 7 February Emiliano's body was found. Our next game was against Nîmes three days later. We wore all black. It was the most emotional game of football I've ever played in my life.

Emiliano was gone. But he will never be forgotten.

Fabio – Fight

I'VE BEEN in football long enough to understand and appreciate the way people look at things. I know what people will say about me, what they do say: that my career started brightly and I dropped a level. They'll talk about my injuries. They'll talk about my potential. Football careers are funny. Maybe it goes for all sports. People look at how you start and how you finish – and most of the time how you finish defines a footballer in the perception of most observers.

Robin van Persie, for example. Before he joined Manchester United there was always talk about injuries and underachievement. And then he moved to Old Trafford and had this great contribution to the title we won in 2013 when I was on loan. He suffered from some injuries again after that and moved to Fenerbahçe and then to his boyhood club Feyenoord. Everyone talks about what he did in 2013, and rightly so. His career is almost defined by that. I suppose if you turned my career around – if I'd started in Nantes and ended up at United, playing a part in one of the most successful periods in the club's history, maybe people would look at my career differently. I'm not particularly bothered by that – but it is an interesting observation, something I have thought about.

I have learned to be strong enough to live with the highs and the lows. When I have had the highs I have had my family around to enjoy them with me. When I have had lows, they have been there to support me. It always comes back to them. So whenever there is any conversation about what I might or might not have achieved, I remember the goal my brother and I had at the start of our careers. How we achieved it almost straight away and then everything else has been a dream, a bonus. And, in a sense, I count my time in Nantes just as valuable as my time in Manchester.

Here's why.

Vahid Halilhodžić left the club on the eve of the 2019/20 season and was replaced by Christian Gourcuff. Whatever went wrong, Vahid left behind a squad that had a special unity because of what had happened in the previous months. We lost our first league game at Lille – a good Lille side – but Christian had barely had a chance to work with us and even so, I felt our performance in defeat was strong and encouraging. There was a togetherness.

In our second game we drew 0-0 against Marseille at home. We would have preferred to win but there was a platform, in the clean sheet, to build upon. Then we got a late winner at Amiens and we could feel confidence and momentum building. Christian was working with us closely, everything felt positive. We went on to win three of our next four – all at home by a scoreline of 1-0.

We won by the same score at Lyon and then at home to Nice. There was a moment before PSG played when we were top of the league. We were flying. There was a brotherhood in our defence. Nicolas Pallois, Dennis Appiah, Andrei Girotto and Charles Traoré – there was this bond between us where it felt like we would die for each other. We were so proud of the record of five consecutive clean sheets at home and how crucial that had been to how well we were doing. I have never played in a defence like that – okay, maybe we weren't perfect, but we always had each other's backs. If one player made a mistake there would be another desperate to cover just as if it was his own error.

It seemed as if everybody wanted us to do well because of what had happened to Emiliano. We could feel that from the outside and I think that helped us. I believe strongly in energy like this. We had the goodwill of the world, neutrals in France and even overseas, and you can feel it. When you have this feeling it can push you further than you felt was even possible. Against Nice we scored our winner in the 86th minute.

I had some good moments with Cardiff and Middlesbrough but I have to admit that in September 2019 I had this awakened feeling. Something was stirring. I hadn't competed for a title since I was at Manchester United. I liked it. I loved it. And because of what we had been through, and how close we were, I have to be honest and say I was probably at my most content since leaving Manchester, when it comes to my professional happiness. It wasn't the same as being at United, but then again, Nantes are not United. There was not the same level of expectation. So to be pushing like we were made it very special. I agree with my brother that sometimes it seemed pointless when PSG were hitting their big scores but there is just something about the unpredictability about football, and playing the game. You can take PSG out of it and the French league is competitive with teams close to each other. We felt as though we were a match for anyone on our day and that confidence was, as I say, growing all the time.

We played Monaco in late October. We were controlling the game high up the pitch. Nico pushed high and they played a ball behind him for Ben Yedder to chase. I ran like a crazy guy to catch him. I had to do that to close him down. I also knew his style – he's a player who likes to cut back to get his shot away. So I stopped in what I thought was good time to get my position right. Right as I did, my tendon snapped.

I collapsed on the floor with my back to the goal. I knew instantly I had done my knee. Andrei and Nico came to me and asked me what had happened. 'It's my knee, my knee,' I said. They could see my patella had popped out of position. They knew how serious it was. I was in that strange moment where the pain hadn't yet set in but I knew it was bad. 'Did they score?' I asked. 'No, no,' Nico said. 'They didn't.' There was a strange silence in the stadium so I didn't know what to think.

While the club doctor was coming on to the pitch I looked up to the scoreboard. It said 0-1. 'Sorry boys,' I said to them. I could see they were upset, but for me more than the score.

The doctor moved my patella back into position – okay, now I feel it.

I was more devastated about the result and the loss of our proud record. Momentum is one of the hardest things to build in football. We had such a strong moment. In his post-match interview Christian said that losing the match wasn't the problem – losing me for the season was.

Shortly afterwards, Nico picked up an injury – it really upset our pattern in defence and all the positive steps we had taken were derailed. This is football, it happens, but it was very hard to take.

I'd been injured before. Some bad ones, some bad luck. I knew this was different. In the days after I was very pessimistic and I was trying to pass that off as being realistic. I couldn't find out much about the injury and what I did learn was not good. Ronaldo – Il Fenomeno – had suffered it and his doctor had said it was the worst injury he'd ever seen. It was unusual to break the tendon in the way I had.

I remembered what had happened to Ronaldo. He'd been 23 with his career in front of him, and even though he returned and even won the Ballon d'Or and World Cup in 2002, people said he was never the same as he was before the injury. I was nearly 30. There were moments I allowed myself to believe my career was over. I read about what to expect once I'd recovered. I would lose my speed. I would lose my ability to jump. These were two of what I believed were my best qualities.

I had the operation and spent six weeks with my leg in a protective cast and cases. My wife did everything – everything. I thank her so much for that. I was having medication because the pain was so bad, and even when it was time to start my rehabilitation, the pain was still there. I talked to the doctors about it. After three or four months I could still feel the pain and I was convinced I couldn't play football again.

I couldn't bend my knee without the pain being severe. The doctors were reassuring me that it was part of the normal process for this type of injury. 'Are you sure?' I would ask them. It didn't feel normal. It couldn't be. They asked for trust. I kept working. I did trust them. I allowed myself to see the light.

Then in February, the coronavirus pandemic hit the world. In March the French president enforced a lockdown and all football was cancelled. It was terrible news at the worst possible time for my recovery. The physiotherapists and doctors sent me a schedule of training and exercises. I got all the equipment I needed to have at home. The club sent some. We talked at length – I needed this. I had only just allowed myself to feel positive. I could not stop.

The routine helped me incredibly. I started to jog. I started to run. In football you are used to this as part of your recovery. But you usually have other team-mates with you. Here I was going to be alone – until my wife said she would support me by running with me. She'd never done anything like that before but now she was going to be my team. I went out every day. Then I went out twice a day – once with my wife and once without. She pushed me. And I did not want to stop. When I wasn't running I was working on my upper body strength. I don't even think a Tony Pulis pre-season could have been more demanding of me than I was of myself. I know that there was a moment in the summer of 2020 when I felt more physically fit than at any point in my life. But that wasn't enough. I wanted to keep working.

The pandemic meant lockdowns and lockdowns meant responsibility. We couldn't travel. It was a very tough decision. Things were changing all the time. Where could you go – how could you get there? Isolating if you went anywhere. Then there was the responsibility of perhaps catching the virus and not being aware but going somewhere and passing it to a vulnerable relative. I couldn't do that. When it was permitted, my brother and his family came to stay with us.

I told him that I was in the middle of my recovery schedule. He insisted he was working hard too. I said he could come with me if he was sure. First day, we went out running on the road.

My pace was good. 'Nenê,' he says. 'You're going to have to slow down. You cannot keep at this pace.' I think he was trying to look out for me. I told him this is what I did every day. He told me to continue – I ran so much faster that when I looked back I couldn't see him. I had to run back to him. 'Nenê, you're crazy,' he says.

We've always called each other Nenê. It's our nickname for each other. Mum and Dad say it goes right back to when we were very young. Whenever people would see us they would say what nice babies we were – that's what it means in Portuguese – and we thought that's what our names were. It might have been confusing for you to read, though, if we referred to each other that way for the full book!

We were running to Andrei Girotto's house. It was around seven kilometres from my house, up and down hills. When we finally got there I said hello to Andrei and then goodbye after a minute – I intended to run straight back home, like I did every day. 'You're kidding,' Rafael laughed. 'Not a chance!'

I will be fair to him. From that day on for five weeks he joined me. All the time. He, too, ended up in the best shape of his life. Every day, without fail.

I can't say that my injury was a good thing but it did help me. Something good from something bad – my diet, my routine. I convinced myself that I could not let the injury beat me. I needed to come back for myself and for my family. I could not let that moment be the moment that finished my career; the moment I went out on. I wanted to prove to those who loved me that I could come back.

When I arrived back for pre-season everyone was surprised – the doctors, my team-mates. The truth was that I could still feel the pain. I was told that was natural. But my development and recovery meant that physically, overall, I felt better than I had before the injuries. My muscles were strong. I could run.

When I was finally back on the pitch for the first game of the following season at Bordeaux, I don't think I've ever been as proud. It was a better feeling than the first game of my career. I was born again. There was a time when I was my own biggest doubter. I needed to prove to myself that I could do it and play football again.

Of course it was more than that. I know people would have looked from the side. They would have said 'poor Fabio'. Another injury, a really bad injury. They would have understood. They would have been sympathetic. But I didn't want sympathy. I wanted to prove that I was good enough to still be there. It was important to me that I could play for Nantes and play well; to be worthy of my place and contribute to the team.

I did not want the injury to define me. I didn't want it to be the final thing. I didn't want people to talk about what could have been if not for injuries. To be completely honest, yes, maybe I could have had a better career. But I look at the injuries and say they didn't change anything. I'll never complain about them because in some moments they helped me develop physically and mentally. They were challenges I was able to overcome.

I can't change how people think or how perception usually works in football. I know people won't necessarily look at my career as a whole from start to end, just like they do with everyone. I know they'll probably compare it to my brother's career and say something. But I cannot control that and I'm at peace with that. I know that I started at the biggest club and I moved eventually to Nantes. I know people won't say everywhere is smaller than Manchester United – they'll look at Nantes and be critical. Maybe they'll use the word failure. Like I say, that's for other people. Maybe if I played ten years in Nantes and the last one at Manchester United people might say it was a great career.

If you cannot play for Manchester United then you can hope for one of two things – to compete to win trophies or to find a place where you enjoy your life and have a strong connection to the club. Nantes is a historic club in France with one of the greatest supports. It has been a while since they have won something and we would love to change that. What we have been through as a club brought us together and it really strengthened the bond between us as players and the supporters.

I was grateful that I had the opportunity to play my first home game back in front of a few thousand, before fans were not allowed to attend again due to renewed concerns about the pandemic. I was so excited. I played well against Nîmes – I got a yellow card early on and after around 30 minutes I was fouled for a penalty. It turned out to be the winning goal – Imran Louza scored the kick, and then was sent off just after half-time. It meant we all had to work that bit harder in the second half. I was never less than 100 per cent committed. With a couple of minutes to go I went in for another tackle – this time the referee thought it was worth another yellow card. Sent off!

After the game the press were asking Christian why he kept me on when I was already on a yellow card and playing with such enthusiasm that I was not going to back away from any challenge. 'I couldn't take my best player out of the game,' he said. I was upset because of the red card but those comments made me very happy.

It was vindication for myself. It was everything I worked for, everything I had hoped for. Every step of that journey of the last year. I could play again. I could belong in this company. I could thrive.

French football had been cancelled so we had escaped, mostly, having to play in empty stadiums. I was hoping I would not have to do it but unfortunately the restrictions were imposed again and most of the season was played without spectators. I don't think I can be any clearer than this – football, without fans, is nothing. Nothing. It is not the same. For me it's like playing with your friends. No atmosphere means the energy is completely different. You cannot enjoy it the same way.

For a team like Nantes who have a bond with the support I can say with some certainty that it had a huge impact on our season. More than half of our league games were either drawn, or lost by a single goal. Our team was much better than the 2020/21 season suggested. We did not have luck on our side. Just as we had benefitted from this surge of positive energy before my injury, we seemed to be suffering from the opposite, and we just couldn't turn things around. When things aren't going your way you look to the manager for guidance and as much as I love Christian, I could understand that there were a few players who were concerned that he didn't have the answers to turn it around. He couldn't find the click.

Raymond Domenech was brought in to replace Christian on a permanent basis. Or, so we thought. Raymond had been manager of France for six years but hadn't managed at club level in the 21st century. So much had changed in the game since then. We spent a lot of time watching videos when Raymond was there – in the moment, we needed something to try and turn the small margins in our favour. Raymond was not a poor coach but I think our squad needed someone with lots of aggressive encouragement. Our confidence was low and getting lower by the week because results were not turning around. The directors made a quick decision – Antoine Kombouaré was hired as Raymond's replacement. Antoine had plenty of recent managerial experience and had spent seven years at the start of his playing career at Nantes.

His first day was an experience. He made no excuses about the squad to the press or to us. He told us how bad it was; no dressing it up. We needed discipline. He provided it. Players were coming in late for training. It was all too casual.

Breakfast was 9am and people were arriving at 9.40am. He put big fines in place. No more late breakfasts.

It sounds simple but sometimes you need to go back to basics. Get the squad together and you'll eventually build togetherness. Emphasise the need to work hard for yourself and for your colleague and you will eventually see the results on the pitch. Sometimes it is eventual but the best things in football rarely happen with the flick of a switch. You need time for things to grow naturally and that's when the best results come. It didn't happen for Antoine straight away but then it did. Sometimes, when you're putting that work in, you need a moment to elevate you to the next level.

I have a fantastic relationship with Antoine. I had a minor injury when he arrived and had missed a few weeks but was so keen to play that I tweaked a muscle when I was back against Lyon. We lost that game. I said it was no problem – I was just so desperate to play to help the team.

We were at Strasbourg. They scored just before half-time. I was on the bench – Antoine agreed to take me to the game but said I wasn't going to play because of the advice of the doctors. He didn't want me to risk rupturing my hamstring but appreciated my commitment to being around the team. At half-time in this match I was devastated. I couldn't play, we were losing – I felt for sure we were doomed to relegation. Nothing was going right.

And then it did.

In the second half we showed courage to turn the game around. We won late on. There was a weight lifted from the shoulders of the players, who started to believe they were much better than their position in the table. We were four goals up at Brest and won 4-1. We scored three against Bordeaux and four against Dijon. I had recovered but Antoine didn't want to change a winning team – I understood.

From being almost certain of relegation, we managed to fight to get to the relegation play-offs. We were relieved to come through that on away goals.

As we prepared to say goodbye to a very difficult season, I asked Antoine what he had planned for the future. I must admit that sometimes the romantic thought of teaming up with my brother again appeals, but at the same time, I have a connection to Nantes that I do not take for granted because I know just how difficult it is to find in football.

'Forget this season,' Antione said. 'I want you here 100 per cent.'

It was what I wanted to hear. I'd played over 20 games. Every game was a special reward. Just to be there.

It was a tough year. I always felt we were too good and too together to be relegated. At QPR we had players but no unity. At Cardiff and Middlesbrough, even though hopes were high, expectations were always more realistic – those two clubs were always favourites to go down. With Nantes, we knew we were much better than what we went through. We look at a club like Lille who went from fighting relegation to winning the title and we can use them as inspiration. I don't say that we expect to win the league, but, anything is possible. I hope that when we have our supporters back we can give them a successful and special reward. Anything seemed possible in October 2019 and I hope we can return to a similar moment. Within the squad we spoke about the strength that would come as a consequence of winning the fight we had at the end of the season. We have the capacity to do something great.

I don't know what the future holds. As my brother and I have both said in this book, we had this objective to help our family. So the bond I have with Manchester United will always be extra special, in ways that go beyond what we achieved on the pitch. The club changed our life. No title we ever won could compare with what we were able to give our parents. But I know that establishing a connection with a club is a rare thing. Not every player is fortunate to have that. I know that my brother and I have been popular players with the clubs we have played for and, trust me, I appreciate that deeply. It is a privilege. At the moment I am here in Nantes, my family love the life here, and although I hope that this doesn't happen for a while yet, I feel that my connection to this club will continue in some capacity after I hang up my boots – although I don't think I want to be a manager!

No, I don't know what the future holds for me. But I do know I will be able to play football – and that for me is a blessing. I want to enjoy every minute.

Rafa – Turkish Delight

OUR NEW manager at Lyon in 2019 was Sylvinho, the former Barcelona, Arsenal and Brazil left-back. Just like Bruno before him, he had no managerial experience before taking the job – though to be fair, again, I wouldn't have held this against him. And, although I only got to play one game under him because of some injury issues I was suffering, I felt he was a good coach from my limited experience of working with him. I liked the way he went about his business.

Apparently, not everyone at the club agreed, and two months into the new season he was sacked. We won just one of our first nine league matches. We had established ourselves as a team competing for those Champions League places and the league was a little more competitive now – the directors felt a change was needed immediately to turn it around.

So what went so wrong that we had to change our coach so quickly? I think it was a case of something which would be considered a positive in another scenario being considered a negative in this one. As a consequence of his journeyed career, Sylvinho spoke many different languages: English, Spanish and Italian as well as his native Portuguese. The main language he didn't speak happened to be the language of the country he was coaching in for the very first time. He didn't bring many people with him – just one guy to assist him. So he found it difficult to articulate and explain his ideas very well to the people who mattered. My brother spoke about the balance at Middlesbrough being so far the other way – this is one of the difficult issues facing modern managers, with the capability to go to any country. I could not say he was an unpopular manager. But in the time he had, the most important matter was not even tactics – it was that he didn't get enough time to properly express his vision. As a squad we didn't get enough time to work with him to fully understand. You can't criticise the tactics because he had only a couple of months to work. Perhaps it was harder for the domestic players to be motivated in the same way the multi-lingual players in the squad seemed to be.

I do not say this is a criticism – I'm not saying any of the French players objected to him. It's a natural consequence of time, or in this case, not having enough time. Results help – or don't. You could say that the directors should have known about the issues before they hired the coach, and that would be fair. I think Juninho had a strong influence in his compatriot getting the job. Maybe he felt a sense of responsibility – and the poor results, in fairness, suggested something big needed to happen.

It was clear that Champions League qualification was imperative so Sylvinho lost his job and was replaced by Rudi Garcia, who had experience of managing in Italy as well as in France with Lille and Marseille.

I can't write here that my relationship with Garcia was the greatest. But I won't describe it as being difficult in the same way as with Louis van Gaal. I think there were a lot of factors – he was new in his job and needed to get to know the players. We had some right-backs at the club and they got chances. I got a chance but maybe I wasn't in my best form. I can accept that there was probably a moment in which I wasn't very happy about the situation.

Neither of us had much of a real chance to impress anything upon the other before the coronavirus pandemic changed the world; one of those changes was the suspension of competitive sports across the globe. Another was the prohibition of travel. For many people the consequences were much more severe. So many loved ones were lost. So much loss without the opportunity to say goodbye.

I was approaching my 30th birthday. It is a time when you reflect upon things, particularly as a footballer, because you are so much closer to the end of your playing career than the start of it. When we were not allowed to play or train, I realised just how much I loved football. I looked at myself harshly in this period. If I had trouble at Lyon, it was normal for a footballer – a new manager comes in and perhaps doesn't see you as part of his plans. All this time by myself gave me the opportunity to be introspective and take responsibility. Maybe I'd put on a few extra kilograms. Maybe I'd become comfortable. But life was proving to be unpredictable – and being without football made me appreciate that once you retire, it's gone forever. I looked at what I could do and what I wanted to do – I felt that I should aim for at least four or five years playing top-level football. I wanted to enjoy it. I wanted to be at my best. I was having some niggling issues with my knee and I knew that losing weight would help with that.

It is without question that I drew inspiration from what my brother was going through, and I would be lying if I said that that hadn't influenced my own way of thinking, even in the months before the pandemic. The medical staff were hard with him at first. They admitted they didn't know if he could play again. So you think about two things – the severity of the injury, and the stage in your career at which it occurs.

France was one of the countries that seemed to be hit harder than most by the pandemic. I thank God that my brother was in the country at this time, even though he was experiencing such a difficult moment. I was able to visit him and spend time with him, so even though we knew we would not be able to go home and see our parents, we would have each other. We spoke all the time but I wondered what being around him would be like.

He was training like a mad person. We went for a run. He was jogging without getting tired – I was panting like a dog! I told him, 'Fucking hell, Nenê, you need to slow down.' He says, 'No, this is what I need to do to get back.'

I stayed with him for 35 days. Every single day we were running. Running, gym, running, gym. How could he be like this after what they said to him? I love my brother of course. But I was so inspired by him in this time. And the simple truth is he that was the one who made me better. He made me achieve my own goal. More than that, he made me realise a new thing. Because we were a bit older we needed to work harder. We had always worked hard, but age meant needing to work harder to keep up. It was a valuable lesson and I thank him for that.

I write this in the early summer of 2021 a year later, on the better side of the pandemic. There were options with travel windows to go to Brazil but we made the decision not to – and of course it was not just my family, but my wife's family, and my brother's wife's family. It was hard on all of us but I think it was the responsible decision. Now I am in

Brazil with my parents who are vaccinated and it has been an emotional reunion. We had never missed a summer coming home before 2020. But we'll treasure them more for the one we did miss.

The months in which football was cancelled – well, as you know, it was not the first time that we had been excluded from playing for a long period of time. Older, and with a greater appreciation of time and opportunity, I know I would have gone crazy without kicking a ball. My brother and I played footvolley, which is a combination of beach volleyball and football. He had a net at his house and we were at least able to play that together – so many people around the world at this time were not able to engage in this sort of recreation. I came from a background in which playing with a ball on the street was a privilege so I understand and appreciate the fortune I had. Without my brother, both as a competitor to help inspire me and as someone who had a place where we could play some footvolley, I don't know how well I would have been able to handle the pandemic.

The French league was postponed indefinitely on 13 March, and on 28 April it was announced that the matches would not resume and current positions would be final. It was hard on Lyon: we had improved from that tough start and were on the edge of the European places. Nobody would have caught Paris realistically, but with a good run we might have challenged for the Champions League spots. Every player on every team would say the same, and would feel hopeful of their chances.

At the time I felt it was the right decision to cancel the league. There were bigger things to worry about. But then I saw how other leagues made arrangements to resume their competitions so they could complete their seasons and France remained the biggest major league to keep its cancellation in place. Of course, this is with hindsight, but I felt we could have continued. You can change your mind and I did – and at the same moment I can appreciate and understand what a difficult decision it was to make. Many people had different opinions. At the time, when it mattered, the people in charge made a responsible and cautious decision, and you cannot complain about that.

Some competitions did resume and Lyon were still involved in those. We had qualified for the Coupe de la Ligue Final to play against PSG, and we had also got a good result in the first leg of our Champions League round-of-16 game with Juventus. I was thankful that we had the chance to see these competitions through to the end, although by the time we were back on the pitch it had become clear to me that my future would be somewhere other than Lyon. I was feeling as fit as ever and was still only a substitute for the cup final – Rudi brought me on with four minutes to play, and to be honest, in normal times, he wouldn't have brought me on at all. Because games were played in a more condensed period to complete the season quickly and not disrupt too much of the following season, rules had been relaxed to allow more substitutes, so more players could rest. I was the fifth of five permitted subs.

The game ended 0-0 in regular time and in the last seconds of extra time, Ángel Di María went through on goal with the game and trophy in his grasp. I chased him. I didn't think I could get the ball. In the moment, you have to calculate everything. How long is left? This is probably their last attack. Can I get to him to foul him before he gets into the box? Will I get sent off if I do? How likely am I to take a penalty in the shoot-out? With all of this considered, what is my most valuable contribution?

I have no regrets about fouling Ángel. The ball was too far but I got to him just before he got into the box. I was sent off. Looking back I'm not sure it was bad enough to deserve a red card because I wasn't the last man but I knew the risk I was taking.

Perhaps this was one final moment of French football and my tackling not really having the best relationship. I remember, after being sent off in a derby game a couple of years earlier, speaking about it after the match. It's easier to speak when you win, as we did on that occasion. I said football is a contact sport and if you don't want contact you need to play another sport like tennis. They laughed. I guess they thought I was joking. But I was serious. If you want to make a tackle most of the time you are going to have to make contact with an opponent. It's normal. But we are entering a period – and it's not just French football – where it seems you are only allowed to touch the ball. Some people want football to be like that.

Unfortunately, even though my risk on the night was calculated – and a decision I would take again ten times out of ten in those same circumstances – we were not lucky in the penalty shoot-out. All ten of the regular kicks were scored. Bertrand Traoré was the unlucky one in sudden death and Paris had another trophy.

We were both still in the Champions League, and we played our second leg with Juventus in August. Cristiano Ronaldo scored twice and they won the game but we went through on away goals. I had mixed feelings because I was now firmly out of Rudi's plans and could only watch from the bench. Mixed feelings because we lost and because I didn't get to compete against my friend, but mostly because I wasn't out there helping my team-mates. I was happy that we went through to the quarter-final – from that point, all of the knockout ties would be played in single games over one week in Portugal. We were drawn against Manchester City. Again

I didn't play, but this time I don't mind admitting I was more happy because of who we beat!

We got to the semi-final against Bayern Munich, the biggest game of my time at the club, and I could only watch from the bench. It was tough. I had all the motivation to help my team – everyone in the team needs that. And I felt that defeat just as if I was on the pitch. We started well and should have scored. But we were against a good and clinical Bayern team. They scored after 15 minutes and then controlled the match. We were eliminated but could be proud – this was as far as the club had ever come. You don't celebrate losing but at the same time you can be happy for writing a new page in the club's history, especially after such a difficult year.

It was obvious that I would have to write a new page in my own history, too. It was another tough choice. My family loved France. My daughter, son and wife – who was pregnant again – all adored where we lived. I did too. But of course Rudi was going to stay, and that meant I wasn't going to play. I had conversations with the directors and they were keen for me to stay, but I stressed how much I needed to play and I have to be thankful to them because they made it very uncomplicated to move on.

If I had a sadness with the way I left Lyon – and United, for that matter – it's that I didn't get a chance to say goodbye to the fans on the pitch. But that's asking for a lot when you have been blessed like me. Not many footballers get the chance to say goodbye. And at least there is social media now, where you can communicate directly – and I'm sure supporters of both clubs know how proud and happy I was to have represented their team. And who knows if those goodbyes are final? Maybe one day you'll return.

I had offers from different clubs in Turkey. İstanbul Başakşehir had something compelling happening. They were champions and were in the Champions League. They had some former Premier League players I was familiar with. I felt wanted; I felt needed. The decision was straightforward.

I'm a very lucky guy. I would say I'm modest with my ambitions. When I was younger I surpassed them all because it was difficult to really know what expectations to have. As the years passed you realised how fortunate you were to experience those days. You realised that luck has a lot to do with it. Your fate can come down to someone putting their hand in a bag and drawing a ball out – no different to a lottery. It's the same principle. Within days of moving to Turkey, my new club's ball was drawn out of a bag with Manchester United and the dream I'd held since leaving them six years earlier – to one day play against them – was finally going to happen.

Before that, we had domestic business to get used to. And it was difficult to get used to it, I admit. The first thing is – as I've said earlier – Turkey is a country in which everybody knows how loud the supporters of any team can be, especially in Istanbul. But because of the coronavirus most games were still being played behind closed doors – there were some trials, and in European competition we were allowed a few hundred fans in, but mostly it was empty stadiums.

It was a difficult season on the pitch. A year before winning the league, Başakşehir had come very close, only to lose it late on. Their victory in 2020 was the culmination of two years of work with players pushing themselves to the limit. Football is energy. That, coupled with the new circumstances everyone was having to adapt to, made it a strange experience. But when we finally got to play in front of supporters at Trabzonspor, we picked up our first win of the season. After that, we put in a great display against Antalyaspor at home. We were 4-1 up at half-time and I had a hand in two of the goals – we were winning so comfortably, the coach Okan Buruk took me off to let me rest for the visit of my former club that coming midweek.

I'll never forget that night. Of course many of the faces had changed since I left – Ole Gunnar Solskjaer, someone I did know well, was now the manager, with Mike Phelan his assistant and Michael Carrick on the staff. To see them all again was great. And, of course, I was someone the press were talking about beforehand. There was an extra determination to play well. I put everything out there – we won and I was named man of the match. Some of our fans were there to see what I'm sure was one of the greatest nights in the club's history. My old team-mate Rio Ferdinand tweeted about my performance and I had so many graceful United fans congratulating me, even though their team lost. It was a supernatural feeling. That evening I went home to my wife and said that moving to Başakşehir was the best decision I'd ever made in my life. It couldn't have been more perfect. I hope that God gives me the grace to allow me never to forget it.

Three weeks later I returned to the city, to the club that had given me everything. My new awareness of time made me realise just how rare this chance was. I was conscious about it. It was different arriving in the away dressing room – for a moment I almost walked towards the home room!

The win at home had given us an unlikely chance of qualifying if our results improved but unfortunately we were beaten at Old Trafford, where their new talisman Bruno Fernandes was in good form. As I came off the pitch, Karen – the United media officer – came up to me and told me to follow her. I was still in my kit and boots and walked with her to a room where Sir Alex was waiting for me. I sat talking about things with him for 15, 20 minutes. Just conversation, like friends. We hardly talked about the game. We talked about life. He asked me how I was, how my brother was, how my family was. You know I admired him before. It went to a different level after this. He didn't need to do it. But he did. What a man.

Those three weeks were a highlight but, in spite of the tough results on the pitch, I would say my decision to move to Turkey was something that felt even more right as time passed. Istanbul is amazing. I didn't know what to expect – I was maybe a little apprehensive, a little scared, before we went. I can say that the incredible first few weeks helped but also that I have enjoyed my time in the country. I am still trying to learn the language, but so many people speak English.

We changed coaches in January – Okan had won the title and had at least been given the opportunity to take us into the Champions League. His replacement was Aykut Kocaman and under him we finished the season strongly, winning four and drawing three of our last seven games. We finished 12th in the league, but for sure everyone will remember that we played in the Champions League and beat Manchester United. It is just a shame more of our supporters weren't there to see it. For us as players, we know what the club is capable of, and hopefully Başakşehir will be challenging for honours again.

Harmony

Rafa: This is how it went. Our parents left to go back to Brazil in 2010. Fabio made the decision to move to London temporarily a year later. My first daughter was born a year after that, around the same time of the Olympics. Our lives had been shaped by our close relationship with our family. And yet when my daughter came along everything felt like it changed for me. It changed the way I was as a person, the way I thought about things. After playing football, my goal in life was to have a family, to have a happy family. All of my career I had played for my family but having a child of my own made that feeling very different. I really was playing for her. I think it helped me settle.

Fabio: It was similar for me. My first-born came at a time when things were changing in my life. I was at a new club by myself, so I was experiencing a lot of new feelings. I was never afraid of playing before I was a father but now suddenly I was. I asked myself why and I think it was simply the thought of always needing to be there, to support and protect them. You think about these responsibilities. I am as close to my brother as any sibling possibly could be but because we were the same person it was never a case of needing to protect him and look after him. We could do that ourselves.

Rafa: We were already uncles thanks to our brother who, like us, had a girl first. That was when he was living with us in Manchester. We were different uncles as we became different fathers. It was nice for us to learn when we were all together.

Fabio: It was a good learning experience. We were very involved.

Rafa: When our parents moved back to Brazil, I think the following years were harder for them than they were for us. Their children and grandchildren were growing on the other side of the world, having this life experience, and we were all together away from them, especially in the pandemic.

Fabio: I think Dad had an easier way of dealing with it. He was very pragmatic. Of course he missed us but I think he could deal with it as a part of life. For Mum it was very difficult, emotionally. She didn't want to let us go.

Rafa: I'm not saying it was good that they went home. We missed them like crazy. But we became very mature, very quickly, because we had to. We learned a lot in the first year after they left. Mum was so intense. She loves being a mum. She wants to do everything to take care of everyone. We had to learn what real life was like when she went home.

Fabio: In Cardiff it was like I was with my new family by myself. I wanted to have children at the same time as my brother but it took us a little longer – everything seemed to happen as we moved to Wales. I thought my wife was joking when she told me we were going to have a baby. Everything had been so busy! After trying for almost two years my next dream was coming true; it was coming at a time we were going to be by 'ourselves' for the first time.

Rafa: It was hard being away from our parents and then being away from each other. But Dad was right and we had been preparing ourselves for the moment we would be separated. The dream was that we would play together forever for Manchester United.

Fabio: We did achieve that dream. It could be forever, because the chances of us playing for United, as twins from Brazil – I don't know what percentage the chance is of that happening.

But it has to be lower than one. What we accomplished already was further than anyone could expect.

Rafa: My smart brother, he's right. He always is. We are realists. We were prepared for the realities of life and knew that one day we would have to move on; I think that helped us appreciate what we had in the moment, even as young boys, and then also to appreciate the next step, and that we'd had that moment for as long as we'd had it.

Fabio: I think that is where having this large family helped us. The moves away were easier. I felt sympathy for my wife, who was an only child, so when she moved to Manchester she was away from her family. They didn't move to England. It was very difficult for her parents, and for her. I appreciated the sacrifice that she made and I still do.

Rafa: I can remember when you got married. My girlfriend came over to England a year later. I was so anxious to get married too because Nenê had. I joked with my girlfriend that she had to get my brothers presents because I was the only single one left. Thank you, God, that she agreed to marry me. She has been such a great support to me, especially in the moments when my brother couldn't be there. It was not easy for her, it's been difficult to be away from family.

Fabio: Our marriages helped us stay grounded and focused. A lot of young players get lost in the game because they are not as fortunate as we were to get that. Being apart has made the time together even more special because you have a concentrated period of time where you just want to stay with family.

As I write this, tomorrow I will see my parents for the first time in almost 18 months, because of the way the football season works and because of the coronavirus pandemic, which has had such an impact on international travel. I normally spend every summer back home and I enjoy letting our mum getting her way for that period of time. She can mother us all she wants. It's a special time. Our connection and bond feels like it gets stronger during these periods. It also gives us an opportunity to reflect on what we have accomplished.

Hopefully there is still plenty more to come from football. I don't mean from a sporting perspective, I mean, from the objective of working to ensure our parents wouldn't need to. We were lucky enough to do that when we were young. And now we could be in the position where our children don't have to work to struggle to make money. Speaking now as a father, that is a difficult thing and I can understand my father's struggle with similar issues.

Rafa: Our children are lucky. They have been born into a good lifestyle with good opportunities for education. But we still try to let them know that life is not like this. They do need to work. Things don't come from the sky. They don't need anything. Sometimes we get embarrassed by the things they have, that we weren't fortunate enough to have. And sometimes I do feel scared by that. Like I said, life is not like this. You don't always get what you want when you want it. People are going to say no. I say no to my kids all the time because of this. Life is usually no.

Fabio: I agree with that. I am usually no, but I would say I am more open. That is a complexity with my own personality – I have always had a hard time saying no to people. I say yes to please people. I do try and educate my children, to help them appreciate their privilege in comparison to the poverty that is the reality for too many people. It is one of my intentions to be more proactive to help them understand and appreciate it.

Rafa: I think this is a lesson for everyone, though, because the perception of privilege against poverty isn't just a case of the distinction between rich footballers and people who cannot afford to eat. It's obviously more complex than that. Real life is also, now, a pandemic which has caused millions of people to lose their jobs, their lives. Nobody wants to project bad impressions, especially in a world where so much influence is governed by what people see on social media. People want to say their life is perfect. People want to see good things on Instagram. I'm guilty too, I know. I'm the best golfer in the world on Instagram. Sometimes it makes us aspire to things that aren't realistic because they aren't real. I know people look at things on social media and ask why they don't have it. They tell themselves they want it. It changes your perception of your own blessing. To have food when someone else doesn't is not a blessing. The extra we have is a privilege. We could be those guys fighting to eat. If we didn't play football, who knows. And I sincerely mean that. Who does know? We were very lucky. We didn't grow up dreaming of playing for Manchester United and winning league titles. It all came from the desire of wanting to win whatever we were competing at.

Fabio: That is exactly how it started. Everything else — league titles, Champions League games, final appearances — happened because we wanted to win whatever game of football we were playing. So when we left United, and maybe I speak for my brother as well with this, it was this that was the ambition. Win every time you step on to the pitch. You can't afford to not think like that.

Rafa: I have seen so much talent not make it in the game because they don't have that quality. You have to have that at Manchester United.

Fabio: It comes with wearing the shirt. To have that badge on your chest. What a feeling.

Rafa: I just could not understand *not* having that feeling. You're playing for the best club in the world, man. You get older and you learn more about the history of the club. It makes you proud that your heart is beating behind the badge. And then, when the time comes to move on, you can't be anything less than that. I just could never understand how anyone who had the privilege to be at Old Trafford could not appreciate the opportunity they had. The saddest things I have seen in football come when I see a player is not showing complete commitment for that club. You can miss a pass. You can miss a shot. That's not a problem. If you are not running – this is a big problem. If you play poorly, I don't care. But you have to try. Over time that has changed. It's not just at United. It's a privilege to play professional football. You are rewarded. You have to show everything for the badge you are wearing – that's the commitment you agree to when you sign for that club.

Fabio: Life is what it is. It presents challenges and obstacles. In the time I was injured, coinciding with the pandemic, I had so much time to think. About life, my career. And I've reflected upon it all writing this book. Looking back with the perspective I now have, I would give every penny I have for one more go with Manchester United; for the opportunity to go back as a teenager and do it again. I think it would be so different. My brother and my wife always say to me that I'm too nice. If that is a personality trait, I can't change that, and I wouldn't want to. But I think I would change how I was on the pitch. I would be more aggressive.

Rafa: Too nice? Maybe with everyone else. You're a pain in the ass! With everyone else, the nicest guy on earth.

Fabio: It's just – I carry it. If I hurt someone it would devastate me. I would be sorry a million times. I'd be overbearing, annoying with my apology. Maybe it's a quality to offer an apology but I know I'm too apologetic. An example: we had some friends over. I was so eager to ask if they were okay, if they had everything, my wife said I'd unsettled them and made them uncomfortable. So I know it's too much. I try to stop it. But I know this was part of my problem at United. I know that there were 70,000 in the stands, and I don't know what it was, or why. I just didn't want to let them down. The shirt was sometimes heavy.

Rafa: That is why, in my opinion, my brother never played well for Ole at Cardiff. He was calling me all the time saying he didn't want to disappoint him. He had it in his head that he couldn't play poorly.

Fabio: It's true. That's how it was with Sir Alex. He did so much for us. He changed my life. He changed the life of my family. I know I carried the pressure of that, and I know he wasn't the one giving me the pressure. He gave me the opportunity. I just didn't want to disappoint him.

Rafa: After leaving United, and after Ole left Cardiff, that was a period for my brother to think about the reasons for why he felt like this. It was an advantage for him to know that it was a problem because sometimes people don't. But he had to learn for himself that nobody had given him anything he hadn't earned. We had so many conversations. I'm not saying it disappeared from his game. But when he would tell me that he was afraid to play poorly, I told him that thinking like that was inviting it to happen. Look, I know butterflies are sometimes healthy. I read that Cristiano had admitted that he sometimes gets them still. But you have to control it or it will control you.

Fabio: When I arrived in Manchester I had to prove that I was worthy of my place. And then when I left United I was *from* United so I was having to live up to that, too, in my own mind. When we first came to England everyone spoke so highly of me; of us both. They really liked us. They said I was going to play for Brazil for a long time. You listen to it. You want to prove yourself. But the setbacks come and the doubt creeps in. The shoulder injury. It takes some time to get a chance. *Maybe I'm not good enough.* You do it to yourself. You add more pressure on yourself. I could not play with freedom as I was restraining myself.

When I was younger I thought that admitting the truth about my anxiety was a weakness. So I kept it in. Now I am older, I understand that it wouldn't have been. The weakness was holding it in. Applying pressure to myself. If I knew in advance I'd be playing, I would be anxious as far as three days before a game. I couldn't enjoy it. And I was playing for the best club. Now I know it's just 90 minutes. I just wish I could go back to tell the teenage version of myself that same thing. I'm not saying it's cured, that I'm perfectly at ease. It's a battle. But I try to remind myself that feeling this way is restricting my freedom to enjoy one of the things I love the most. I want to enjoy playing football in the time I have left to play it.

Rafa: My career has thrown a couple of unexpected highlights my way in the last two years or so. So I think I'm just trying to embrace the unpredictability of it all and see where it takes me. I couldn't have expected to have played a Champions League semi-final with Lyon and then a couple of months later be playing against Manchester United for a team from Turkey. I get chills when I think about playing against United. That was the time I got real butterflies – I'm experienced enough to not really get nervous or anxious before a game, but this was special. They're my team, I'll support them forever now. But I was delighted to win against them. I tried my best. I wanted to prove that I was good enough to still play for them. That I belonged there. I felt I proved myself in that 90 minutes. Football is like this – it provides disappointing moments as well as good ones.

It was a shame that I left in the way I did. But I wasn't the first or last to play and leave. I was blessed to have played for them at all. Life took me to Turkey, one of the countries in the world that is so passionate about football – an opportunity to play in front of those fans. As an emotional player, that's an experience I am grateful for. It's still a dream of mine to want to play for Botafogo.

Fabio: Mine too, one day in the future.

Rafa: After I finish playing I will coach. I will never forget how difficult it is to play the game. It's not a video game. It's a human experience. Players have lives and families and sometimes they're not having a good day for whatever reason. I will be empathetic to that, but I also think the game has changed so much in the generation we've been playing that coaches are almost afraid of players. Why should that be the case? It won't be for me, that's for sure – I think you're preparing to lose your job the second you're afraid of the players. Respect is a two-way street. My vision of football is simple. The game is, after all. I think the media has changed the way the game is played. It influences coaches to be pragmatic and negative. You have to be strong enough in your own mentality to survive the outside influence. That's how you'll survive. You have to have conviction. I will want my teams to play well and score goals. Concede ten if you want, as long as you score 11. Of course I don't want to concede ten – I want to win. We can't have football where teams are afraid to play.

Fabio: I'm a little different. I can understand caution. What I can't understand is creating opportunities where you are likely to make mistakes. Teams playing the ball around the defenders and goalkeepers when they're not comfortable doing it. I like taking risks, but that's taking risks in the wrong way. I won't be telling my goalkeeper that if the opposition is pressing him he should still try and play it from the back. In normal football conditions you can't play like this. I also don't think it's good to take those sort of risks. It's negative.

We learned with the best: Sir Alex Ferguson. Football is simple. Players complicate it. You have to understand your players as people and that's why he was so good. That's why he was the master. He had everything – the mood of the player, the mood of the opposition. The mood of the moment. We will try every day when we are coaches to pass on his lessons. Just as we do in our every day life.

Acknowledgements

FABIO AND RAFAEL would like to thank all of the people who have made a positive impact on our careers.

We would like to thank Wayne Barton for working with us on this book.

Thank you to Paul and Jane Camillin and all at Pitch Publishing for sharing our story.

We are both indebted to Edgar Pereira for looking after us as we were growing into footballers. We are grateful to John Calvert and Paul McGuinness – and many, many more – for helping us to settle into Manchester.

We are so thankful for the incredible support we have had the privilege to play in front of for all of our careers.

Words do not exist in Portuguese or English to express our gratitude for our father in football, Sir Alex Ferguson. We were educated by the greatest football teacher there has ever been, and learned so much about life along the way.

ACKNOWLEDGEMENTS

To our parents, our wives, children, all of our family and friends – you are everything to us.

==

Wayne Barton would like to join the twins in thanking all at Pitch, as well as the following: First of all, thank you to Fabio and Rafael for giving me the privilege of helping to tell their story. Paddy Barclay, Rob Smyth, Danny Taylor. Eifion Evans, Mark Foster, Barney Chilton, Ben McManus, Tony Park, Matthew Galea, Nipun Chopra, Oyvind Enger, Matthew Smallwood, Phil and Mikiel Gatt, Gem and Steve. Thank you to Daniel, Kim and Alex Burdett. Thank you to Dave Murphy. A big thank you to my family, especially my nephews Freddy and Noah who we adore. Thank you to Stacey, my beautiful wife.

Also available at all good book stores

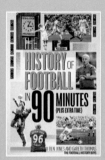

9781785318399

9781785316869

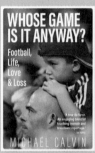

9781785318849

9781785318528

9781785316722

9781785318627

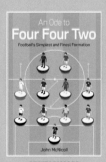

9781785318382

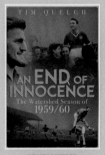

9781785317583

9781785317736